BROKEN KALEIDOSCOPE SYNDROME

Daughter of the Soviet Union

BY MILA KRAABEL

Suite 300 - 990 Fort St
Victoria, BC, V8V 3K2
Canada

www.friesenpress.com

First Edition — 2021

Editor: Beth Jusino

ISBN
978-1-5255-9254-6 (Hardcover)
978-1-5255-9253-9 (Paperback)
978-1-5255-9255-3 (eBook)

1. BIOGRAPHY & AUTOBIOGRAPHY, CULTURAL HERITAGE

Distributed to the trade by The Ingram Book Company

In the memory of my parents,
Valentina and Ivan Kondeykin

TABLE OF CONTENTS

The Union of the Soviet Socialist Republics, 1968

Unbreakable Union of freeborn Republics,
Great Russia has welded forever to stand.
Created in struggle by will of the people,
United and mighty, our Soviet land!
(from the Anthem of the Soviet Union)

PROLOGUE

1947 was an eventful year: India and Pakistan gained their independence from the British Empire; the United Nations partitioned Palestine between Arabs and Jews; the Communist Party seized power in Hungary; President Harry Truman introduced the Truman Doctrine to stop the spread of communism and signed the National Security Act of 1947, which created the CIA and the US Air Force; Joseph Stalin launched a new wave of political repressions in the Soviet Union; Bell Laboratories demonstrated the first transistor; the AK-47 assault rifle went into production; French fashion designer Christian Dior presented his first collection; and pilot Kenneth Arnold spotted flying saucers over Mount Rainier.

That was also the year I was born in Ashkhabad, Turkmenistan. Nobody knew or cared about this event except for my parents and their extended families. For the rest of the world, I was just one of the 175 million small cogs in the enormous machine called the Union of Soviet Socialist Republics.

PART I

1: The Kondeykins

When Mama brought me home from the delivery ward, my Aunt Nastya, Papa's eldest sister, unfolded my blankets, checked my tiny body from head to toe, and said that I hadn't long to live. My heels, she said, were too skinny, and that was a sign that I didn't belong to this world.

Mama cried all evening. She wrapped and unwrapped me, staring at my heels—they were skinny all right. She listened to my breathing—too labored, she thought. She pressed her lips against my forehead—hot, she panicked. To make things worse, I screamed nonstop, and that was proof that something was definitely wrong with me.

Late that night, when Papa came home from the restaurant where he worked as a bartender, he found her sitting on the bed, her face swollen from tears. Stuttering with sobs on every word, Mama told him about his sister's dire prediction.

The story, as I heard it, ends there, but I suspect that my Papa went straight to Nastya and blurted out everything he thought about her stupid behavior. Nastya probably shouted back that she didn't mean to upset Valentina; that it was just what people in their village used to say about new babies. The whole family of Kondeykins was short-fused but easily-appeased, so the emotional eruption would have exhausted itself quickly, and my aunt would have come the next morning to calm Mama, bringing her something nice to make up for the mistake. She was a kind and generous woman, my Aunt Nastya.

Mama didn't hold a grudge against her sister-in-law, but the silly superstition stuck in her head for a long time, making her wary at any sign of trouble. Fortunately, I was a healthy baby, but I was a handful, especially in a house full of noisy cousins.

Although I was my parents' first child, I was born into a big clan. My Grandpa Mikhail and Grandma Praskovya Kondeykina, their four sons, and their sons' wives and kids all lived in a big, one-story adobe house on a quiet, shady street of Ashkhabad, the capital of the Soviet Republic of Turkmenistan. My father's sisters and my Mama's three brothers also lived in the city, not far from us.

We were not native Turkmens. Both my parents had been born in small Russian villages and had come to Ashkhabad with their families at the beginning of the 1930s. Although Turkmenistan was part of the Soviet Union, its culture was distinctly Central Asian, and the hullabaloo of exotic-looking bazaars, cacophony of languages, and pungent aromas of melons and herbs was utterly foreign to them at first.

By the time I was born, though, they were used to Turkmen men in big furry *telpek* hats and women in long red or green *koynek* dresses and colorful head scarves. The fortissimo of braying asses tied to telephone poles and the occasional regal caravan of one-hump Arabian camels strolling down the street were normal. My family embraced low houses fenced in clay, arteries of *aryks* (irrigation canals) bubbling with clear water, and shady parks for weekend strolls.

Ashkhabad became their home.

Ivan, my father, was the youngest of his parents' thirteen children—only six of whom had reached adulthood. He married Mama in January 1946, eight months after he came home from what we called the Great Patriotic War and the rest of the world called World War II. The Kondeykins all liked his young wife,

Valentina, for her nice temper and friendliness, her eagerness to help, her contagious laughter, and the tears that surfaced in her eyes without warning.

Mama, for her part, had been orphaned at seventeen and was happy to have a family again. Her new in-laws were less educated and had different values than her own family, but they were generous, down-to-earth people with strong survival instincts. They accepted her as a daughter and sister, and when in February 1947 she brought home an infant, the women showed her how to swaddle me, how to take care of her breasts, and how to nurse.

My young parents looked so much alike that people sometimes thought they were siblings. To prove they were spouses, they had to show their Soviet passports with the marriage registration stamps. Although Papa was much taller, they both had slender, strong figures with thin waistlines and long legs, high cheekbones, big foreheads, and chestnut eyes. Their friends and family called them Vanya and Valya, common short names for Ivan and Valentina.

My parents called me Ludmila, a popular Slavic name that means "beloved of the people." I had two cousins with the same name. Like all Russians, besides my first, patronymic, and last names—Ludmila Ivanovna Kondeykina[1]—I had many nicknames: short Mila, affectionate Milochka and Milenka, and chummy Milka.

When I was a toddler Mama called me "jingle bell." She always knew where I was playing or what I was doing just by listening. My voice and laughter stood out in any crowd. If she didn't hear me, it meant trouble.

At fourteen months, I could recite simple children's poems and fairytales, and my proud Papa dragged me everywhere with him

---

1 Russians use three names: first name, middle or patronymic name, which is derived from their father's first name, and the family name. Women's last names add an *a* to the masculine form of the name.

and made me recite *Kurochka Ryaba* (Specked Hen) for anyone looking for amusement.

The Kondeykin brothers had lots of fun with me at that age, as well. On hot summer evenings they would drink beer under our grapevine arbor. I would sit on my Papa's lap while Mama was busy cleaning up in the kitchen.

One of my uncles, Nikolai, was deaf-mute since a bad case of measles when he was three. He sat with his brothers at the table, but unlike them, he never drank or smoked. "Mila, ask Uncle Nikolai if he wants to take you to the movies," Papa would say, lowering me to the ground.

I'd pitter-patter to my uncle and tap him on his side to attract his attention. He'd look at me, and I'd rub my thumb and two fingers together in the air. *Do you have money?* He'd nod, then rummage in his pocket and give me a coin or two. Clenching the money in my fist, I'd move an open palm of the other hand several times in front of my eyes and then wave it. *Let's go to watch a movie.* He'd laugh his strange coughing laughter, and I'd join in with my high-pitched glee. I don't know if I ever went watching movies with Uncle Nikolai, but I loved "talking" with him. The two of us were buddies.

Papa and his brothers spent many hours at that table, talking and drinking. As in most Russian homes, no supper went by without a bottle of vodka on the table. Alcohol, Mama realized shortly after she got married, was a problem in the Kondeykin family. Three of the brothers had fought in the war and returned home loaded with wounds, trophies, and booze. Long after their wives went inside to put kids to bed and make preparations for the following day, they continued their carousing. Sometimes the evening ended in a heated exchange or a fistfight, which only Grandpa Mikhail could stop.

★ ★ ★

When I turned one, Mama went back to work waiting tables during the day at Ak Altyn Restaurant, where Papa worked the night shift. At first, he took care of me when Mama was at work. But she soon had reason to question my presence in men's company.

One evening, to keep me busy while the women cleaned the table and washed dishes after supper, Mama gave me a piece of paper and a pencil, put me at the end of the table, and asked me to draw a picture for her.

Apparently, I decided that there wasn't enough room to do my art. I reached forward and swiped the dishes out of my way. The sound of breaking glasses was followed by my loud, "Get the fuck out of my way. I'm going to draw a picture for my Mama."

Mama froze. Her two sisters-in-law covered their faces with their aprons, choking with laughter.

"My first reaction was to come up and slap you," Mama told me years later. "But you continued scribbling with such an innocent expression on your face that I knew you didn't have any idea what you had said. I didn't draw your attention to it, and I never heard it from you again."

The same week, Mama found me a nanny. Papa was dismissed from his duties as caregiver.

2: October 6, 1948

It was a warm October evening, the beginning of the best time of the year in Ashkhabad. The sweltering summer had given way to the long, deliciously warm fall. Grandparents sat on benches in front of their houses until dark, chatting with neighbors and watching noisy children romp around. Young lovers strolled by, holding hands. From behind tall clay fences came the sounds of dominoes banging on wooden tables and surges of men's laughter.

My family gathered in our yard for their usual after-dinner tea. While the women bustled around, setting the table, the men talked. Grandpa Mikhail—a strong, broad-chested man of sixty-seven with a bald head and carefully trimmed gray beard and mustache—sat at the head of the table, surrounded by his sons, Peotr, Mikhail Jr., and Nikolai. They were making plans to build an extension to the house for my father, my Mama, and eighteen-month-old me.

Neither of my parents was in the yard with the family. Papa was working and wouldn't come home until long after midnight. Mama was inside, caring for me. Several weeks earlier, I had come down with a bad case of whooping cough, and she kept me in our tiny room, isolated from my numerous cousins. For a while, I had such terrible coughing fits and difficulty breathing that the fear of losing me had snaked back into her heart. But a pediatrician who had come to visit me that afternoon said that the worst part of my infection was over, and I was on my way to recovery.

Still, I know just what it all looked like. A copper samovar polished each morning by Nikolai's wife, Marfa, with a mixture of tooth powder and soda, stood in the middle of the table, puffing with steam. Surrounding it were two colorful teapots, glasses in metal glass-holders, lump sugar, and a big jar of homemade apricot jam. Finally, Grandma Parasha came out with a big bowl of *pyshki*, a type of doughnut sprinkled with sugar. At the sight of her, my cousins rushed to the table and sat with their mothers. Three generations of Kondeykins sat at the long table. As always, the stories, jokes, and laughter flew.

When I fell asleep in my small metal bed, Mama came out to have a cup of tea with the others. The Kondeykins welcomed her news about my pending recovery with loud cheers.

Eventually, the women went inside to put the older children to bed and prepare their school uniforms for the next day. The men stayed outside, smoking and talking in hushed voices. Soon they also retreated, having agreed to meet in the morning and talk to Ivan about the construction.

By eleven o'clock the house was cloaked in black.

Mama tried to wait up for Papa so that she could tell him the good news about my health, but she fell asleep on top of the bedspread, still fully dressed. She was exhausted from weeks of sleepless nights with her sick baby.

She woke up to a strange commotion outside her open window. Grandma's chickens were cackling in their pen as if someone had scared them.

"Vanya, is it you?" she called. Nobody answered.

Mama turned on the light and looked at the alarm clock beside the shaded lamp. It was five minutes past one. Vanya's shift was over, and he would be on his way home soon.

The clatter outside increased. Our small dog, Sharik, began howling, long and plaintively. *Sobaka voyet k pokoiniku* (a dog howls for the dead), Mama recalled the Russian superstition and shivered. How foolish it was to think about such nonsense at night. She tried to compose herself. But then I burst out coughing, sat up in my bed, and began crying.

Mama lowered her feet to the wooden floor and felt with her toes for her slippers. She heard a growing rumble as if a dozen heavily-laden trucks were passing by our house. She stood just as the room began shaking, and she felt the floor moving under her feet. Trying to stay upright, she clutched the metal headboard of her bed, but a powerful jolt broke her grip and slammed her to the floor. The lamp went out. In darkness, she heard me scream once, and then I was silent.

"Milenka! *Dochenka* (little daughter)!" she begged into the darkness. "Wait a little. Your Mama is coming."

She attempted to pull herself up, but another enormous jolt shook the house. The world around her cracked, crashed, and crumbled to the ground. Something heavy fell on top of her and pinned her to the floor. The air was thick with dust that clogged her nose, mouth, and lungs. She felt like she was suffocating.

The shocks stopped as suddenly as they began. For a few seconds, everything was quiet. Then Mama heard somebody's muffled moans. The shriek of a baby. A woman begging for help. She recognized the voice of our neighbor, Mona, a Korean woman who lived next door. Mona was calling her older son repeatedly, with increasing despair in her voice.

Much closer, she heard her brother-in-law, Mikhail, and his wife, Dora. Dora was sobbing.

"Mikhail! Dora!" she yelled. "Help us! Please tell Ivan that we are here." But the voices moved away.

Mama tried to free herself from under the wreckage that pinned her. Scratching her hands and breaking her nails, she pushed aside pieces of adobe, dirt, and broken planks. She didn't know how long she had been there. Minutes? Longer? It seemed like an eternity. She groped for something sturdy, grabbed it, and pulled with all her strength. Sharp pain pierced her lower back, sending lightning through her legs and abdomen. But her body had moved.

Blindly, she squeezed herself through the wreckage to my bed. Bracing herself for the worst, she reached for my pillow. Her hand bumped into a huge timber that pinned my pillow right in the middle where she expected to find my head. Frantically, she felt around the narrow space between the beam and my mattress. This time, her fingers came across something soft and warm—my tiny foot.

Mama's heart swooned as she touched my legs, and then my body and head, checking for injuries. There was dust and pieces of plaster in my hair, but she didn't feel any blood or broken bones. She pulled me closer, and I stirred and started crying.

"The whooping cough saved your life," Mama would tell me years later. "When you coughed in your sleep, you would sit up in bed, then lie down in a wrong direction. I often found you sleeping with your head at the foot of your bed. That saved you from the ceiling beam. When it fell on your bed, one end squashed your pillow and the other rested on the metal footboard, making a nice shelter for you to sleep."

Mama held me through the dark hours. She heard muffled knocks, dull scraping, and the sounds of heavy things being pulled across the ground. She heard familiar voices. She called for help over and over again, but nobody could hear her.

Then the thumping noises moved closer. Pieces of plaster and dirt fell on her head, and through a tiny opening where the ceiling used to be, she saw a faint ray of light. Someone was coming at last.

"Vanya, we are here!" she called, crying and laughing at the same time. "We're here. Please get us out!"

Whoever was there remained silent. All Mama heard was labored breathing and the knocking of a tool against a hard surface.

The opening to the sky became larger, and a dark figure of a man squeezed halfway into our shallow grave. When he saw us, he made a loud, guttural sound. Nikolai!

The noises her deaf-mute brother-in-law made had scared her when she first moved in with Papa's big family. Now they were the sound of her salvation.

She let my uncle take me from her hands. He disappeared for a few seconds and then returned. He clasped her around her chest with his strong hands and heaved her from under the ruins. Mama choked with pain and lost consciousness.

3: The Aftermath

Papa staggered home at dawn, clutching at his hair to keep his head upright. The earthquake had caught him at the moment he was locking the restaurant's front door. The beam that held the awning over the entrance fell and knocked him out. A coworker, Kira Yakovlevna, pulled Papa out of the rubble. "She saved my life," Papa would acknowledge later.

Dizzy and disoriented, Papa had left the ruins of the restaurant and started down the hill toward home. The pain in his head and neck left him swaying from side to side like a drunkard.

He understood the extent of the catastrophe as soon as he entered the residential area. In the weak light of the nascent morning, he didn't recognize the city where he'd lived since he was nine. He once knew every building in this part of the city. Now, wherever he looked, the picture was the same—ruins, ruins, and more ruins.

There are two ways to measure the size of earthquakes. Russia, as well as many European and Asian countries, uses the intensity scale, which measures the severity of shaking produced by the earthquake. The Richter scale, used by other countries, measures the size of an earthquake's seismic waves and amount of energy released. The magnitude of the Ashkhabad 1948 earthquake was 7.3 on the Richter scale, and its intensity was IX–X(Violent-Extreme).

Thousands of people—crushed, broken, bloody, and dead—lay on the road. They moaned, calling for children, spouses, and parents still trapped in the rubble. In four years of fighting the Great Patriotic War, Papa had never seen so many dead and wounded in one place. Survivors in undershirts and nightgowns, some of them completely naked, searched for family members in the ruins.

Stumbling down the road, Papa passed the wreckage of *Krasnyi Krest*, the biggest city hospital. Patients' blue robes mingled with white medical smocks as everyone who could move threw themselves into search and rescue.

Papa turned right on Chekhov Street and headed down to Engels Street. He was almost home. His heart constricted with a premonition. He leaned against a tree and closed his eyes, trying to delay the unavoidable.

When he finally arrived, the damage to his own house exceeded all his fears. Piles of crumbled adobe, broken planks, wooden beams sticking out from the debris, and wires scattered around the place that had been his home just a few hours earlier.

A slim young man in striped pajama pants—Nikolai—rummaged in the ruins. Papa waved his hand, trying to attract his brother's attention, with no success. On the sidewalk, he found a small group sitting around a smoldering fire. Dora and Nyura, his sisters-in-law, were disheveled in torn and dirty nightgowns. Each held a sleeping baby on her lap. Three half-naked boys, his nephews, were stirring dying embers with sticks, whispering among themselves.

The boys noticed him first and began yelling that Uncle Vanya was alive. The women rose, clutching the babies to their chests. They began weeping and wailing like simple peasant women.

"Oh, Vanya. What a grief. What terrible misfortune befell us."

He searched the shadows frantically with his eyes. "Where are Valya and Milochka?"

Choking with tears, the women told him that Mama and I were both alive. Valentina was injured and taken to the road where she was safer from the aftershocks, they explained. Then Dora pulled a blanket from the baby she held. My face and hair were covered with dirt, but I slept peacefully in my aunt's arms.

"Where's the rest of the family?" Papa asked.

Dora jerked her chin in the direction of the sidewalk, where several men perched on the rubble of the fence. Papa's brothers Mikhail and Peotr—bruised, covered with blood, and gray with dust—were among them. They were silent as he approached.

Before he reached them, he saw the bodies lying just across from the ruins of our house, their faces covered with pieces of a torn, white sheet. He faltered closer, weak in the knees. His brothers trailed behind him.

Papa froze when he saw the stark, broad-chested frame of a man in black shorts and the woman in her long nightgown lying next to each other. Her left hand, awkwardly twisted, rested on the man's right thigh as if she was afraid he would leave her. Papa closed his eyes, unable to bear the sight of his dead parents.

Someone pulled the sleeve of his shirt. Nikolai stood next to him, desperately grunting and gesturing. He was two years older than Papa, and throughout their childhood they had been best friends. Though Papa was younger, he was taller and stronger, and he protected his voiceless brother from swaggering ruffians during their teenage years.

Look at this! Nikolai gestured. He sank to his knees beside the bodies of his wife Marfa and his eight-year-old daughter Toma, and bellowed like a dying animal. Nikolai's ten-year-old son, Kolka, hung over his father's neck, joining with his own lament.

Papa couldn't stand seeing their misery. Grief, anger, and frustration from his helplessness mingled with his terrible physical pain. But there were more bodies to consider.

The two dead girls at the end of that terrible lineup were his nieces, Irina and Anna—eleven-year-old cousins, classmates, and best friends. Their skinny, tanned legs stuck out from under a single sheet, covering their half-naked bodies. The "Jolly Grasshoppers," as Papa had nicknamed them for their skipping and dancing all day long, remained inseparable even in death.

Six broken Kondeykins lay on the ground, and their grief-stricken mothers, fathers, sons, and daughters-in law stood or knelt over them.

"Your Mila is the only girl in the house who survived. She's the lucky one," Dora interrupted his heavy thoughts. She still held me in her arms.

Papa looked at her. Something didn't fall into place. "Where's *your* baby, Dora?" he asked.

"She's still there." She waved at the ruins that had been their home. "Her crib is under that pile, but we couldn't get to it with our bare hands." Dora sighed heavily and shook her head. "Anyway, she's already gone."

Papa turned to his brother. "What if your daughter is alive? You cannot give up hope until you know—"

"The girl's too small to survive," Mikhail interrupted him. "Look at our father. If this oak is down, our baby didn't have any chance. She's only six weeks old. We have been digging all night. Dead children . . . ," he choked. "Dead parents . . . I can't take it anymore."

"What if she's still alive?" Papa repeated stubbornly.

He headed to the ruins. His family followed him. Papa walked slowly, measuring something with his eyes. He stopped a little short of the big pile of adobe. "Dig here," he said.

"No, Ivan. This is where the entrance into our bedroom was. Her crib is closer to the wardrobe where that pile is now."

"Dig here," Papa insisted.

While his brothers shoveled bricks and pulled broken planks and boards, Papa sank onto a piece of rubble and watched. The pain in his injured neck had spread to his right shoulder and arm. His head felt split open. Even speaking was painful. Yet the night was not over yet.

After some time, the men found the crib. Mikhail pulled out the lifeless body of his daughter, tightly swaddled in a diaper and covered with a thick layer of dust. Dora started wailing again.

Papa stood and came closer. He put his free hand on Luda's tiny neck. Under the layer of dirt, she felt warm and soft.

"Open her mouth," he ordered.

The baby's toothless mouth was clogged with dirt. He stuck his pinky inside and, piece by piece, began removing the ooze until he cleared it all. The baby's airway was free, but she still showed no signs of life.

"Unfold her," he told Dora. She obeyed silently, removing the baby's swaddling.

Papa examined his niece, feeling the brittleness of her birdlike neck and ribcage. His brother was probably right; the baby didn't have a chance in this terrible mess. Losing hope, Papa shook and slapped the little girl's limp body as if she was a rag doll.

"Leave her alone, Ivan!" Dora screamed, trying to pull her brother-in-law from her daughter. "She's dead!"

Suddenly, the baby inhaled with force, produced a weak cry, and started vomiting.

While Dora was busy with her baby girl, Uncle Peotr's wife Nyura showed Papa to Mama's temporary shelter on the road. She led her two-year-old son Mishka and me by our hands through the tangle of prostrate bodies, stepping over somebody's legs and arms.

Mama lay on her back, covered with a blanket that someone from the family had dug out and put over her. Her eyes were closed, but she was moaning. Slowly, Papa lowered himself next to her and took her hand. She opened her eyes.

"You're alive," she whispered. They looked at each other for a long time, unable to speak. Both felt like a whole century had elapsed since they last saw each other.

I started screaming then, demanding my parents' attention. Aunt Nyura tried to calm me, explaining that Mama and Papa were sick and could not hold me. She let me get closer to kiss my parents.

"I want to go home," I told them. "I am hungry."

"There is no home any more, baby. Everything has fallen down. See?" Mama said.

"I want a sausage," I demanded.

"The meat factory is ruined."

"I want beer," I screeched. "Beer, beer, beer!"

"The brewery is not working either, my darling."

Woeful, hurting people around us started to chuckle, forgetting their own pain and grief just for a moment.

"Why did a silly toddler's babble on such a terrible day stick in everybody's memory?" I asked Mama once.

"I don't know," she said. "Probably because you made people smile when they thought their life was over."

I don't know how many times I heard these earthquake tales during family gatherings in the following years. My memory soaked them all so well that I can see the scenes vividly, and sometimes I wonder if I really remember it firsthand.

4: The Day After

After the long night of terror, aftershocks, and screams, the dawn finally came. Bewildered survivors looked at their city, trying to comprehend what had happened. There were speculations that the Americans had dropped an atomic bomb, and it was the beginning of World War III.[2]

With the light came word that all of the hospitals and medical clinics in the city were destroyed. Injured people should be taken to Karl Marx Square, where citizens of Ashkhabad had jubilant demonstrations during political holidays. Now, a makeshift hospital was set up in the open air to provide first aid to victims.

An endless stream of people—limping, holding their broken limbs, carried on blankets or pushed on carts—moved towards the city center. The Kondeykin brothers found their wheelbarrow, nailed a wooden door onto it, and placed Mama on top. Nikolai wheeled his sister-in-law to the Square when it became clear that Papa was too injured to take her himself.

---

2 While writing this chapter, I learned there was another opinion, too. On his radio show, US Admiral Ellis M. Zacharias, former Deputy Chief of The Office of Naval Intelligence, purported that the cause of the earthquake was the first Soviet atomic bomb test.

As the wheelbarrow started moving, Mama cried, "Vanya, what will happen to Milochka? She hasn't recovered from her whooping cough yet. How is she going to be without me?"

"Don't worry," he assured her. "I'll find Nastya and ask her to take care of the baby. She's probably on her way here now. I'll find you soon."

People were told that trucks would come to pick up the badly injured and the dead. My uncles started to make coffins from any material they could salvage. Sweat mixed with tears rolled down their dirty faces as they worked intently, turning floor boards, doors, and tabletops into boxes that would hold their children, parents, and wife.

Nobody came to pick up the dead as promised. There was more urgent work to do, and the dead could wait. What else could happen to them, anyway? Only at the end of the second day would a string of trucks start hauling their terrible load to cemeteries. The convoy would continue for a week. Those who didn't have surviving relatives to identify them were buried in mass graves.

Papa didn't realize how long it would take him to keep his promise to find Mama. When a truck delivered him to Karl Marx Square that evening, it was packed with thousands of mangled, injured people. Improvised operating tables made from salvaged desks and doors stood next to military field hospitals sent from nearby Turkmen cities. Local doctors and medical students, survivors themselves, applied make-do splints, put dislocated joints back in place, and cleaned contaminated wounds. Military paramedics sorted out who needed urgent surgery, who could wait until the next day, and who required hospitalization. As the hours passed, more medics arrived from the neighboring republics. Surgeries continued all night under battery-powered floodlights and the headlights of military vehicles.

Papa had to wait until the end of the second day after the earthquake, when a medic from an Uzbekistan medical team examined him and put his name on the list of patients to be taken to a hospital. My teenaged cousin, Viktor, managed to find Papa on the Square and brought him "a painkiller"—a bottle of vodka that had miraculously outlived its owner, my Grandpa Mikhail. Viktor reported that he'd combed the Square for his Aunt Valya, but he could find her neither among the injured nor among those who had died before help arrived. At Papa's request, a young Uzbek nurse checked whether his wife's name was on the list of patients flown to Tashkent, but did not find it.

It would take three months before the three of us met again.

5: The Reunion

Aftershocks continued for days. Survivors forgot not only how to laugh, but also how to cry. They slept in the open air, because even the houses that remained standing were unstable and dangerous during aftershocks. The smell of decaying bodies hung around us all. A week after the quake, Red Army forces were still digging out bodies. The number of survivors decreased with each passing day.

On October 11, five days after the earthquake, city authorities announced that coupons for bread and other food products would be distributed through workplaces. Those who hadn't returned to work had to go immediately to register and get coupons.

October was warm, but with winter approaching, people needed shelter. Hastily built huts, called *vremyanki*, started sprouting next to destroyed houses. Families began to settle into a new normal. Trade resumed, money regained its significance, men built, women rattled their pots and pans, children chased each other along dusty streets. The city came out of its prostration.

"We humans are creatures that can get used to everything—wars, natural disasters, even deaths of our loved ones," Aunt Nastya would say, recalling that time. "What else could we do? We had to live."

Both of my parents were in distant Soviet hospitals for three months—Mama in Baku with multiple pelvic fractures and Papa in Tashkent with a broken neck. I remained in the care of my Aunt Nastya, the one who had predicted my death in infancy.

The oldest of the Kondeykin siblings, Nastya didn't have a family of her own. Long ago, when they still lived in Russia, she was married and had a daughter, but her little girl and husband both died from typhoid fever. She remarried once, but her second husband turned out to be a scoundrel who stole her savings and disappeared. After that she devoted herself and her unspent love to her siblings and their families.

During those tragic days, besides me, Aunt Nastya also had to watch after her younger sister.

The night of the earthquake, Aunt Nastya had been at Aunt Pasha's home, helping with her kids. Tanya, Pasha's eighteen-month-old daughter, had a fever. To give Aunt Pasha some rest, Aunt Nastya took the girl to her bed. When the first violent jolt awakened her, she grabbed the girl and tried to get up, but falling rubble pinned them to the bed.

She always cried when she remembered what happened next. "Dust was so thick that it was almost impossible to breathe. Tanya's face was pressed against my chest. She was suffocating, but I wasn't able to move a finger to help her. Her body stretched, she peed on my nightgown, and went silent."

They found Aunt Nastya and Tanya on the third day. My aunt had a permanent dark spot on her chest where her dead niece's head had been pressed for such a long time.

Aunt Pasha's older daughter, Lida, slept in her own bed. When the earthquake hit, a carpet that hung on the wall fell on top of her. She didn't have a scratch on her body when they found her. Like her younger sister, she died of asphyxiation.

Distraught with grief over losing both of her strawberry-blond, blue-eyed daughters, all Aunt Pasha could do was stare off into nowhere and call out their names. Sometimes she suddenly began laughing, which scared everybody even more. They say there were many people like her in the city after the earthquake. Time cured some of them, including Pasha, while others were never the same again.

In the middle of December, Papa returned from the hospital. Two weeks later he went to Baku to bring Mama home. My reunion with her was emotional for both of us. She reached out her hands to me, tears running down her cheeks.

"Milenka, come to your Mama! Don't you recognize me?"

I cried, clinging to my Aunt Nastya's skirt, scared of this strange person who looked like a boy in women's clothes. Aunt Nastya gently pushed me forward. "Don't be scared, dear. It's your Mama. Go and give her a hug."

"No," I yelled, hiding my face. "No, my Mama is pretty. She has hair."

"Don't get upset, Valya," Aunt Nastya comforted Mama. "Give her some time. Three months is a very long time for a baby. Besides, it's hard even for me to recognize you—thin like a stick and no hair. You do look different."

Mama sighed. "They were too busy to think about our hair. There were hundreds of us, and people were dying. The first thing they did was shave every bedridden woman's hair to avoid lice. Actually, they sheared me like a sheep, using scissors."

They sat silently for a moment, watching me suspiciously peek out from my hiding place.

"How is she doing? Does she still cough?" Mama asked.

"She is fine. Her cough is gone, and she doesn't let me sit for a minute. Now, instead of the *Kurochka Ryaba* fairytale, she lists all our dead by name. 'Grandpa died, Grandma died, Aunt Marfa died . . . ' All nine of them, and she repeats 'died' after each name. She doesn't have any idea what it means. She recites it like a poem and laughs, pleased with herself."

"You said nine? Who else?" Mama asked.

"Sorry, Valya. I didn't want to write you about it while you were in the hospital. Boris's daughter, Lyuda, was also killed."

"Oh, no." Mama closed her eyes and kept them shut until she could speak again. "My poor brother. Have you seen him and Nina?"

"No. They left Ashkhabad soon after they buried their daughter. A lot of people have left since the earthquake. They're scared of another one."

Aunt Nastya and Mama grew silent.

People left Ashkhabad by the hundreds every day. My Papa, Mama, and I joined them in January, shortly after Mama came home from the hospital. We moved to Kuybyshev, one of the largest Russian cities located in the southwest of Russia, on the east bank of the Volga River. I don't know why my parents chose that place, in the middle of the freezing winter. The winter clothes my parents brought from Ashkhabad were "made of fish fur," as Mama would say, not nearly warm enough for the severe Russian climate. While it snowed sometimes in Turkmenistan, the temperatures rarely stayed below freezing.

In that frosty Kuybyshev winter I turned two, and was oblivious to all the difficulties my parents went through. Mama's short hair had grown back, and she became the most beautiful mother in the whole world again. She and I stayed in a rented room in a house on the outskirts of the city. Papa found a job as an aviation mechanic at the aerodrome.

He walked three kilometers to and from work every day. He left in the dark of early morning and came back home when Mama was putting me to bed. Within days, Papa's ears and toes were frostbitten, and my parents spent much of his first paycheck on a rabbit fur hat with flaps and a pair of warm boots that were too small for him.

We stayed in Kuybyshev for five long months. My parents struggled the entire time with weather and loneliness. Letters from Ashkhabad described a life that was picking up again. The surviving Kondeykins lived in a barrack they built from whatever material they could salvage from the ruins. They went to work in the morning and came home in the evening to the kids who made it through the disaster. They cooked, washed their clothes, and started again the next day. It helped them pull through the grief and slowly come back to life.

Reading the letters from their loved ones, my parents realized that though they were born in Russia, their roots had grown deep in Turkmenistan—that remote, torrid land which was now dear to them not only because of their childhood memories, but also as the place where their parents lay in rest and where their friends and relatives continued their everyday struggles.

When Aunt Nastya wrote that the Turkmen government was giving subsidies to earthquake victims to build new houses, that settled it.

"I cannot stand it anymore," Papa said at dinner, looking into Mama's red eyes. "We don't belong in Russia. Let's go home."

Days later, we listened to the measured clicking of train wheels on rails and watched the landscape outside the window change from the mighty Volga River and small, wooden houses of the Russian countryside to the vast steppe of Kazakhstan, and then the plains of Uzbekistan, and finally the boundless yellow sands of the Kara-Kum Desert of Turkmenistan.

As our train slowly rolled into Ashkhabad, my parents stood in the car vestibule with their luggage on the floor and me on Papa's forearm. They saw building carcasses with empty window sockets, chimneys of destroyed factories, and piles of rubbish. Eight months was too short a period for the wounds of the earthquake to heal. But Papa and Mama also saw children walking home from school, men and women busily working in their yards, trucks loaded with building materials, and city buses running along the streets. The warm air, heavy with the fragrance of blooming acacia trees, wafted inside the train car. Ashkhabad was alive.

It was June of 1949. We were home again.

6: The New House

The Kondeykins settled us in a tiny room of the rough building where all of Papa's siblings and their families lived. The men were reserved when they were sober, but at supper, when vodka loosened their tongues, they remembered their dead parents and kids. They talked about their vanished friends and drank for the repose of their souls. For centuries, vodka had been a painkiller, a tranquilizer, and a sleeping pill for all troubles and injustice in Russia. Once again, it helped them if not forget, at least to dull their dolor.

A few weeks after we returned to Ashkhabad, Papa came home with a smile on his face. He scooped Mama up and danced her around our small room. "I'm done with the paperwork," he laughed. "On Monday I will get a lot and a plan of our house. Then we can start building."

"Oh, it sounds like a fairytale." Mama laughed, as well, for the first time in a long time. "We'll have a house of our own."

"I got an adjacent lot with Peotr," Papa told her. "Mikhail and Nikolai have lots next to each other just a block away."

The happy smile on Mama's face faded. "No, Vanya. Please don't do it. We need to have a life of our own. I want to live separately."

"Why? Don't you like my family?" Papa asked, his own mood darkening.

"Don't start that again. I just don't want our daughter to grow up listening to your drunken talks and seeing your fights with each other."

"You want me to tell them, 'Sorry, brothers, but my wife doesn't want to live close to you'?"

"Listen to me, Vanya. It's not about me, it's about our daughter. I know how much you love Mila, and how much you care about her future. You're twenty-eight years old, and you have your own family. You can be a good brother without sitting with them and drinking every night."

Mama won. When Papa came back a week later, he had a government-issued blueprint and an address—108, Bagirskaya Street—a block away from Mikhail and Nikolai and two blocks away from Peotr, Pasha, and Nastya. There would be lots of walking back and forth, but from then on, we had our own private branch of the big Kondeykin clan. Mama became its tireless guardian angel and Papa its reliable benefactor.

When my parents went to see the plot the government had given them, they found three small *vremyankas* (temporary structures) already there, with families of earthquake survivors residing in them. Papa was told that the squatters would be relocated from our lot as soon as they received government housing.

It sounds strange today, but at the time, there was never a question about making squatters move. The people of Ashkhabad had been through hell together, and there was a sense of fraternity among us. Besides, there was nowhere else for the survivors to go until the government gave them a new home. My parents simply built our house beside their shacks, encircled all of the structures with an adobe wall, and shared the small yard.

It would take over a decade before two of the squatting families were finally relocated to new, government-built apartment complexes. The third family stayed even longer.

Ded Vasiliy and Baba Masha were too old to move out. Although the couple had no children of their own, everyone—even my parents—called them *Ded* and *Baba* (grandpa and grandma). He was a tall and lean-as-a-stick old man with a shy smile and soft voice. One of his legs was broken during the earthquake, which left him with a permanent limp. He died when I was in middle school. Baba Masha looked like a puffy cotton ball, slowly rolling along and talking to herself if there were no spare ears around to listen. She lived in the clay hut in the corner of our yard for two decades until her death.

Papa began the construction of our new house at the beginning of October, one year after the earthquake. We were the last family on the block to be given a lot. When he started, most of our neighbors had the foundations of their houses finished. But Papa soon caught up.

"Look, Dusya," said a neighbor to his wife. "See? That tall guy is here again."

"Which one? That one with the hat?" his wife asked. Papa became well known on the block for his straw hat, which was replaced with a felt one later in the season. The Hat came and went, bringing truckloads of sand, bricks, and planks. The Hat shouted orders, helped to unload a truck, carried beams, measured something, then disappeared and came back with a helper or a tool he needed. Neighbors watched the speed with which our house progressed and shook their heads.

We celebrated my third birthday in our new house. It was still under construction, but there was a roof above our heads, and

Mama declared that was all a person needed for a home. It was a sturdy brick building consisting of a bedroom, living room, kitchen, and small veranda. Papa reinforced it with metal rods and seismic belts in case of another earthquake. We shared an outhouse in the yard with the squatters.

A Holland heater—a brick oven built into the wall between our two rooms—kept our house warm on cold winter days, and this is the first memory that I am sure is my own: a frosty morning when I woke to the sounds of Mama getting ready to start a fire—opening and closing the front door, clanging a metal scoop against a bucket, and thumping the heavy bucket of coal down on the metal sheet nailed to the floor in front of the burner.

In the darkness, I climbed down from my battered metal bed and pitter-pattered with bare feet across our wood floor.

"Oh, Milenka, it's freezing here. Why don't you stay in bed until I'm done?" Mama snatched me from the cold floor, wrapped me with a plush jacket that still bore the warmth of her body and perched me on a stool to watch.

The cast iron door of the heater made a squeaky sound when she opened it, reminding me of the gaping maw of a wild animal.

I watched Mama put small slivers of wood on top of wadded old newspapers and light a match. The fire quickly burned the paper, spread to the thin slivers, and started licking bigger pieces of wood underneath. She closed the door of the burner, wiped the metal sheet and the floor around it with a damp cloth, put all the utensils in the bucket, and took it back outside.

The crackling of the wood, the hissing of the sap, and the smell of the burning fire filled the room with life and warmth. I sat on my stool waiting for Mama to come back. I knew what would happen next. She reappeared and removed the down shawl from her head. "Now I'll warm up my hands and help my little girl get dressed." She turned her back to the heater and stood there, touching its shiny warm surface with her palms, her eyes closed.

It is one of the very few memories I have of Mama in an idle pose.

That first winter in our new house, Mama became pregnant. Smells of food made her feel sick, so she was not able to continue her work as a waitress. When the restaurant where she worked offered her a temporary position as a cashier, she gladly accepted it.

Mama's responsibility was to collect the profit the restaurant made each day, complete the receipt vouchers, sum everything up on a deposit slip, and turn over the proceeds to the restaurant's accountant. Mama was sharp and quick to learn. Before her mother died, she'd studied in a financial school and still remembered some of the basics. When some of the financial transactions in the restaurant didn't make sense, Mama asked her new boss.

"Don't bother with it for now," the accountant told her with a sweet smile. "When you come back from your maternity leave, you'll learn some specifics of our work. Now, concentrate on your pregnancy and your future baby."

Five months later, the restaurant was audited by the OBKhSS, the Department Against Misappropriation of Socialist Property. The department's purpose was the prevention of economic crimes against state property. As there were no private businesses allowed in the Soviet Union, everything from a tiny barber shop to a powerful factory was state-owned and state-controlled. Any financial violations were considered crimes against the state.

Just mentioning the OBKhSS terrified people, especially those who worked in a field involving any kind of financial transactions.

The OBKhSS discovered the discrepancies that Mama had noticed and arrested the accountant on suspicion of financial fraud. Several days later, they summoned Mama and the director for questioning.

Mama was terrified. In the Soviet Union, being questioned for a crime was the same as being charged. The OBKhSS officer who conducted interrogations pressured her to confess that she was a part of a criminal group engaged in money embezzlement. He threatened Mama that if she didn't admit her guilt, he would make sure she didn't see her children and husband for a long time.

"I was innocent," Mama would tell me later. "I was young and naïve, and that accountant set me up. I became her accomplice."

Mama cried through the last trimester of her pregnancy, fretting about what would happen to me and to her unborn baby if she was convicted. She was heavily pregnant when the trial took place. The accountant was convicted and sentenced to prison. Mama was found guilty of criminal negligence, forced to pay restitution to the state to cover a part of financial losses, and prohibited from working in the financial system for ten years.

Years later, I discovered that everything would have been much worse, but my father bribed a high-ranking OBKhSS official.

Shortly after the trial, Mama delivered Igor, my baby brother. He was born with a congenital heart defect and died nine months later. My parents buried him in the same grave as our grandparents and cousins, adding his name on the metal plaque below the long list of earthquake victims. Mama never talked about Igor, except to say that he was a beautiful baby with huge, sad dark eyes, as if he knew his fate.

"It was you who brought me back to life," she would say to me. "You were a small, happy ball of energy who needed lots of love and attention. You wouldn't let me sit there and brood over my misfortunes. I had to go on."

7: They Won't Bite You

I was four years old when our family's life took a sudden turn. As a result of Mama's trial, my parents had incurred debts. They were broke, the construction of our house was frozen, and Mama was jobless. Looking for a way out of this situation, Papa made the risky decision to leave his job, borrow more money, and start a honey business.

Stepan and Dusya Scherbakov lived one lot past ours, and they quickly became my parents' close friends. They had two children, twelve-year-old Alla and three-year-old Anatoliy, who everyone called Tolik. He was a gentle child with lazy movements and a soft smile, and he became my first real friend.

The Scherbakovs were beekeepers, and Stepan convinced Papa to buy a small apiary and become his partner.

Although no private businesses were officially allowed in the Soviet Union at that time, beekeeping was a unique case. The Soviet Union had one-third of the honeybee population of the entire world, and our honey was a source of national pride. In 1919, Vladimir Lenin signed The Decree on the Protection of Beekeeping, which gave every Soviet citizen the right to own an apiary of any size and to place them on state land in any town or city. All special taxes were abolished.

This was unheard-of freedom in a tightly-regulated society like ours, but not everyone could afford buying bees and all the necessary equipment to engage in beekeeping. In addition, beekeeping was a hard business, especially in Turkmenistan. Exhausting weather conditions, poor roads, the absence of beehive trailers, and the need to move frequently from place to place without basic conveniences scared people off. But not my fearless Papa. I never saw him back down from a challenge.

"Who doesn't venture gets nothing," he told Mama when she expressed her concern.

Beekeeping would make us a half-nomadic family. From October to April, Papa explained to me, we would live in our house, and the rest of the time we would move with our apiary, taking it from one field to another in search of a good honey harvest.

Stepan and his wife, Dusya, were happy to help my parents and, at the same time, acquire reliable business partners. They lent Papa money to buy ten beehives with two bee colonies in each, and the most essential equipment to start the business—an old military tent, wooden barrels for keeping honey, and a honey extractor. The Scherbakovs shared other equipment—bee-wax comb foundations and frames, a smoke fan, and special knives—until my parents had enough money to buy their own.

One morning, I woke up to find a row of long boxes in our yard. Each beehive was painted in two different colors—half white and half light blue or green. The design wasn't for beauty, Mama explained, but for the bees. Because two different colonies lived in each hive, the colors made it easier for them to find their own homes.

The bees were busily entering or exiting their houses through long, shallow slits at the bottom of the hives. Each slit had a small latch, which Mama showed me she could slide to make the entrance wider or narrower, depending on the weather conditions or the traffic of bees. Several bees sat at each doorway.

"Why aren't they flying?" I asked.

"They're guards," Mama said. "They check that every bee entering the hive belongs to their family. If they find a stranger, they don't let her inside their house."

I was hesitant to get too close to the hives.

"Don't be afraid of honeybees," she said. "They're kind. They'll never sting you if you don't threaten them. Don't hurt them, don't wave your hands when you're around them, and don't try to catch them."

She was right. Over the twenty years I spent around honeybees, not one of the multiple stings I got was due to their aggression. Our Caucasian bees (originally from the high valleys of the Caucasus) were good-natured and gentle species. They became agitated only when they were hungry because there were not enough flowers for them to feed their families.

That spring went by quickly as my parents prepared for our first long business trip. While our honeybees worked busily on blooming ailanthus trees in the city, Mama sewed covers for the beehives, mended the old military tent that Papa had traded for two bottles of vodka with a Soviet army officer, bought and packed dry food, and cooked lamb *kaurma*, which could be stored in jars in its own fat for a long time. Papa made tent pegs, fixed hives, checked that the latches on the bee entrances slid properly, and prepared the barrels.

Having worked in a beer bar, he knew exactly how to handle the big barrels, which bulged in the middle. Papa said that would make it easier to roll and turn them, even when they were full and heavy. He tightened the metal hoops to close small chinks between the staves, so they wouldn't leak.

Excited with the prospect of going somewhere new, Tolik and I "helped" by running around, gathering our toys and books, and putting them into big cardboard boxes.

It took weeks for Papa and Uncle Stepan to get passes from the Ministry of Internal Affairs for us to travel into the Kopet Dag

Mountains, where we would take our apiaries each spring. This was a frontier zone that separated the Soviet Union and Iran. It was guarded by Soviet border troops, and no one could get into the mountain area without special permits. Every year, Papa had to go from one bureaucrat to another, filing papers and waiting in lines until, at last, he came home with the passes.

We left in the middle of April. Just before dusk, when the last bees had returned home after their busy working day, Papa went around the beehives with a flashlight, a hammer, and a box of tiny nails. He closed and secured the notches while Mama used a bee smoker to force the remaining bees inside the hive. From time to time, I heard Papa's muffled curses and Mama's yelp when one of them was stung.

It was well past my bedtime when Papa and Uncle Nikolai, who had come to help, finished loading the truck that waited to take us away: first beehives and apiary supplies, then cots, multiple crates with dishes, food supplies, a kerosene primus stove, and our clothes and bedding. When the truck was full, they tied everything with ropes, and we were ready to go. Mama lifted me into the cabin beside the driver and then climbed in herself. Papa instructed the driver to follow the truck with Scherbakov's apiary, and then he climbed on top of the load in the back. Off we went into the darkness of the night.

My memory of that night is of bumpy, dusty country roads, uncertain beams of light searching the way, frequent stops to check if we were on the right track, turning back and finding the right road if we were lost, fear that we could tip over when the track careened down hilly slopes, and the wail of a tired engine.

We were bound for the Kopet Dag mountains, which were covered with a lush carpet of bright green grasses and wildflowers.

We were close to the border here, and checkpoints were a worry. Even at age four, I knew that something important was happening. I sat wary on Mama's lap while Papa showed young guards in green uniforms our documents and passes. When they came up to our truck, flashing lights in our faces, Mama stopped talking with the driver. Feeling the importance of the moment, I tried to make my best and most innocent face.

The checkpoints were never quick. The guards would take our papers to their small booth so that they could call somebody somewhere. While we waited, Papa would throw in a name or two. "I know the boss of your Komarovka outpost. Just last week we sat in a restaurant and drank vodka together." Papa didn't lie. He knew half the population of Ashkhabad, and he was friends with all kinds of people, including military, militia, and KGB officers. And they did drink together—a Soviet man couldn't call another man a friend if they'd never shared vodka.

Eventually, a *shlagbaum* (border barrier) would be raised, and our trucks would continue deeper into the mountains. I woke and fell back to sleep to the sounds of an engine straining up the hill while Mama tried to shift me to the other side of her lap when her arm got numb holding me.

At last, our truck stopped. I sat up, awakened by a sudden stillness.

"We have arrived, Milenka," she said.

The driver turned the lights off. In the pitch dark, Mama opened the truck door and lowered me to the ground. After hours in the howling truck, the silence was deafening. Slowly, I started distinguishing strange sounds—the singing of crickets, barely audible sounds of insects, soft gurgling of water, and the rustle of grasses in the breeze. Above the dark silhouettes of the mountains, I saw the sky.

"Mama, what is that?"

"Stars, my dear."

"Why are they so close?"

"Because we're in the mountains. The air is clean here and there are no city lights, so you can see them better."

The men untied the ropes and pulled the boxes from the trucks. Mama and Aunt Dusya carried everything to a tarp they spread on the ground. The first thing they did was pull out a mattress, covers, and pillows to make a bed for me and Tolik. They told us to crawl inside.

"I'm still in my dress, Mama," I said.

"Never mind, my dear. You'll sleep dressed tonight."

I fell asleep on the spot and didn't see how our apiary was unloaded. Our exhausted parents carried our beehives and put them in two neat, parallel rows, then installed the tent, made beds, and carried me inside. Mama and Papa didn't sleep all night, and when dawn broke they still had a lot of things to do—open the beehive notches, bring water from the quick and shallow mountain river, cut back the tall grass in front of the apiary and the tent, and put an awning above the living area that would become our kitchen and dining room.

In the morning, I woke up alone and couldn't understand where I was. I heard the singing of birds, the soft buzz of honeybees, and my parents' voices.

The sun was already high in the sky, and when I came out of our tent, I had to squint. The trucks were gone. Our apiary was in a narrow valley surrounded by mountains covered with tall grasses and flowers. On one side of the apiary there was a dirt road, and on the other, a shallow mountain river. Weeping willows hung low over the water, reaching their long, drooping branches to the cold stream. Both the river and the road wound away and disappeared in the distance where the mountain ranges came together.

All day, Tolik and I played, following our mothers' order not to wander from the apiaries. Our parents were too busy and too exhausted to pay much attention to us.

The next morning, after we finished breakfast, Mama took me for a walk. It was warm, but not as warm as it was in the city, and I had to wear a thin jacket. Startled by our approach, grasshoppers sprang in all directions: small green and gray ones hopped, larger, brown ones flew away with a rattle, suddenly revealing their bright red underwings. Because of that color, Tolik and I would later call them firefighters.

Mama and I stopped several times to watch honeybees working on the flowers. Some of them gathered nectar, going deep inside flowers with their proboscises, while others worked on stamens, collecting pollen in orange and yellow balls around their tiny legs.

We meandered up a narrow path created by unknown animals. I picked small flowers and handed them to Mama. She admired their color and fragrance and collected them in a bouquet, which, she said, we would put into water when we got back.

I was several steps ahead of Mama when I saw something gray lay coiled in my way. I stopped, thinking how to pass it, when it started moving, slowly uncoiling itself in front of me. The thicker end of it lifted and I saw two small eyes staring at me. It made a hissing sound, moved its triangular head forward, and froze.

"Mama," I cried out. "Look! It has eyes!"

"Don't move!" Mama said firmly. "Give me your hand." She spoke like this only when she was displeased with me, but I didn't know what I had done wrong. Mama took my hand and slowly pulled me back.

"It's a snake," she explained, her voice steady. "Let's show her that we don't want to hurt her."

"Will she bite me?" I asked.

"No. If you don't run or make noise, she won't bite you." Cautiously, without taking her eyes off the snake, she reached down and scooped me off my feet. She didn't put me down until we reached our tent. There, she sat me on a folding chair, took a kettle, and poured herself a cup of water. Her hands were shaking.

When Mama described our encounter to Papa, he said that it was *gjurza,* a blunt-nosed viper, one of the world's most venomous snakes.

Like our honeybees, Papa assured me, a snake would not bite me unless I threatened it.

"It's some people you have to be scared of," Papa said that day. "They can bite you without reason. A snake would never do it."

"Why?" I asked.

"Never mind, Milenka," Mama said. "Papa was just joking."

When the mountain flowers began shedding their blossoms and the grass on the slopes lost its gloss and turned brown, it was time to move our apiary. One early morning, Papa and Uncle Stepan went in search of a new place. Mama and Aunt Dusya spent a day inserting small pegs between honey frames in the hives so they wouldn't press into each other during transportation and smash the bees.

The men returned the next day and began dismantling our tent and the canopies. Mama packed boxes. Before dusk, two trucks arrived from Komarovka, a nearby settlement, to take our apiaries to the Kara-Kum Desert, where the camel thorn was about to start blooming.

8: Wind, Wind, Calm Down

In the mornings, when the sun began its business of searing the Kara-Kum Desert, the cool night air clashing with the warm front often gave birth to whirlwinds. They started waltzing around, coming closer to our apiary, passing by, and going away. Small cyclones sucked and spun dust, dry grasses, and pieces of shed snake skins before they died out. The large ones looked like giant pillars between the earth and the sky, slowly rolling over the plain. Those drew our attention. My parents watched them, commenting on the direction they moved and guessing their distance from us.

The whirlwinds didn't bother me as much as *sukhovey*, the dry wind of the desert, which came out of nowhere and raged for hours and sometimes days. The honeybees all stayed in their hives when the *sukhovey* picked up. It lashed my skin, threw sand in my eyes, and pricked my cheeks with billions of tiny needles. Its writhing fury made me miserable.

During one stormy afternoon that first summer in the desert, I lay on my stomach on my camp cot inside the tent. My face was buried in a pillow, palms pressed against my ears, and eyes shut tight. It was hot and difficult to breathe, but I was afraid to move. With every raging gust, the walls of the tent shuddered and its edges beat against the ground. The reed canopy over our beehives was untangling, slamming against the metal poles, and my parents had run into the storm, trying to catch the loose ends and tie them back before the whole structure collapsed. I could hear them shouting at each other over all the noise.

"*Veter, veter, potikhon'ku* (Wind, wind, calm down)," I chanted into the hot pillow. "*Veter, veter, potikhon'ku.*"

I kept pleading until all sounds became muffled, my parents' voices melted away, and I fell asleep.

When I woke up, the wind was gone. In the stillness, I could hear the singing of the birds and the droning buzz of our bees, back outside and at work. My parents sat next to the tent, drinking tea and talking in half voices about how to repair the damage.

"Mama," I called, "is it over?"

"Yes, Milenka. You've slept through it all. Come out. We'll be having supper soon."

A month after we returned from our first summer in the fields, the November weather was still balmy. The sun warmed my back and neck through my plush jacket, and the bittersweet smell of burning leaves hung in the air, tickling my throat and stinging my eyes.

Mama was inside, measuring, cutting and sewing on her Singer machine, making baby-size straw mattresses to put under the lid of each beehive to keep our honeybees warm during winter. Papa had gone with Uncle Stepan to the railway freight yard to buy coal for the winter.

"I'll be back soon," Papa had said. "If a truck with the coal arrives before us, tell the driver to unload it in front of the gate. When I come, we'll carry it into the shed."

The trucks arrived. They dumped the coal in two big, shiny piles on Bagirskaya Street, one in front of the Scherbakov's house and the other one at our gate. The drivers got their tips and drove away.

When our fathers didn't show up by the middle of the afternoon, Mama and Aunt Dusya started worrying. "If we don't carry the coal inside the shed by dark, we won't find half of it here tomorrow morning," Aunt Dusya said. "Where are those husbands of ours?"

"Let's start moving your pile without them," Mama suggested. "They'll finish the rest when they come."

Aunt Dusya brought buckets and shovels. Mama went home to change and returned wearing black breeches, an old jacket, and galoshes. While our mothers loaded and lugged the heavy buckets to the shed at the far end of the yard, Tolik and I ran along with our toy pails, trying to help. "Good job," our mamas praised us, laughing at our smudged faces and black hands.

Soon, Tolik and I found more important things to do. Our mothers moved slower and didn't laugh anymore. Sweat ran down their faces, leaving dirty streaks on their cheeks. They stopped from time to time to rest their hands and get their breath back.

Only after half of the heap had disappeared into the shed did our fathers show up, reeling up the street. Aunt Dusya saw them first.

"Look at our helpers," she whispered. "Drunk as pigs. The street isn't wide enough for them."

"Papa!" Tolik and I shouted as we chased each other to meet our fathers. Mine reached into the pocket of his pants and pulled out a chocolate bar, disfigured by his body heat.

"Here, Chocolate Baby. It's your daily ration," he said slowly. "Show me how you love your Papa." He pulled me up. I threw my arms around his neck and hugged him with all my strength. Holding me in his arms, he continued to weave toward Mama.

"Valya, your husband came home," Papa announced.

"Such happiness," Mama said, but she didn't look happy at all. "Vanya, let the girl go. You're drunk. You can drop her."

"I wouldn't drop her even if I were dead," he said, grinning widely. "She's my little daughter. I'll kill anyone who would even think of hurting her."

"Mila, come to me." Mama reached to Papa to take me.

Probably he was still holding me when she pulled and that made him lose his balance. It all happened quickly. Papa swayed and then flopped onto the heap of coal—first on his butt, and then his shoulders and head followed in slow motion. His felt hat slipped from his head and rolled down the pile.

"Oh, my God," Mama cried out. "Your new suit!" Both women burst into nervous laughter.

Slowly, Papa struggled up to his feet, trying hard to keep his balance. He was no longer smiling. His teeth and fists were clenched, and his glassy eyes froze on Mama.

Her smile faded from her face.

Back on his feet, he charged towards her, like an outraged bull.

"Run, Valya," Aunt Dusya shouted. "Run inside."

Mama, still holding me, rushed into the Scherbakovs' house. Aunt Dusya followed with Tolik in tow. She shut the door and turned the key just a moment before Papa grabbed its handle. Through their veranda windows I saw him wrench it again and again. The door trembled under his pressure.

"Open the door," he roared. "Open the fucking door, Dusya, or I'll break it!"

"Calm down, Ivan. I'll open it if you promise not to hurt your wife," Aunt Dusya shouted back.

"Leave the women alone, Ivan." Uncle Stepan tried to pull Papa aside. "Let's go and have another drink."

Papa cursed and pushed him away. "Come out, Valya, or I'll break the door. I will count to three."

Mama pressed me tighter against her chest and stepped back. She was shaking. A moment before, everything had felt like a game, but now I was terrified.

"One—" I heard him counting.

"Two—" Mama darted like a frightened bird and froze again.

"Three!"

Without waiting another second, he head-butted the door, and with a loud thud, wooden planks and pieces of glass flew in all directions. Through an opening in the broken glass, he stuck his hand inside, turned the latch, and barged into the room.

Terrified, I screamed.

Papa stopped. His huge fist froze in midair. He stared at me.

"Put her down," he ordered. Mama didn't move. "I said put her down," he repeated.

"Do you want to kill me?" Mama's voice rang with emotion. "Then kill both of us. I don't want our daughter to be motherless with a father like you."

Horrified, I gripped Mama's neck and buried my face into her shoulder. "*Veter, veter, potikhon'ku,*" I started my chant, believing it would carry me away to a safer place, as it always did when I was scared.

I don't know what happened next. When I came to from my trance, the storm was over. Mama hugged me, crying quietly. Aunt Dusya swept pieces of glass from the floor, and Papa was gone.

Mama and I spent that night at the Scherbakovs' house. I could not fall asleep for a long time, and I don't know if she ever went to bed. Every time I closed my eyes, a monster with bloody eyes appeared and reached his arms to grab me. I shuddered and opened my eyes.

I heard Mama and Aunt Dusya talking in the living room.

"If I had a place to go, I would have left him long ago," Mama said. "But he and Milochka are my only family."

"Your Ivan is a fool only when he is drunk. Look at my husband—he can be mean even when he is sober. I have to swallow his insults and stay nice to him."

"A spoonful of tar spoils a barrel of honey," Mama said. They went silent, and I wondered if they were drinking tea with honey there.

Aunt Dusya finally said, "Look at the other families. Husbands drink. They don't care if their kids have enough food or nice clothes to wear. They work only to satisfy their own throats. Ours are good family men, and they're great fathers."

"That's true," Mama said. "But I'd be the happiest of women if Ivan didn't drink."

When I got up in the morning, Mama was not there. She came back later and took me home. Papa sat at the dinner table with a pitcher of water and a glass in front of him. He wore a clean shirt and pants, and his head was bandaged.

For a couple of days, Papa didn't play or kid with me. He avoided Mama's eyes and looked guilty all the time. Her lips were pressed and her voice had metal when she spoke. My fear went away. I felt sorry for him.

9: Honey for Uncle Stalin

Tolik and I had two friends who also lived on our street, Borka and Tolyan. The four of us were all about the same age, born shortly after the end of the Great Patriotic War when our fathers came back from the front.

Tolyan was the son of one of the families squatting in our yard. His mother worked as a janitor at a local school, and his father was some kind of laborer who often came home drunk. Borka lived over the fence from Tolik with his grandmother, older sister, and his senile great-grandfather who always sat on a bench near their house and greeted passersby, lifting his hat over his head. Borka's parents died in the earthquake when he was two years old.

We spent our days doing all the silly things five-year-olds do when their parents let them loose—running, jumping, climbing, or digging in the dirt. Our mothers grew alert when we became quiet. As soon as we had a good idea, Mama would be on the porch, shouting, "What are you doing? Why are you hiding, Mila? What's in your hands, Tolik? Come here and show me that thing!"

The rest of the children on our street were either much younger than us or much older, like my friends' teenage sisters. They were the prematurely grown children of the war, with eyes too serious for their age and memories of times too hard for us to understand.

The older kids often talked about the birthday "cakes" their mothers made for them during the war—a piece of heavy black bread barely sprinkled with sugar. For my fifth birthday, Papa brought home a tall layered cake baked in the shape of the Kremlin Tower, with a red caramel star on top. It was made by a pastry chef who used to work at the restaurant with my parents. While not all of my peers' parents could afford to order a cake like mine for their kids' birthdays, they could all buy a simple one at the bakery or buy the ingredients to make a cake at home. My friends and I didn't know what it was like to go for days without food. We were a new breed of Soviet children, the happy and carefree sons and daughters of the victorious country.

Uncle Stalin was our *Vozhd'* (Leader). We had loved Uncle Stalin for as long as we could remember. Waking up in the morning, we heard his voice on the radio. We saw his portraits everywhere. We recognized his figure on pedestals in squares and parks. We sang songs and memorized poems about him. We couldn't imagine our lives without him, as we couldn't imagine it without our mamas and papas.

A normal afternoon found us sitting in a circle in Tolik's backyard. "My Papa is brave. He shot down millions of German planes. He beat the whole army," I said.

"Your father is not a general. Only generals can beat the army," objected Tolyan. He was the smartest of us. He knew all the letters of the alphabet and could read. His mother sometimes brought home books from the school where she worked. The books were old and some didn't have jackets, but they had lots of pictures, and Tolyan sat for hours, turning pages. At first, he just looked at pictures, but then he learned letters and started slowly putting them into words. Even his mother was surprised. "Nobody taught him how to read," she told Mama.

"Stalin is the most important general," Tolyan continued. "They call him *Generalissimus*." He pronounced this difficult word slowly and deliberately, as if it was made of glass and he was afraid of breaking it. "He defeated the Germans and killed all their commanders. He won the war."

"Yes, I know," I agreed. I had heard Papa saying that if it was not for Stalin, we wouldn't have won the war. "But my papa helped Uncle Stalin win the war. Uncle Stalin gave him many orders and medals for it."

This time, no one objected. Papa's war medals and orders were stored in a shoebox in my parents' bedroom chiffonier. When we played in our house, I'd bring the box out, and we'd hang those medals on our chests, imagining ourselves as war heroes.

"Stalin is the strongest man in the whole world," Borka said. "All enemies are afraid of him."

"And he's the most handsome," added Tolik. "When I grow up, I'll have a mustache like his." I looked at Tolik, trying to picture Stalin's bushy mustache on his round, dainty face. I wished I could also say something like that, but girls didn't grow mustaches.

Instead, I got up and loudly recited a poem from my picture book called *Ya Zhivu v Moskve* (I Live in Moscow). Mama read it to me so often that I had memorized almost all the poems in it.

У стен кремлевских	At the Kremlin wall,
Запели трубы.	Trumpets burst into singing.
Столице славу	The glory to our capital
Горнист поёт.	The trumpeters sing.
Еще сильнее	We love Moscow
Москву мы любим	Even more,
За то, что Сталин	Because Moscow is
В Москве живет	Where Stalin lives.[3]

---

3 *Ya Zhivu v Moskve* was written in 1949 by Soviet poet and children's writer Agniya Barto. The translation is mine.

"I love Stalin so much," said Borka. "More than anyone else."

"Me too," the boys echoed.

"When I grow up a little, I'll take a train to the Kremlin and bring Uncle Stalin a present," I said.

"What present?" the boys asked in unison.

"Flowers and a big jar of honey."

The boys sat silently, thinking.

"Can I go with you?" Tolik asked. "I can help you carry the honey."

"All right, let's go all together," I agreed. "Uncle Stalin will be so glad to see us."

We promised not to tell anybody about our upcoming trip and, pleased with ourselves, started to run around the yard, chasing one another.

10: The Deficit

"Valya, they've thrown cheese into our store," our neighbor shouted from her yard. "I'm running there to get a place in line. Do you want to send Mila with me?"

"Milenka," Mama called me. "Go with Aunt Maria and get in line. Hold two spots. I'll come when I finish ironing. Take an *avos'ka* with you." She handed me a string shopping bag. *Avos'* in Russian means "maybe." People in Ashkhabad always carried a "maybe shopping bag" with them in case they got lucky and could *maybe* buy something during their lunchtime or on the way home from work.

Cheese was something I knew was a *deficit*. As a child, I thought the word *deficit* meant something delicious or special, because people were always eager to run and buy it. Later, I understood that the adults used *deficit* to refer to anything that was often missing from our stores—soap, toothpaste, lightbulbs, linen sheets, towels, toilet paper, children's stockings, and many food items. We never knew what would go missing next.

Everyone scoured stores for the products they needed, and if they were lucky enough to find it, they would buy as much as possible in case it disappeared again. Because stores were only permitted to sell a limited amount of deficit goods "in the same hands," which meant to a single person, standing in line became part of every Soviet child's life. We were an extra pair of hands to buy an additional portion of whatever was in short supply. I was particularly proud when I could help Mama buy ten bottles of cooking oil or twenty lightbulbs at a time.

Papa refused to stand in the lines. Instead, he acquired deficit items from his acquaintances and friends, or he got things like a fifty-kilogram (110-pound) sack of flour "from the back door" by overpaying.

When a missing item suddenly appeared, we said it had been thrown into the store. News would spread around the neighborhood, and a stream of people, adults and kids alike, would rush to get in line. Depending on what was missing and for how long, queues could be several hours long. The mood of a line depended on the quantity of the product in the store—would it be enough for everyone? The crowd grew irritated when rumor said that the commodity was getting short. There was nothing more annoying than being in line for half a day, and then seeing a deficit sell out right in front of your nose, sending you home empty-handed.

Some people tried to hold lines in two, three, or even more queues of different departments or neighboring stores. They walked back and forth between them, holding their place in all locations. So even visibly short queues sometimes moved slowly. Tempers flared and accusations erupted. "You were not standing here!" Then there were the people who tried to sneak a friend or relative into a line, making everyone behind them furious. Angry, impatient adults would start to push and name-call. It scared me to death.

More than once, I lost my place in line. It was difficult for children to stand still for a long time. We often left our spots to run around and play with each other. Adults generally let us back into our place when the queue moved forward. But I had difficulty remembering faces, so I tried to notice something special about the clothes of the people standing in front of and behind me—a green beret, a checked jacket, a mustache, or a woman with red hair—so I could find the right place when I came back.

It was December, the only time of year when our stores sold mandarins. We were all preparing for the New Year's celebration, with its decorated *yolka* (New Year tree), *Ded Moroz* (Father Frost), and *Snegurochka,* his granddaughter and constant companion. And, of course, there were the presents! We would find them under our trees early in the morning on January 1, and *Ded Moroz* handed a present to each of us during a school party. Inside each crispy cellophane bag, tied with a ribbon, would be caramel candies in colorful wrappers, a few waffles, a handful of walnuts, and always a couple of mandarins with their intense sweet-and-citrusy smell.

Losing the queue for anything was bad, but losing my place in the mandarin queue was a catastrophe.

I ran along the line, trying to find a woman in a dark green jacket with big patch pockets. A couple of times I thought I recognized people who had been standing next to me, but when I tried to insert myself into the line, the angry crowd pushed me out, shouting that I didn't belong there. With tears streaming down my cheeks, I went along, scanning the queue for the last time. Suddenly, a woman in a black fur coat grabbed my hand.

"Have you lost your line, girl?" she asked.

"Yes," I confessed through my tears.

"You were standing in front of me. Don't you remember me?"

"Behind me was the woman in a green jacket," I said.

"Right. It's me. I was freezing, so I went home and changed to a warmer coat," she said. I still didn't recognize the woman, but I was happy to be in line again.

I bought my mandarins, but as I left the store, holding a half-full *avos'ka* in my hand, I saw the woman in the green jacket. This time, I recognized her. She was still in line, way behind the counter. I felt like an imposter. I lowered my eyes as I walked past her, fearing that she would see me with my purchase. That woman in a fur coat had probably confused me with another girl, I thought.

Years later, remembering that softhearted woman, I'd repeat her trick more than once to save a miserable kid who had lost her place in line.

11: An Orphaned Land

On the sixth of March 1953, less than a month after I turned six, I stood in our living room, barefoot and wrapped in Mama's old flannel shirt that served as my nightgown on cold winter nights. The sun had not yet risen, and in the dim light, our white-washed walls looked ghostly blue. I was supposed to be sleeping, but something had woken me.

In the corner of the room, our radio was on. Yuri Levitan—the famous Soviet announcer with the rich, velvety baritone—was talking about Uncle Stalin.

I knew that Stalin was seriously ill. The news about his stroke had shocked us all two days earlier. Since then, my parents kept the radio tuned to the Moscow station all day and night. Soft classical music floated through our house between the news announcements. My parents spoke in half voices. When Yuri Levitan started to speak, we all raced to the living room, scarcely daring to breathe as we listened to the latest government bulletin on our Beloved Leader's condition.

Shivering from the morning cold, I listened to Levitan's solemn, brimming-with-emotion voice. I only understood a little of what he said.

". . . with deep grief . . . on March 5 at 9:50 p.m., Josef Vissarionovich Stalin . . . died after a serious illness. The heart of the collaborator and follower of the genius of Lenin's work, the wise leader and teacher of the Communist Party and of the Soviet people, stopped beating."

Levitan continued speaking, but I couldn't hear it. How could it be? Stalin—the Father of the Nation, the Great Helmsman, the Best Friend of Soviet Children—could not just die like an ordinary person. I had heard stories of death as long as I could remember. People talked about the Great Patriotic War and the Ashkhabad earthquake. I knew that those who died never came back again. But Stalin? How could he never come back?

"Mama! Mama!" I ran into my parents' bedroom. "He said Uncle Stalin died!"

"I know, Milenka." Mama hugged me, her body still warm from the night's sleep. She was sitting on the edge of her bed, crying. Papa, already dressed, stood beside her. His face showed confusion, as if he didn't know what he was supposed to do. I had seen Mama cry before, but I had never seen that look in Papa's eyes.

"What's going to happen, Vanya?" Mama asked.

"I don't know," he said. "We'll live and see."

"How can Stalin be dead?" I wailed. "He is Stalin!"

"Unfortunately, there are no eternal people," she said.

"What's eternal people?"

"Those who never die."

"Like Lenin?"

"Lenin died long ago," Mama said.

"Then why do they say 'Lenin lived, Lenin lives, Lenin will live?'" I asked. "Will Stalin live, too?"

"I don't know, Milenka. He probably will live like Lenin. In our hearts."

"Don't cry, then. He'll come back," I assured her.

In the days after Stalin's death Ashkhabad mourned. Red flags trimmed with black ribbons stood at half-mast. Big, black-framed pictures of our *Vozhd'* filled the front pages of newspapers. Adults and schoolchildren alike wore red and black armbands. Joyless music, closed movie theatres, vacant parks and dance floors, and solemn meetings submerged everyone into depression and nationwide grief. Everyday life froze.

"What will we do now?" people asked each other. "How will we live without him?"

"Probably it will be another war. The damned capitalist sharks are just waiting for their chance to swallow our country."

"What if Beria comes to power?"

"God save us from him."

Lavrenty Beria was the powerful Chief of the NKVD, the Soviet Security and Secret Police. The first time I remember hearing his name was shortly before Stalin's stroke, when Papa took me to visit his eldest brother, Peotr. While the two of them drank vodka, smoked, and talked in the kitchen, my cousin Mishka and I played hide and seek. When we used all the hiding places in the living room, we spilled into his parents' bedroom, then into the corridor, and at last I sneaked, unnoticed, into the kitchen and under the table.

I sat between two pairs of long legs and huge boots. *Mama would never allow my father to wear his dirty boots in the house*, I thought, trying to avoid their shuffling feet and keep the hem of my dress from soiling.

Mishka stuck his nose into the kitchen, looking for me, but his father shooed him away.

Papa and Uncle Peotr were talking about the Great Patriotic War. Whenever they came together, I knew, their conversation inevitably turned to the war.

"We defeated Hitler because of Stalin's wise leadership. If not for him, the whole world would be under the fascist boot today," Papa said.

"I know," Uncle Peotr agreed. "We rushed into attacks and threw ourselves at German tanks yelling, 'For Motherland! For Stalin!' My friends died with his name on their lips. He is the greatest man on Earth."

"Let's drink to our *Vozhd's* health, brother," Papa proposed.

I heard the gurgling of vodka as they poured it in the tumblers, the clinking of glasses, and their grunting and heavy breathing.

"I don't get one thing," Uncle Peotr said, lowering his voice. "How Comrade Stalin doesn't know what's going on. Beria has already imprisoned half of the country. I believe that some of them are the people's enemies and spies, but there are many innocent people among them."

Papa agreed. "They're both Georgians," Papa said, "and Stalin trusts Beria like his own brother. You know how those southerners are. Stalin is too busy to know everything that's going on in the country. If he knew, he'd never let it happen."

Knowing that Papa would drive me out of the kitchen if he saw me hiding under their table, I sat quiet as a mouse and held my breath.

The brothers continued their conversation, pausing only to drink more vodka. Their voices rose, and they began arguing about something and swearing. Papa used words I never heard him say in our house. I knew he was drunk.

I got tired of sitting there. As I tried to make a plan to escape unnoticed, the boots withdrew from under the table, the chairs slid back, and the two pairs of legs stumbled across the dirty kitchen floor. I heard the front door open and close, and it was safe to crawl from under the table.

When Papa and Uncle Peotr came back from the outhouse, Mishka and I were in the living room, playing cards.

The next morning during breakfast I declared, "Beria is a bad man."

Mama put her spoon aside. "Why do you say that?"

"I know. He kills people, and Stalin doesn't know about it."

"Where did you hear that?" She looked at me intently.

"Papa and Uncle Peotr were talking about it yesterday."

Mama turned a frozen look to Papa's face. Silently chewing his buckwheat kasha, he stared into his plate.

"Milenka, Papa and Uncle Peotr were talking about something else." Mama hammered every word into my ears. "You just didn't understand. Please forget about it and never repeat it. Do you promise me?"

"Yes, Mama," I said. I didn't understand why she suddenly became so stern.

"*Never* and to *nobody*," she said again.

After breakfast, Mama sent me to play in the yard. Through the open windows of our veranda, I heard my parents arguing.

"Truth?" Mama was saying. "She doesn't need to know the truth. You realize what will happen to us if she repeats *truth* in the wrong place?"

The funeral of Comrade Stalin took place in Red Square in Moscow on March 9, 1953. Mourning processions and rallies were held all over the country, including in Ashkhabad.

Papa and I wore red-and-black mourning bands on our sleeves. I took his hand, and off we went. Mama stayed home. She had been feeling sick in the mornings and couldn't join us.

We walked in a stream of people all moving in the same direction. It was almost like the October Revolution parade that I had marched in with my parents the previous fall, only this time, there was no festive music, no flowers or balloons. Nobody danced or sang. Dressed in black, the crowd was silent and somber. Loudspeakers played slow, mournful tunes. I clung to Papa's hand, afraid to let it go.

We walked for a long time, but at last the crowd thickened and we stopped. I didn't know where we were. Perhaps Stalin Avenue, the longest and most beautiful street of Ashkhabad, or Karl Marx Square in the heart of the city. Squeezed among strangers, I could see only men's trousers and women's skirts. People talked over the loudspeakers, but I couldn't make out their words.

The long speeches bored me to the edge of sleep. I wanted to go home.

"When will they stop talking and start burying Uncle Stalin?" I yelled, so loudly that a woman standing next to us flinched and looked at me nervously.

"Hush!" Papa said, lifting me from the ground. "Sit tight. They'll be done soon."

As Papa promised, the speeches were soon over, but we didn't go home. Radio dishes on the poles began broadcasting the events from Moscow, where Stalin's coffin was carried to the Mausoleum and laid to rest next to Lenin, the founder of our Soviet country. The Great Leader of the World Proletariat and his genius follower were together again.

The funeral march sounded soft, then swelled in a powerful crescendo to an overwhelming fortissimo. People around me started crying—women sobbed, men silently brushed off their tears. That universal anguish was so deep and genuine that I got scared and began weeping too, so bitterly that Papa had to console me.

Mama was right. Stalin didn't die. He was still alive in the minds and hearts of the Soviet people. He still watched us from portraits and monuments. The imperialists didn't start a war, and Beria didn't become our new leader. Our life continued under the watchful eye of our dear Communist Party.

12: Sweat and Honey

In April, the Scherbakovs and my family left again for our nomadic honey hunt, moving our two apiaries from the wildflowers of the Kopet Dag Mountains to the thistles in the foothills, to the clover fields of the collective farms, to the camelthorns in the Kara-Kum Desert, and finally to the cotton plantations of the Tejen region.

Each move took us deeper into rural Turkmenistan and farther from our urban home. There were no newspapers here, no transistor radios, and no people around to tell us what was happening in the world. Only when Papa or Uncle Stepan went in to the city to get food, medications, and vodka and cigarettes for themselves did we have any connection with the outside world.

One evening in July, Papa returned from a city trip on the back of a collective-farm truck that happened to be passing near our apiary. While Mama helped him unload the boxes of new supplies, he told me to go and fetch Tolik's parents. Uncle Stepan and Aunt Dusya didn't make him wait long.

"Beria was arrested," Papa declared as soon as they sat down.

"No!" Aunt Dusya pressed her hands to her lips.

"It's here in the newspaper." Papa pulled out a copy of *Pravda* and dropped it onto the table. "They say he led criminal anti-party and anti-Soviet activity that was deeply concealed and masked."

All four of them were silent, and I expected somebody to say, "You kids go and play while the adults talk," as they always did. Nobody paid any attention to us, though, so we stuck around.

"At last this scoundrel will get what he deserves," Uncle Stepan said. "His hands and arms are in human blood up to his elbows."

The conversation continued long after Tolik and I went to bed, and I fell asleep in our tent to the sound of Mama reading a *Pravda* editorial.

The next morning, Mama and Papa were still discussing the news. But soon their conversation turned to our bees. National intrigue was important, but the only thing that really mattered out here in the desert was the next honey harvest.

Every time we moved our apiary to a new place, my parents put one of our hives on a flat commercial scale, weighed it, and wrote the number on its side in chalk. They called it a control hive, and it remained on a pedestal. Every day after supper, when our bees had all settled in their homes, Mama or Papa weighed the control hive again and calculated the difference from the previous day. That's how they knew what the daily nectar flow was.

When the control hive had added about twenty kilograms (forty-four pounds) of weight, it was time to extract the honey. That usually happened every two or three weeks, depending on how opulent the place was.

The day before harvesting, Tolik and I were sent down the dirt road with instructions to gather *kizyak*, the dry cow, sheep, or horse dung used as a fuel for our bee smokers. *Kizyak* didn't burn; it smoldered, producing a cloud of smoke that made our bees calmer and easier to work with. We each carried an old pillowcase and a stick. Before picking up a piece of dung with our bare hands, we turned it over with the stick to see if it was completely dry. The dry dung smelled of the last year's decayed hay, dust, and the sun.

When we had enough *kizyak*, Tolik and I returned to our apiaries, proudly spilling our catches outside the tents.

The next morning, after a quick breakfast, my parents carried the beds out from our tent and brought in the honey extractor and a table. Mama arranged a dripping pan and long uncapping knives on top of it. She heated water in a tall, narrow Turkmen kettle called a *tuncha* and put the knives in it to keep them warm. While she was doing that, Papa got two carry boxes for the honeycomb frames, a big soft brush, and began preparing the bee smoker.

The smoker was an empty cylinder with a bellows attached to its side and a curved lid with a spout. Papa filled the smoker with *kizyak*, added pieces of crumpled paper, and lit it. The paper burned quickly, creating enough heat for the dung to smolder and smoke to come out the spout when Papa pumped the bellows.

From a safe distance, I watched Papa approach the hives. He wore a long-sleeved shirt, buttoned all the way up to his neck, and a hat with a veil covering his face. His movements were quick and precise. He opened a hive, and the bees, disturbed by the sudden intrusion of air and light, started an angry buzz. To calm them, Papa pumped smoke inside the hive. He lifted a frame and inspected both sides of the comb for honey and brood. If it was ready to take, he shook the bees off with a brisk movement and put it into the carry box. He repeated this several times until the box was full and ready to carry into the tent for Mama to extract the honey.

She lifted one comb frame from the box at a time, lowered one of the shorter sides onto a drip pan and, holding it upright with her left hand, slid a warm uncapping knife smoothly along the thin layer of white wax sealing the cells. The gooey mixture of wax and honey slipped lazily to the bottom of the pan, exposing a honeycomb pregnant with amber ambrosia. She turned the frame around and scraped the wax from the other side, then put the frame into holders inside the honey extractor. When four frames had been uncapped and loaded into the extractor, she began turning the handle of the extractor's crankshaft, first slowly and then gaining speed. The frames inside spun around, and the sound of the whirling centrifuge, accompanied by the soft tap of new honey raining against its walls, was the music of the day. When the bucket was full, Papa poured the viscous fluid through a wide funnel into the huge barrel outside the tent.

Sometimes Mama allowed me to spin the extractor. "Turn it smoothly," she taught me, putting her hand over mine on the handle. "If you jerk it or spin too fast, you can ruin the brood." No matter how careful I was, there were always a few small larvae floating in the honey at the bottom of the extractor or caught in the strainer underneath the spigot.

Not far away, Tolik's parents were following the same steps with their hives. Tolik and I ran back and forth between the apiaries, doing small chores, arguing about whose turn it was to open the honey release valve, or sitting next to the extractor eating warm honey. We dipped our index fingers into the warm golden liquid and made quick half circles with our wrists to keep the honey from dripping.

Harvesting days were always festive, but by evening my parents' faces were haggard. They collapsed at our small table, too tired to eat, and I understood why the honey business was not for everyone.

Honey production could be unpredictable. There was one summer that Papa and Mama had to harvest honey every three days, because the bees were producing so quickly. More often, though, the control hive wouldn't gain weight quickly enough. Sometimes, it would even lose weight. The flowers, for whatever reason, weren't producing nectar, and the bees were forced to start digging into their honey reserves for sustenance. They grew irritated as they flew around in search of food.

The sound of hungry, irritated bees was different from their regular buzz. It was higher in pitch, louder, and almost peevish. If there was no gain for several days in a row, our gentle laborers turned into vicious robbers. They invaded weaker neighbors and stole their food. Fights broke out, and there were lots of dead bees on the ground around the landing boards. Mama would move the sliding doors of the hives to make the entrances narrower, so that it would be easier for the guards to protect their colonies from thieves.

My parents didn't look happy on those days. It meant lost opportunity and more hard work ahead. Papa would go in search of a better place and a big truck to move our apiary. Mama would start securing the frames in the beehives, folding the awnings, disassembling the tent, and gathering and packing all our belongings.

Tolik turned seven, which meant that he would start school in the fall. I was a year younger, and I couldn't stand listening to his bragging about everything he would do at school without me.

Sometime in the middle of August, he told me that he was going to Ashkhabad soon with his mother to buy clothes and books, and they were not coming back to the apiary. I was desperate to go to school, too.

During supper, I waited impatiently for a chance to insert a word into my parents' conversation. Surely I could convince them to let me go with Tolik. But before I had a chance, Mama's words caught my attention.

"Mila and I will leave on Friday when the collective farm trucks go to the city," she said.

"Am I going to school like Tolik?" I seized my chance.

"No, you have to wait until next year. But we'll go home with Tolik and Aunt Dusya because I have some business to do in Ashkhabad."

"Perhaps we should send her to school," Papa interjected. "Mila knows all the letters, and she can count better than Tolik. What's the point to wait?"

"She can have another year of childhood," Mama said. Then she thought a little. "Although it might be good timing."

"Exactly. You're going to stay home anyway. She'll be at school all morning, and you'll have more time with the baby. I'll bring the apiary at the end of September, closer to the day," said Papa.

"What baby?" I asked, school now forgotten.

Mama got up to check something in the trunk where we kept our dishes.

"Remember you told us that you wanted to have a little brother?" Papa asked. "Well, Mama and I decided to buy you a baby brother or sister."

Mama lowered herself back onto her chair and pulled me against her rounded tummy. Her eyes were full of tears, but she was smiling.

On Friday morning, Tolik and I walked to the country road with our mamas and waited for a passing truck to give us a lift to Tejen, a dusty district center located 220 kilometers east of Ashkhabad. A couple of hours later, all four of us were jostling on the back seat of a dirty, battered bus that rumbled and clattered, threatening to disintegrate from its old age and fatigue. It was packed with people from nearby Turkmen villages. The ride was long and torturous, full of Turkmen men in shaggy ram skin hats and women in long red and green dresses, with galoshes on their bare feet and flowery shawls covering their heads and mouths. Carrying big sacks and small babies, they sat on the floor, on the stairs, and on each other's laps, talking loudly. The men smoked and the women nursed their babies. The hot, dusty air blowing through the open windows didn't bring any relief. It smelled of sweat, unwashed bodies, and something sour. At the end of the trip Mama's face was pale, and I felt sick.

Finally, we stepped down into the havoc of the Ashkhabad Intercity Bus Station, a dirty and crowded place across from the Tekinskiy Bazaar. Mama didn't feel like taking another bus, so we walked home. After almost five months of peace and quiet in the middle of nowhere, the noise of the city was overwhelming.

13: A Schoolgirl

On the first of September, the sweet smell of pastries woke me earlier than usual. I opened my eyes and saw my new school uniform. While I was sleeping, Mama had attached a white collar and cuffs to my dress and ironed my white pinafore-style apron and two white ribbons.

During our shopping for school supplies, Mama had bought me two aprons, one white and one black. She explained that the black apron would be my everyday apron, and the white one was for special occasions and holidays. The first of September was a special day for all Soviet schoolchildren—the first day of a new school year.

I leapt out of bed and ran to the kitchen.

"Mama, let's get dressed. We'll be late!"

"Good morning, Milenka," Mama said with a smile. "Don't worry. It's still early. Go brush your teeth and let's have our breakfast first."

I pulled my old baby chair from under the sink and climbed onto it. Our outhouse didn't have running water, so we used our kitchen sink for all our toiletries. I took a toothbrush, wet it under the stream of cold water, and pressed it against white powder in a round carton. The chalky taste of it filled my mouth. I hated brushing my teeth. It made me gag. But that morning I didn't have time for dramatizing. Everything was different now—I was a schoolgirl.

In a hurry, I finished my breakfast and ran to get dressed. Mama helped me put on my brown uniform and white apron.

"Be very careful not to stain it," she said, turning me around to tie the long straps on my back. "Nobody likes untidy girls."

I felt like a birthday girl, excited with anticipation of surprises and jittery of the unknown. I could hardly stand still while Mama combed my hair, braided white ribbons into two pigtails she called mousetails, folded them into loops, and arranged two huge bows on the sides of my head. When I was ready, she put a small handkerchief into my apron pocket and stepped back to examine me.

"You look like a real schoolgirl now," she said. She came up to the mirror, quickly adjusted her hair, and touched up her lipstick. "Let's go, Milenka. We have to make a stop on our way to school."

My school, Middle School #4[4], was located on Engels Street, a ten-minute walk from our house. On the way, we made a small detour to the Startsev's garden to get the flowers Mama ordered on the day I was accepted to school.

Holding a heavy bouquet of white and purple asters in one hand and my black school bag in the other, I proudly marched with Mama along Engels Street. Acacia and ailanthus trees grew along the *aryks* on both sides of the road, casting long shadows on the sidewalk.

The closer we got to the school building, the more crowded the street became. Boys in white shirts and dark pants with freshly cropped hair headed to the nearby all-boys schools. Older girls, whose uniforms looked like mine, walked in small groups, chirping with each other.

The schoolyard was packed with schoolgirls of all ages, and the buzzing sound reminded me of a bee swarm on an early summer day. Mama and I found a group of first graders with their

---

4 Elementary and middle schools in the Soviet Union resided in the same building and had unified administration.

parents, standing near two teachers with "First A" and "First B" signs in their hands. My First-A grade teacher's name was Vera Aleksandrovna, which the children shortened to Versanna. She was a tall, bony woman with gray hair gathered into a knot at her nape. Mama told me that she was the oldest and the most experienced teacher at school. Our class, which she would teach for four years, would be her last before her retirement.

After the girls all lined up with their classes, the principal, Tatyana Yaropolkovna, congratulated the children and their parents on the beginning of the new school year. She said that all the girls had grown taller and looked rested, and now they could start their new school year with renewed energy and enthusiasm. She told us how much our Communist Party and Soviet government cared about us, the Soviet children, and how they did everything so that we would grow up free and happy.

"It's important," she said, "that you study well to become worthy followers of our dear Communist Party and patriots of our Motherland."

At the end of her speech, she addressed the first graders. "Yesterday, you were just small children," she said. "But today you become schoolgirls. Today you start your new life. You'll have a lot of new friends and new responsibilities. You'll learn how to read and write and count. But most important, you'll learn how to love your Motherland. You'll grow up to live in a happy time, the time which is called Communism. Study well so that our Motherland, your teachers, and your parents will be proud of you."

The director said that our celebration was over and, after the school bell rang, we would all go to our classrooms. "I award the privilege of starting the new school year to a new member of our big school family, one of the youngest students of our school—Mila Kondeykina." The sound of my name pierced me with an electric shock. I froze and didn't know what I was supposed to do.

Someone lifted me high in the air. Another one gave me a heavy bell, decorated with a big red bow, and helped me to wiggle it from side to side. The sharp and powerful *di-ling, di-ling, di-ling* rang in my ears long after we went inside our narrow, one-story barrack school. My school life began.

After that, at eight o'clock in the morning, six days a week, the school bell called us to morning lineup and exercises. When we were gathered in lines according to class and the noise had subsided, the physical education teacher, a short woman in her early thirties wearing a navy tracksuit, began the warmups.

"*Raz, dva, tri, chetyre* (one, two, three, four)," she counted as we stretched, bent, and jumped, raising small clouds of dust under our feet. After fifteen minutes, when we had perked up, the head teacher or the senior Pioneer Leader greeted us and made announcements for the day.

At eight thirty, Baba Grunya, our maintenance lady, emerged from the front door with the big brass bell and started shaking it above her head, announcing the beginning of the first lesson. In pairs, keeping our formation, the classes entered the school building. We all covered our ears and started to run when we passed Baba Grunya and that bell.

In the beginning, my class had only three forty-five-minute lessons a day—arithmetic, ABCs, and penmanship. Letters and counting were not as stressful for me as cursive writing. In specially-lined calligraphy notebooks with horizontal and slanted vertical lines, Versanna taught us to write dots and lines, then hooks and circles with a pencil. When we mastered this, Versanna said, we would start using dip pens and ink. I knew that a tiny box of metal tips, Number 11, an inkwell, and a bottle of ink were waiting for me at home, and I dreamed of the time when I would be allowed to use them.

Finally, Versanna told me I was also ready for a dip pen. If I only knew what torture waited for me, I wouldn't have been so happy. Using ink proved to be terribly difficult. Each letter I wrote was supposed to have two different strokes—thick and thin. On a downstroke, I had to exert pressure to the pen, making that part of the letter thicker. Going upwards and releasing the pressure, I was supposed to achieve a line as thin as my hair.

"Press—hairline, press—hairline," I echoed Versanna's voice, writing letter after letter in my exercise book. If I pressed too hard, tines of the nib split in the middle and caught on the paper fiber, dragging it through the hairline and making it look truly hairy. Blots in my calligraphy notebook multiplied like flies in our school outhouse.

Mama watched sympathetically as I spilled tears over my homework. She held my new baby brother, Andrey, who was born on the first day of October.

"Don't be so frustrated, Milenka. You'll get it," Mama said, looking over my shoulder. "Don't press too hard. Brush the excess ink against the side of the inkwell. Use your blotter. Good. You see, it's much better. Look at this letter. It's come out beautifully."

After the first graders got used to sitting at our desks for three lessons, Versanna added painting, crafts, physical education, and singing lessons to our schedule. On Saturdays, we had a social class hour, the theme of which was left to Versanna's discretion. She talked about how we should behave in public places, what it meant to be a good friend, and how to cross a road. Sometimes we planned upcoming events, like a trip to the movies or to the zoo.

One day Versanna explained to us that our country, the Union of the Soviet Socialist Republics, was the biggest and the best country in the whole world. It was the only place where all people were equal and happy, because we didn't have rich people or poor people. "We're all rich," Versanna said, "because everything in our country belongs to the people—fields, forests, factories, schools, planes, every small bench in a park. Everything we see around is ours. Your parents don't need to pay for kindergartens, schools, textbooks, or doctors because everything is free in our country. But you should remember that not all children in the world are as happy as you."

By the end of December, we had all learned all thirty-six letters of the Russian alphabet, and we had a "Farewell to ABC Book" celebration. After the winter break, we started a new subject—Reading. Our new text-book was called *Rodnaya Rech* (Mother Tongue). Along with reading poems, fairytales, and stories about school, family, domestic and wild animals, nature and seasons of the year, we soaked up knowledge about our great leaders Lenin and Stalin, our Motherland, and the Soviet Army.

On April 22, just a month before the end of the school year, we celebrated Lenin's birthday. Versanna hung a picture of a small boy with curly hair and clever brown eyes on the blackboard.

"Children, who is this?" she asked.

"Vladimir Ilyich Lenin," a student answered.

"How old do you think he is here?"

"Four . . . five . . . three," we started guessing.

"The picture is called *Lenin at Age Four*," she said. "View the picture carefully. Could you describe his face?"

"He has a nice face and blond, curly hair," we volunteered.

"Right. And what can you say about his eyes?"

"He has clever eyes. They're big and brown."

"Have you noticed anything else about his eyes?" she prodded. When the right answer didn't follow, Versanna helped. "He looks directly at you. He is not glancing or glaring. Are these the eyes of an honest boy?"

"Yes, they are," we agreed enthusiastically.

"Good. What else do you know about Volodya that proves he was an honest boy?"

"Only once he lied, when he broke a pitcher at his aunt's house. But later he told his mother that he had done it," a girl remembered.

"Good. From the stories about Lenin we have read, can you tell what kind of boy he was?" Versanna asked.

"He was inquisitive and curious. He broke his toys to see what was inside."

"What features of Volodya's character do you like the most?"

"Honesty!"

"Bravery!"

"Curiosity!"

"That's right. You girls need to cultivate the same character traits in yourself if you want to be like Lenin."

I wanted to be like Vladimir Ilyich. I had never seen pictures of Stalin as a small boy or heard stories about his childhood. But young Lenin—a mischievous little boy, happy and noisy—was very much like me and my friends.

Like us, he could be naughty,	*Как мы, шалить умел он*
Like us, he loved to sing,	*Как мы, он петь любил,*
He was truthful and courageous	*-Правдивым был и смелым -*
So our Lenin was.[5]	*Таким наш Ленин был.*

The school year ended at the end of May. I was one of three girls in our First-A class awarded a Certificate of Merit for excellent grades. Mama was proud, and that was what mattered to me the most.

---

5 From poem by Soviet children's poet Margarita Ivenson (1903-1977)

On the first day of June, Papa came from the apiary and took Mama, eight-month-old Andrey, and me to the Kopet Dag Mountains, where our bees had been foraging for honey since April. My three-month summer vacation began.

14: The Gazha School

Our mamas brought Tolik and me home from the apiaries in time for us to start our second year of school. This year, they told us, we would be schoolmates. After separating the genders for more than a decade, in 1954 Soviet schools switched back to coeducation. All children from Bagirskaya Street were assigned to a brand new, two-story brick building called the Seven-Year Secondary School Number 4.

Our new school district included Gazha, the neighborhood of steep streets that climbed into the hills a few blocks to the south of the school. Most of Ashkhabad was flat, located in a picturesque valley in the foothills of the Kopet Dag mountain range. But just beyond the city's public outdoor swimming pool, the city's face changed: the pavement ended, and narrow dirt streets without sidewalks wound past crooked, makeshift huts with rubbish-strewn courtyards. The whole place felt as if it had been glued together in a hurry, and the higher the streets climbed, the poorer and more crowded the dwellings became.

The inhabitants of Gazha were known as *gazhintsy*. They were generally low-level workers who, after the earthquake, were stuck in line for state housing. Decades after most of us received subsidies to build houses of our own or moved to subsidized apartments, *gazhintsy* continued living in the slums where alcohol, drugs, fights, and theft were part of their everyday existence. Gazha was a notorious world of its own.

The boys from Gazha were bold and scrappy. At first, they kept to themselves, staying away from other children. They were not good students. Many were raised only by their mothers, because their fathers were "in places not so remote," which is what adults called prisons (as opposed to the "remote places"—labor camps in Siberia and the Far East). Having a father in Gazha wasn't always a benefit. When a teacher summoned a parent to school to complain about a son's behavior, fathers often went home and "took measures." The next morning, the boy would show up at school decorated with bruises and stripes from his father's belt. Teachers often preferred to deal with Gazha boys without their parents' "help."

When I returned home that afternoon, I excitedly told Mama about my new classmates. When I mentioned that one of them was named Misha Shishlovskiy, she puzzled me with a question.

"Is he a Jew?"

I didn't know what to say. I thought that *Jew* was a bad word, because when Papa didn't like somebody, he would say "he's probably a Jew," or "he's stingy like a Jew." I once heard him refer to a friend as a good guy, even though he was a Jew.

"It's a nationality," Mama said, and she pulled out her passport to show me the column that said *Natsional'nost: Russian.* "We're Russians, Nina Verdiyants from your class is Armenian, Gulya Ovezova is Turkmen, and Kostya Anastasiadi is Greek."

"I thought we are all Russians," I said, still puzzled. I knew that Turkmen people were different than me. They spoke a different language, they dressed differently, and their children went to Turkmen schools. I knew that everyone said the woman in the long, puckered skirt who sold *matsoni* (homemade yogurt) on the corner near the zoo was Kurdish. But how could the kids in my school, who all spoke Russian and dressed alike, be different?

Mama explained that nationality, as we used the word, was not about what language we spoke or where we were born. It was our ethnicity, which we inherited from our fathers along with their last names. Kostya Anastasiadi, for example, was Greek because his father's family had been Greek, even though his mother was Russian and both his parents were born in the Soviet Union.

The whole idea of nationality seemed complicated, but it gave me an idea.

Kostya Anastasiadi was the cutest boy in my class. All the girls fell in love with him the minute he walked into our classroom, and I was no exception. Now I knew how to attract his attention.

I started teasing him about not being Russian. He chased me around during our breaks.

Once, while Versanna was explaining something at the blackboard and Kostya and I were sitting side-by-side, I took a piece of pink blotting paper from my exercise book, put it in the middle of the desk, and wrote a big letter "G" on it. Kostya looked at it and waited.

"R," I added. He showed me his fist under the desk.

"E," I drew, grinning. His fist moved closer to me.

"E," I started again, but before I finished writing the letter, Kostya punched me in the ribs.

"*Oi!*" I screamed.

"What happened, Kondeykina?" Versanna stopped the lesson and turned to me.

"He hit me," I said.

"Anastasiadi, why did you hit her?"

"She called me Greek."

"No, I didn't," I lied. "I wanted to write "green."

"Kondeykina, you don't pay attention to what's being said and distract your neighbor. Stand up and repeat what I was telling the class before you interrupted."

I got up trying to remember what Versanna had been talking about, but I couldn't.

"Shame on you," she said. "Give me your gradebook."

In silence, I carried my gradebook to Versanna's table. A school gradebook was "the face of a student," as our teachers used to tell us. Anyone leafing through it could see the daily, weekly, or quarterly progress of its owner. It had everything—our daily schedule, a short description of every day's homework, and, of course, our grades. At the bottom of each page was space for our teachers to write their comments and complaints, mostly about our misbehavior.

When I picked up my "face of a student" from Versanna after the bell, a red scar of handwriting on the bottom of the page said, "Your daughter didn't listen to my explanation and distracted her neighbor during the Russian Language lesson."

Trudging home with that heavy load in my schoolbag, I made up stories in my head about what I would tell Mama to justify my behavior. But I had barely entered the house when she asked, "What happened, Mila? Why are you hiding your eyes?"

I once overheard Mama telling Papa that she could see right through me. Now I wondered if she could also see right through my schoolbag to my gradebook.

"Versanna wrote a note for you," I mumbled.

"Why? What have you done?" Mama's eyes became alert.

"I didn't do anything. Kostya hit me during the lesson, and I screamed."

"Give me your gradebook," she ordered. Reluctantly, I pulled it out of my schoolbag and handed it over. She flipped it open to the right page and scanned the note. "Vera Alexandrovna wrote that it was *you* who distracted your neighbor. Who is telling the truth—she or you?"

"She is. But I'm telling the truth, too. Kostya did hit me."

"So, what—he hit you for no reason at all?" she asked. Silently, I studied my fingers.

"You see? I knew that," she continued. "The fact that you did not listen to your teacher during the lesson and distracted your neighbor is bad. But what upsets me is that you don't have courage to admit your mistake. You blame it on Kostya." Mama took a fountain pen from the table and put her signature next to Versanna's note. Without saying another word, she gave me my gradebook back and turned away from me.

All day I felt guilty. Trying to please Mama, I cleaned the dishes after dinner. I played with Andrusha, who was already a toddler. I did my homework without her reminder. But despite all my efforts, I only came across her cold eyes. I suffered. I wished she would spank me, as my friends' parents did, and be done with it. Her stern face and silence made my punishment unbearable.

15: The Piano

"*Bolyat moyee bely ruchen'ki so rabotushki, schemit moye retivoe serdse so zabotushki* (My white hands are sore from the work, my ardent heart aches from concern)," Mama sang while she ironed. A stack of pressed and neatly folded towels, sheets, and underwear sat on two chairs next to the table, and a huge bundle of clothes waited its turn in a pile in front of her. She looked tired.

The lump of pity in my throat made me cry. Mama put the iron on the metal stand.

"What happened, Milenka? Why are you crying?"

"I feel sorry for you because your hands are hurt," I sobbed.

Mama came up to me and pulled me close. "No, my dear. That was a song of Russian peasants from Tchaikovsky's opera *Eugene Onegin*. I heard it on the radio."

"Why did they work so much?" I asked, wiping my tears.

"Because they had to feed their children, and buy clothes so they didn't freeze in winter, and pay doctors when they were sick. The lives of simple people are difficult."

I thought about our long summers with the apiaries. "Do your hands hurt from hard work, too?"

"Sometimes they do," she said with a sigh. "Papa and I didn't have a chance to get an education when we were young, so now we have to work hard to earn money."

"Did you want an education, Mama?"

She smiled a little and looked away, past me. "When I was small, I did. I dreamed of many beautiful things I could do in my life, but the times were different then. My father died, and your grandmother had to feed four children. When I was nine, we came to Ashkhabad. Mama found a job as a seamstress at a sewing factory, and they allocated her a room in a communal apartment. She worked hard to feed and clothe us."

I held my breath, listening. Mama rarely spoke about her parents.

"I graduated from middle school and entered technical school when I was fifteen," she said. "I was a good student and I wanted to be an accountant. But then Germany invaded our country, and your grandmother got sick. She died a week after I turned seventeen, and so I had to leave school and go to work."

"Why did your mama die?" I asked.

"I don't know exactly. She became weak. There was little food anywhere, and she gave all of it to us. When I asked, she'd say that she had eaten at work. We believed her. Then one day, she couldn't go to work and stayed in bed. Three days later, she didn't wake up at all. We were told she died from exhaustion and a poor heart. She was only forty-five."

"And your father?" I couldn't contain my curiosity.

Mama looked at me for a long time. Then she shook her head a little, as if to shake away the memories, and stroked my hair. "He was sick, too. I don't know much about him." She sighed again, then stood and stepped back to her ironing.

"Mama, what would Andrusha and I do if you and Papa died?"

"Don't worry, Milenka, we won't die. But you must promise me that you'll be a good student and get an education. Papa and I will do everything so you and Andrusha will have a better life than we did."

In the mid-1950s, it was popular for Soviet children to attend state-run musical schools and learn to play instruments. The most prestigious instrument was the piano, but not many families could afford it. Only one girl in our class had a piano at home. However, the summer after my second year of school, my parents decided that I would take piano lessons.

By the time we came back from the apiary, though, the musical school entrance exam was over. That didn't stop Papa, who always had ways to get what he wanted. He left the house with a bottle of cognac and a three-liter jar of honey, and when he came home I was registered as a piano student without ever taking the exam.

My parents postponed buying a piano for our house, though. A piano cost money we didn't have. Papa said that by the time he sold our honey, it would be clear whether I had enough of a future in music to invest in a piano. Until then, I could practice at Papa's friend's home. They had an old upright, and I was welcome to come and play whenever I wanted.

Papa's friends lived in the Tekinskiy Bazaar area, two bus stops from our house, and I wasn't old enough to go so far by myself. Once or twice a week—I was supposed to practice every day, but Mama said that we could not abuse the kindness of people—Papa took me. He put me in a side car of the motorcycle Ural that he had bought secondhand from another acquaintance, and off we went, my music folder on my lap and my braids flapping in the wind.

The piano was a huge old instrument with a carved face and copper candelabras on each side. Several keys were missing their ivory, leaving brown spots that looked like rotten teeth and felt unpleasantly rough under my fingertips. The sound was rattling and broken, and a couple of keys didn't produce any noise at all.

To make things worse, Papa and the piano's owners sat in the same room where I was supposed to practice, talking, laughing, and drinking. From time to time, they asked me to play something for them, which made me freeze in embarrassment because

I didn't have anything to play yet. The dull exercises and one-line pieces my teacher made me play didn't sound right. I stared at the music in front of me and felt completely stupid.

The lessons were even worse. My piano teacher always seemed irritated with me, pushing me in the back with her bony fingers and calling me dumb. I couldn't see the notes through the tears that clouded my eyes, and I forgot even the little I learned the day before.

At the end of the quarter, the teacher told Papa that I didn't have a gift for music and that it would be better if he stopped spending his money on my musical education. I felt guilty and ashamed that I hadn't met my parents' expectations, but deep down I was relieved that my torture was over.

But my parents' dream of seeing their daughter playing piano, as it turned out, didn't go away.

16: New Neighbors

The autumn of my failed piano lessons, two new families moved into a duplex on Bagirskaya Street.

One day, I saw a girl about my age sitting on a pile of sand left by the construction workers. Her blond hair was cropped so short that I would have thought she was a boy, but she wore a faded blue dress over her skinny legs. She had big blue eyes, and her cute snub nose was covered with freckles. I came closer but didn't say anything. Instead, I squatted on the other side of the pile and started digging a hole, from time to time casting glances at the girl. She looked back and continued scooping up the sand. We continued like this, in silence, for several minutes, until a woman's voice called from the other side of the fence.

"Yulka!"

"I'm here, Ma," the girl yelled back without changing her position.

The gate opened, and a woman in a bright summer dress emerged. "I'm going to work," she told the girl. "The house is not locked. Don't go anywhere until your father comes back."

Then she noticed me. "Hello. What's your name?" she said.

I raised my eyes, ready to answer, but the woman wasn't looking at me. I turned to see who she was talking to, but there was nobody there.

"What's your name, girl?" the woman repeated. Confused, I didn't say anything again.

"I'm asking you," she bent down, bringing her face close to mine.

"Mila," I answered softly.

"And I'm Aunt Vera," she said. "I'm Yulya's mother. We're your new neighbors."

I stared at her red summer shoes, which had beautiful bows on the sides. Mama had never had shoes like these.

"How old are you?" The woman continued questioning me.

"I'm eight," I said to her shoes.

"Are you in the second grade this year?"

"No, I'm in the third grade."

"My Yulya will be nine in October, but she's in the second grade. I'm glad that she has a girl to play with now. You can come to our place any time. Yulya studies piano, and she can play something for you." Her daughter wrinkled her small nose but didn't speak, and Aunt Vera left shortly after.

"She's cross-eyed," Yulka told me after her mother disappeared behind the corner. "Everyone is confused at first when she talks to them." Yulka told me about how, when her mother was a small girl, somebody scared her so badly that her eyes got crossed, and she could never look straight again. Later, I would hear her tell a similar story about her father being bald because as a young man he had lathered his hair and left it overnight to keep his hair slick. She always told her stories with slight variations, and I couldn't figure out if she adjusted them depending upon who her listeners were, or if she just couldn't remember all the details of her forever-changing tales.

Yulka and I became inseparable. We went to school together and we ate at each other's houses—mostly she in ours, because her mother didn't like to cook, and their fridge was always empty. We had sleepovers, we went to the same movies, we read the same books, and my friends on the street became ours.

Three or four months after I met Yulka, Papa mentioned that he had met the woman whose family lived in the other half of Yulka's duplex.

"She is a piano teacher at the musical school," he said to Mama. "I told her I wanted my daughter to play the piano, and she said she also gives lessons at home. She wants to check if Mila has a good ear."

"Papa," I broke into the conversation, which I knew wasn't a nice thing to do. "Can I go to gymnastics instead? My physical education teacher says I'm very good at it and should join a team."

Papa shook his head. "Gymnastics won't feed you, but music can. Don't you want to know how to play the piano?"

"I do," I mumbled. But after my ordeal with the musical school, I was sickened by the very idea of starting it all over again.

"Let's give it another try, Milenka." Mama said. "We'll go and see what this piano teacher thinks."

On Sunday morning, we knocked on the teacher's gate. As we waited for someone to answer, Mama fixed the bows holding my crisscrossed braids and smoothed her own hair. I heard the creak of a door and a voice shouting orders to somebody in the house. When the gate swung open, I stepped back at the sight of the woman. Her face was covered with a gooey, yellowish substance, and a folded scarf supporting her chin was tied in a knot on top of her head. Its loose ends stuck up like rabbit ears.

"Hello. Come in," she said, moving only her lips.

"I'm sorry." Mama took my hand, ready to retreat. "We're looking for the piano teacher."

"It's me. Don't mind my face. It's a mask," the mask said. "Come in."

The woman's name was Tamara Mikhailovna. Her husband was a teacher at the Railway Technical College, and their house belonged to the Ministry of Education. Yulka's father, I knew, was also a teacher, so this made sense.

Tamara Mikhailovna took us down a poorly-lit corridor to the living room, showed us a couch where we could sit, and disappeared. The room was big and nicely furnished. A piano with a stack of sheet music on top stood at the left wall next to the door, and a cupboard full of china was on the right between two windows. But what got my attention was the wall in front of us. From floor to ceiling, it was covered with shelves of books. The spaces between the shelves were filled with more books and magazines. There were so many of them that I couldn't see the wall.

I had never seen so many books in a house before. Most home libraries I had seen in other houses looked like displays—new books stood in perfect order, coordinated by color: fourteen violet volumes of collected works of Jack London between six orange volumes of Thomas Mayne Reid and six brown books of Alexander Pushkin. Jacket colors and authors varied in every house, but the order and untouched look was the same. Here, the books looked as though they had actually been read. I could even tell the favorites by their swollen pages and worn-out jackets.

"You have a great library," Mama said when the teacher reemerged fifteen minutes later. She looked like a different woman now—big dark eyes, olive skin, and dark brown hair. Her pink lipstick matched the color of her blouse.

"Yes, it's my husband's. He likes to read."

She sat on a piano stool, told me to come closer, and started asking me the usual adult questions about my age, my school, and what I liked to do. When she asked me if I wanted to learn how to play piano, I said "yes" because I knew that was what Mama expected me to say.

After Tamara Mikhailovna finished questioning me, she turned to the piano, carefully raised its lid, and started to play. Her fingers flew up and down the keyboard, one melody following another, and a half-smile wandered on her full lips. I held my breath. I had never heard anybody play so beautifully. My previous piano teacher used to talk a lot, explained how to curl my fingers, how to lift my hands and touch keys. She played simple exercises to show me how to do it, but that was it.

I wanted Tamara Mikhailovna to play more, but she stopped, lowered her hands, and asked me if I knew any songs. I said that we were learning a song called "It's Good to Live in the Soviet Country" at school.

"Could you sing it for me?" she asked.

"We've learned only the first verse," I said, embarrassed to spoil the magic of her music by my singing.

"Sing it for me," she asked.

"I don't remember all the words," I mumbled, trying to swallow a lump in my throat.

"Milenka," Mama interfered. "You sang it for me just this morning. Don't be so shy."

The lump grew bigger, and I felt a tickle in my nose, the sign of coming tears.

"Do you know the song called "My Land"?" Tamara Mikhailovna started playing and singing the familiar melody, expecting me to join in. I was silent. But suddenly, someone behind the wall started to sing.

То березка, то рябина,	That birch, the rowan tree,
Куст ракиты над рекой:	Shrub willows on the river:
Край родной, навек любимый,	My native land, forever dear,
Где найдешь еще такой?	Where to find more of this?

The voice was so high and clean that I thought someone had turned on the radio.

"Sashka!" the teacher yelled. "Stop it! I am trying to test the girl." She turned to Mama. "It's my son," she said. "He's six."

The singing stopped, and a boy with huge silver-blue eyes and a head full of curly chestnut-colored hair appeared in the doorway. He looked angelic, but there was something daring in his eyes.

"Are you going to be my mother's new student?" he asked, staring at me. "She is mean."

I looked at his mother. I had never heard anyone speak like that about their mother.

"Stop it, Sashka!" she ordered. "If you want to stay in the room while I am testing her, you have to let me do it."

Without another word, the boy turned around and left the room.

"Come closer," Tamara Mikhailovna said to me. "Let's do it the other way. I'll play a sound, and you imitate it with your voice. Like this: *a-a-a-a*," she sang.

I did what she said, repeating one sound after another, trying to keep the pitch as close as I could. Every time I sang, the boy behind the wall echoed me in his clear voice. The sounds he produced were so precise that I felt intimidated.

"My Sashka has a perfect pitch," the teacher said proudly.

"Now I want to test your musical hearing," she said to me. "Turn around, listen to the sound I'll play, and try to keep it in your head. Then face the piano and try to find it on the keyboard. Don't rush. You can try as many keys as you like before you tell me which one I've played."

That part was easier for me. She played a note, and when I turned back to her, she held two fingers on the keyboard, limiting the range of keys for me to choose from. Pressing one key after another, I found the one that sounded the closest to what I had heard.

"Good," she said at last. "Now I'll test your rhythm." She lowered the lid of the keyboard, took a pencil, and tapped a simple rhythmic pattern with its flat end. I repeated. She made it longer and more complicated. I repeated it again, feeling more relaxed and confident.

At last she turned to Mama. "Your Mila has an ear and rhythm. She doesn't control her voice well, but it's not a problem. It'll come with time. Your husband told me that you don't have a piano. If you want me to teach your daughter, you have to buy her a piano."

"We're ready to buy it, but we don't know anything about pianos," Mama said.

"Tell me when you are going to shop for it, and I'll come and help you choose a good one. But you have to understand that learning how to play a musical instrument is hard work. She'll have to practice every day." Tamara Mikhailovna looked at me, "Are you ready to do it?"

"We will," Mama said before I could answer.

On our way home, Mama was smiling. "Who knows," she said dreamily. "It could happen that this day would change your life." If she had only known how right she was, she would never had taken me to that new house on the corner.

Two days later, we met my new piano teacher at the Univermag, the only department store in Ashkhabad. Musical instruments were sold in the right wing of the first floor.

Tamara Mikhailovna went from one piano to another, trying their sound with several chords or arpeggios up and down the keyboards. At last she stopped at a Red October, pulled up a piano stool, and started playing. People around us stopped, and more customers hurried in our direction.

Mama stood with me on the other side of the piano, listening. In her eyes, I saw a dream. It was not my piano teacher playing. It was me, her daughter, in a long gown on a stage of a big concert hall. Hundreds of people listened in admiration. I could feel her dream hovering in the air and gently entering my head, becoming my own vision.

"That's the one," Tamara Mikhailovna said, getting up and lowering the Red October's lid. The crowd thinned out. Papa reached into his pocket, pulled out a bundle of ruble bills, and went to the cashier to pay for my piano.

With the piano at our house, I made rapid progress. By the next spring, I could play a second-grade program, and Tamara Mikhailovna wanted me to join her class at the Children's Musical School, the same school that had kicked me out a year ago. I went, played my program, and was accepted.

Twice a week after school, Yulka and I took a bus to the Russian Market and walked to the musical school for our solfeggio or choir lesson. After our class was over, we would climb the hill behind the school with other kids, and, in winter, slide back down on top of our music folders. The folders were made of black or brown leatherette with portraits of Russian composers imprinted on one side—Tchaikovsky on mine and Glinka on Yulka's. The snow barely covered the surface of the hill, and after our games the composers, with their scratched cheeks and skinned noses, looked as if they had just come out of a terrible brawl.

Often, my friend and I took our piano lessons at Tamara's house, which we both hated, because at home she didn't hesitate to scream and slap us. Yulka suffered more from Tamara's occasional fits of rage than I did. Our teacher had permission from Yulka's parents to punish their daughter if she didn't learn her lessons, and Tamara didn't hesitate to yell, cuff Yulka on her nape, or slap her hands. When she tried it with me, though, she met resistance from her own son. Every time Tamara raised her voice, Sashka appeared at the door of their living room and glared at his mother. Once, when she slapped my hand because I had not learned the right fingering in one of my pieces, he rushed into the room, grabbed a crystal vase—my parents' present at the end of the previous school year—from the cupboard, and smashed it against the floor.

"You're crazy!" Tamara yelled at him.

"Look what your boyfriend did," she complained when her son left. But after that day, she never lifted a finger to me.

17: Triumph of Socialism

After Stalin's death, Nikita Khrushchev—a short bald man with the looks and manners of a peasant—became the First Secretary of the Communist Party of the Soviet Union. Under his leadership of the post-war economy, Soviet life continued to improve: salaries increased, pensions almost doubled, more food products appeared on store shelves, and shorter queues lined up in grocery stores. My friends on Bagirskaya Street lived in their own houses with yards where their families grew vegetables, tended fruit trees, and raised chickens or even a couple of pigs or sheep. Most people were still poor, but they all had jobs, and no one starved. For the first time, families could add their names to waiting lists to buy furniture sets, refrigerators, washing machines, and even televisions.

The first TV on our street was an event for the whole neighborhood. Every Saturday, all of the children of Bagirskaya Street went to the Utkins' house. We removed our shoes, quietly walked into the living room, lay down on the floor in front of the tiny screen, and, enchanted, watched the same theatrical staging of *Dead Souls* by Gogol, which Ashkhabad Television Studio showed over and over for months.

It would be several years before a TV set appeared in my own house. By that time, it had stopped being a gimmick, and my family turned it on only to watch the evening news. Mama said that only loafers could sit in front of a TV screen for hours.

"When we came to Ashkhabad," Papa would say, "there were no cars in the streets. Only asses moved along the dusty roads. Now I ride a motorcycle of my own. In a couple of years, I'll drive a car like Stepan."

The Scherbakovs, our friends and business partners, were the only family in our neighborhood who owned a car. Uncle Stepan's Pobeda was the first Soviet-made car to have turn signals, a built-in radio, an electric heater, two electric wipers, and a trunk. According to rumor, the manufacturers planned to call it Rodina, which meant Motherland. When it was presented for Stalin's approval, he didn't seem impressed. "How much will you sell your Motherland for?" Stalin asked. Nobody dared to answer. Someone offered to call the car Pobeda, or Victory. "Not much of a victory," Stalin replied.

Still, when Aunt Dusya opened the gate of their yard and Uncle Stepan drove his Pobeda onto Bagirskaya Street, all eyes followed him until the car turned the corner. Nobody else in our neighborhood could afford to buy a car. Even a much smaller Moskvich, which cost half as much as a Pobeda, was a luxury.

"Beekeeper," our neighbors whispered after him. "Capitalist."

Did they say the same about us when we couldn't hear them? Probably. Though we had enough money to be as comfortable as anyone in my neighborhood, neither of my parents officially worked anywhere. This was unheard of in Soviet culture. Mama, when asked about her workplace, lowered her eyes and muttered, "I'm a housewife." People gave her funny looks. Although I knew how hard my parents worked, as a child I felt like they were doing something wrong. I wished they would work at a factory or in an office as did the parents of my classmates.

Papa spent one winter, when the apiary was quiet, building a real bathroom with running water in our yard. It had a utility room, a bathtub, and a modern toilet bowl. Underneath, he dug a large cellar where we would keep our honey, sugar to feed our honeybees, potatoes, and winter melons. Mama's jars of pickled cucumbers and tomatoes, apricot and cherry jams, sauerkraut, pomegranates from our garden, and homemade wine in big bottles filled the shelves along the walls.

Those were good years. Everybody believed that socialism worked, and under the wise leadership of the Communist Party, we moved to the next stage in our history—Communism. Slogans shouted from walls, billboards, and newspapers: "Forward, to the victory of Communism!" "Victory of Communism is inevitable!" "This population of young people will live under Communism!"

The Soviet press boasted about our victories and achievements: the world's first nuclear power plant, the world's first nuclear-powered icebreaker, the new IL-18 passenger plane, the largest-in-the-world TU-104 passenger jet airliner, the launch of the first-ever Soviet satellite Sputnik, and then Sputnik 2 with the first space passenger—a dog named Laika. One breathtaking headline followed another. The Soviet Union led the space race against the United States, which suffered a series of embarrassing failures with their Pioneer spacecraft. When an Atlas missile finally put an American capsule into Earth's orbit, the Soviet press dubbed it the "At Last" Satellite.

We had triumphed, and we would continue to triumph.

PART II

18: The Young Pioneers

For as long as I'd been in school, I'd dreamed of becoming a Pioneer. I couldn't wait for the day when I could tie a red scarf around my neck and march with others in a Pioneer squad. I imagined myself raising my right hand above my head in a Pioneer salute and swearing by *chestnoe Pionerskoe slovo* (honest Pioneer word) to my friends.

We were in the third grade when my classmates started to turn nine, the age when we were eligible to join the Vladimir Lenin All-Union Pioneer Organization. Versanna told us that only the most worthy, well-behaved students with excellent grades would be selected at first. I tried to show that I deserved that honor, even though everyone told me that I could not become a Pioneer until I turned nine in February. Rules were rules, and no matter how good my grades were, I was not invited to join the Pioneers during October Revolution celebration or when the school held Lenin days in January.

My friend Natasha, an honor student who was ten days younger than me, and I watched enviously as our classmates marched around the school in their red scarves. Our class Pioneers called themselves an *otryad* (troop) and had Pioneer meetings to which we were not invited. They collected addresses of elderly people and disabled veterans who lived alone and needed help. They seemed older, with a look of high efficiency and a discipline in the way they moved. The only other people in our class who were not Pioneers were a few of the Gazha boys, who had been turned down because of their poor academics and bad behavior. "You're not worthy to be called Pioneers," the Chief Pioneer Leader told them. "You have to earn this title."

At last, in the middle of April, all of the non-Pioneers of our class—even the loafers and bullies—were summoned to the Pioneer room located on the first floor of our school and told that our admission day would finally happen on May 19, during the celebration of the birthday of the Pioneer Organization. The school's Pioneer Leader instructed us all to buy a Pioneer scarf and to memorize the Pioneer Motto and Ceremonial Pledge, which we would have to recite during our acceptance ceremony.

That night, I sat on my bed and read the text of the Young Pioneer Solemn Promise, which was printed on the back cover of the third-grade grammar exercise books.

"I, Ludmila Kondeykina, joining in ranks of the Vladimir Ilyich Lenin All-Union Pioneer Organization, in front of my comrades solemnly promise: to cherish my Motherland, to live, study, and struggle, as great Lenin-Stalin bade us to, as the Communist Party teaches us!"

Rehearsals for our solemn meeting took place at home with Mama and at school with our newly appointed class Pioneer Leader, a seventh-grader named Tanya. She came once a week after lessons. We practiced how to tie our red scarves so the knot looked nice and square and how to make a Pioneer salute. We read and discussed The Laws of the Young Pioneer of the Soviet Union. One day, she told us that we had to begin following the laws even before we became Pioneers.

"Starting tomorrow, do your morning exercises every day and *always* tell the truth. Liars have no place in the Pioneer Organization."

Her last words alarmed me. Just a few days before, Mama had caught me cheating.

It happened on a beautiful spring day. The weather was so nice that it was almost impossible to stay inside, let alone to stay inside and play the piano for a whole hour. I looked at the alarm clock Mama put on the top of the piano. The long hand did not seem to move at all. I stopped to check if the clock worked; it was alive and ticking. There were twenty more minutes to go.

The window was open, and I heard noises on the street—bursts of laughter and the bouncing of a ball. I couldn't stand it. I got up, took the alarm clock, and quietly moved the minute hand ten minutes forward. When it rang, I bolted up and shouted, "Mama, I am done! Can I go outside now?"

Mama came into the room, wiping her hands on the edge of her apron. She smelled of vanilla powder, and there was a trace of flour on her cheek.

"That was short," she said. "Have you been playing for an hour?"

"Yes, I have. You set the alarm clock for one hour, and it has just gone off."

"Strange . . . " Mama looked at the clock. Her expression changed from curious, to preoccupied, to suspicious, and then to dour, as if someone had been playing with a switch on the back of her head. "This clock is almost half an hour ahead. I've just heard the time on the radio. Have you moved the hands?" she asked.

"No," I said, feeling blood rushing to my face.

"Are you lying to me again, Mila?" she asked.

"No . . . Well . . . I've moved the long hand, but only ten minutes forward."

"Ten minutes? And how many days have you done that?"

"I don't know . . . probably two," I lied.

"Why did you do it?"

"I wanted to go outside and play with the kids," I mumbled.

"If you don't want to play the piano, it's fine. You should have told me."

I didn't know what to say. I had promised Mama never to cheat, but I had done it anyway. *Why couldn't I just play the piano another ten minutes? Now she won't let me play with my friends.*

But I was wrong. Mama came up to the piano, lowered the keyboard lid, and turned the small golden key in the lock. She tucked the key into her apron pocket.

"Go outside and play. I'll tell Papa to sell the piano." She carefully lifted a long crochet cover that hung on the back of one of the chairs, spread it on top of the keyboard lid, smoothed its edges, and left the room.

My desire to go outside vanished. I followed Mama to the kitchen and told her I was sorry. I promised never to lie again. I said that I would play another hour. I cried and begged her to give me the key back. I tried to reason with her, saying that my piano exam was coming soon and I had to practice. She was adamant.

It was two long days before Mama had mercy and gave me my key back. Now I was afraid that someone could find out about my lies. *Will I still be allowed to become a Pioneer? Tanya said "beginning tomorrow always tell the truth." Does it mean that what happened before today doesn't count? I didn't know about the Pioneer Laws then.* "From now on," I promised to myself, "I will always keep my honest Pioneer word."

I recited my Solemn Promise so many times, standing in front of Mama's mirror and rehearsing my salute, and I tried to tie my Pioneer scarf to make its knot and ends look perfect so eagerly, that when May 19 at last came, I felt, as Mama would say, like a squeezed lemon.

Everything happened exactly the way our Pioneer Leaders told us. The whole Pioneer *Druzhina* (squad), about three hundred children in uniforms, lined up in the schoolyard for the celebration. The girls wore white blouses and blue or navy skirts, and the boys dressed in white shirts and dark pants. The red scarves on their chests fluttered in the wind. Students marched with the Pioneer banner to the sounds of a drum and a bugle.

The Chief Pioneer Leader opened the meeting and passed the right to speak to the principal, who greeted the participants on the occasion of the Vladimir Lenin All-Union Pioneer Organization's birthday. After that, to the accompaniment of *bayan* (a Russian button accordion), we all sang "Our campfires raise high into the blue nights." The celebration continued with declarations, singing, and dancing.

When the time for the initiation ceremony arrived, my group of would-be Pioneers walked in single file to the front. Each of us held our red scarf, folded in half over our left forearm and pressed against the heart. The eyes of the whole *Druzhina* were fixed on us as, one by one, we were called forward to recite the Solemn Promise. I waited for my turn, unable to stop the shaking in my legs. When the boy next to me finished, I took a deep breath and began.

"I, Ludmila Kondeykina, joining in ranks of the Vladimir Lenin All-Union Pioneer Organization . . . " My voice rang out across the schoolyard.

After the Solemn Promise was over, seventh-grade Pioneers came up and tied our red scarves around our necks.

The call came from our Chief Pioneer Leader. "Pioneer, to fight for the cause of Lenin and the Communist Party of the Soviet Union, be prepared!"

Our hands soared in our first Pioneer salute. "Always prepared!"

I wanted every neighbor, every dog on the street, and every bird in the sky to see me going home that day in my new Pioneer scarf. "Look at me," I wanted to shout. "I'm a Pioneer!" It wasn't a game, and I wasn't a small girl anymore. My life had acquired special meaning and significance.

19: Cult of Personality

I became a Pioneer in the spring of 1956, unknowingly in the shadow of another, much larger, event. I first became aware of it about a month before I joined the Pioneer Organization, while I was practicing the Pioneer motto at home with Mama. Papa stood in the doorway, listening.

"Young Pioneer," Mama called, "to fight for the cause of Lenin-Stalin, be prepared!"

"Always prepared!" I responded, shooting my hand above my head into a salute.

"I don't get it," Papa said to Mama. "Everyone is talking about a 'cult of personality' and they're taking down his portraits, but children still have his name in their motto?"

"It doesn't make sense to me, either, but that's what they told her to learn," she answered.

"Whose portraits are they removing?" I asked.

"Never mind," he said. "If you know too much, you'll get old sooner." That's what Papa always said when he didn't want to answer my questions.

The next day, our Pioneer Leader told us to cross out the word "Stalin" from our Pioneer Promise and say "Lenin and the Communist Party of the Soviet Union" instead. She did not explain why.

A couple of days later, I heard my parents talking in the kitchen. Papa sounded agitated, and I feared he was drunk. But Mama's voice was soft as she gathered dishes from the dinner table and put them into the sink. I tiptoed closer to the door.

"I don't believe it," Papa said angrily. "We won the war under his command. He resurrected our country after the war and made it powerful. Now they accuse him of killing thousands of his own people? I don't believe it," he said again.

"What if everything is true? What if he *knew*?" Mama's voice quivered with emotion.

"Then they are all liars and cowards, every one of them, including that bald Khrushch.[6] I don't trust him. Where was *he* when all that was happening? Why was he silent *then*?" Papa was almost shouting.

Reassured that Papa wasn't drunk, and uninterested in politics, I went back to my room to finish my homework.

Stalin was denounced by Nikita Khrushchev at the XX Congress of the Communist Party of the Soviet Union in February 1956, accused of fostering a cult of personality and repressions against his own people. Over the next few months, Khrushchev's speech was read at closed local party meetings. The Soviet press was silent, but slowly the news spread among the people.

During our morning exercises in the schoolyard, our teachers gathered behind us spoke in half voices. "Cult of personality . . . repressions . . . Stalin . . ." When we marched into our classroom, Versanna told us to open our books, sit still, and read. She said she had something important to do, but she just sat at her desk and stared out the window. Her eyes were red.

Years later, Mama told me Versanna's story. Her husband had been a Soviet officer who fought in the Great Patriotic War. He

---

6 Nikita Khrushchev's nickname Khrushch means "cock chafer" in Russian.

was captured by German troops during a battle but escaped with two other soldiers a few days later. They made their way to the Soviet front, but were arrested by Soviet troops who declared them deserters and traitors. Versanna's husband was sent to Siberia, where he died shortly before Stalin's death. Soon after that, thousands of imprisoned military officers were released. Versanna's son, who joined the army as a volunteer at the age of eighteen, was killed in Germany in May 1945, a few days before the victory.

That fall, Stalin's portraits on the walls of our school were replaced with portraits of Lenin, Soviet Party leaders, and famous Russian and Soviet writers. He was not mentioned in our new textbooks. Older books in our school library had some pages carefully removed. When the anthem of the Soviet Union played on the radio, it was just the music, without words glorifying Stalin.

It took years for the monuments of "The Leader of All Times and Peoples" to vanish from the streets of Soviet cities and small towns. Factories, universities, collective farms, and schools gradually changed their names from Stalin to Peace, Lenin, Red Star, and Proletarian. The longest street of Ashkhabad, once called Stalin's Prospect, became Freedom Prospect. In 1961, the city of Stalingrad was renamed to Volgograd. The same year, under the cover of night, Stalin's remains were carried out of the Mausoleum and buried at the Kremlin Wall.

☆

20: My Red Scarf

Unaware of the world events happening around me, I threw myself into Pioneer life. No longer a little light-hearted girl, I became an "active builder of Communism and a proud citizen of my country." My favorite color was red and my idol was Lenin. I had to "keep the alignment with our older comrades—Komsomol and Communist Party," follow in the steps of the Great Lenin and Iron Felix,[7] and honor the memory of Pioneer heroes of the Soviet Union who had fought side-by-side with adults against the Nazi invaders.

I knew their names and recognized their faces as if they were my close relatives or good friends: Marat Kazei, Volodya Dubinin, Lyonya Golikov, Valya Kotik, Zina Portnova. I read their biographies and watched movies about them. I dreamed of being a partisan scout, sneaking in the darkness of the night and planting mines in enemy camps. I imagined suffering torture at the hands of enemies and dying a hero, never giving up my Soviet secrets.

But there was room for heroic deeds in peacetime, too. The faces of Pioneers who worked hard, vigilantly guarded our Soviet frontiers, or boldly dashed into a fire to save a child or property

---

[7] Felix Dzerzhinsky, called "Iron Felix," was the founder and head of the Russian Cheka (Secret Police) from 1917 to 1921, a forerunner institution of the Russian NKVD which later adopted the name of KGB.

looked at me from pages of my *Pionerskaya Pravda* (The Pioneer Truth) newspaper. Every issue called on us to "Help the country with our labor," "Decorate our Motherland with gardens," or just reminded us: "Pioneer word—Pioneer deed—Pioneer honor."

My Pioneer squad swept streets, raked debris, and whitewashed trees in spring. We collected metal and paper scrap, and pulled weeds in collective farm fields. If a boy or girl did not attend a planned event or "escaped" early, a reprimand would be added to their gradebook. Once, when I couldn't attend a volunteer event because I was performing in a piano recital, the teacher's message to my parents said, "Ignored the political event."

My favorite "political event" was the annual metal drive. During the war, Pioneers had started collecting metal scrap to help our country build tanks and planes. Now, they told us, the metal we gathered was used for peaceful purposes—making tractors, cotton harvesters, pipelines, and buses.

There were fierce competitions between classes for who would bring the most metal scrap to our schoolyard and whose pile would be the heaviest. Although honesty was one of the main laws of the Pioneers, each class left a guard next to its mound, just in case someone was tempted to snitch a rusty treasure.

More than a decade after the earthquake of 1948, our city was still full of damaged things, rusty fences, half-destroyed buildings, and construction-in-progress.

We ran from one house to another knocking on doors and asking, "Do you have scrap metal?" Then, in noisy groups, we carried old pans and kettles, kerosene lamps, rusty primus stoves, aluminum wires, bicycle frames, and all kinds of unidentified metal objects to our school. When one of us was lucky enough to find something large and heavy, our noisy crew pulled, pushed, and towed the big catch to the schoolyard where the mountains of metal scrap rose like dough in Mama's pot.

It was a proud day for me when Mama allowed me to carry away the metal bed that had saved my life during the earthquake. It had been outside, leaning against our fence, since my parents had bought me a new frame. The blue paint was almost gone, and the deep notch on the footboard, made by a falling ceiling beam, looked like an old wound.

One spring, our Pioneer Leader told us that the Ashkhabad Silk-Spinning Factory needed our help in raising silkworms. Our Pioneer task was to feed a bunch of tiny silkworms until they grew big and wrapped themselves in cocoons.

Mama, five-year-old Andrusha, and I gathered mulberry leaves to feed the small wriggling swarm I'd brought home in a jar. We brought home several leafy twigs and unloaded them in a big cardboard box, and I put my silkworms on top. The box looked too big for such a tiny population.

"Wait and see what happens," Mama said.

The next morning, there were no green leaves left in the box, and that was only the beginning. Those worms ate day and night, and we had to work hard to keep them happy. Our next-door neighbors, a noisy Turkmen family with lots of children, had a huge mulberry tree in their yard, and they let us cut branches full of delicious red berries and big green leaves.

The worms ate voraciously and grew, molting several times. It was the only time they stopped eating, and I would sit by their box and watch them pause and raise their heads, as if they were listening to something. Then they ate again. They didn't stop until each worm was almost as long as Mama's palm, and their fat bodies turned yellowish and sleek.

One morning, when I opened the box to look at my silkworms, I saw several of them sitting in the corners of the box, covered with white web. Mama said it was time to bring bigger branches and leave the worms alone. I watched as they all settled themselves onto branches and began spinning silk threads around their bodies. At first, I could still see them working behind their veils, but soon they all disappeared inside their cocoons. The box looked like it was full of shiny, oblong snowballs.

The school year was over when my classmates and I all returned with our boxes. We proudly showed our cocoons to each other and shared our worm-rearing stories.

When the truck from the silk-spinning factory arrived, a woman began collecting our boxes. When my turn came, she looked pleased. "Look at these! They are the biggest cocoons I've ever seen. You've fed them really well." Then she dumped the contents of my box into the bloated factory sack that stood next to the truck, waiting to be loaded.

"How do they make silk at the factory?" somebody asked.

"The workers will sort the cocoons by size and color. Then they'll put them through a special thermal process to soften the cocoons and make it easier to unwind the thread. We can get up to one thousand meters of the finest thread, called filament, from each cocoon," she said. "We combine several strands together to make thread, which we reel onto spools and ship to a factory in Russia, where local weavers will make beautiful silk fabric from it." The woman smiled at us. "Do you know what could be made out of your silk?"

"Dresses. Blouses. Silk embroidery. Pioneer scarves!" we shouted.

"That's right. You've helped our country make more Pioneer scarves, Soviet flags, clothes, and even parachutes."

"What will you do with our silkworms when they become butterflies?" I asked.

She looked at me as if she didn't understand my question.

"They will never become butterflies," said one of my classmates. "My father said that all our silkworms will be dead soon."

"We put the cocoons in a big tub with boiling water to kill the silkworms," the woman said. "If we don't, the worms would make a hole in the cocoon when they fly away. That would spoil the silk thread."

Our group grew quiet. I felt tears swelling in my eyes and rolling down my face. I couldn't believe how stupid I was. If I had known what was going to happen to my worms, I could have saved them.

21: God and Pioneer

One of the best parts of being a Pioneer, the older kids told us, was the chance to go to Pioneer camp. They told us about hikes in the mountains, bonfires at night, Pioneer games, and dancing parties after supper.

I was almost beside myself when, in the summer of 1957, Papa drove me to Firuza Gorge, twenty kilometers southwest of Ashkhabad, for a month at summer Pioneer camp. I had worried for months that I wouldn't be able to go. In order to reserve a place in a camp, the parents of Pioneers needed to get vouchers from their workplaces, and neither Papa nor Mama had an officially recognized workplace. But Mama had asked my uncle, her brother Boris, for help, and he had acquired a camp voucher somehow through his workplace.

A week after I arrived, though, all I wanted was to go home. I was homesick. Among all these screaming and fussing girls, I felt like a wild daisy I once found on my way home from school. It grew in a dusty corner next to a fence, and I decided to save it. Carefully I dug it out, brought it home, and planted it on our flower bed. I expected it to thrive and bloom next to Mama's flowers, but by evening, the plant had shriveled. The next morning, it lay flat like an ordinary weed Mama had pulled out and left in the sun to dry. Now I felt uprooted, too. I wanted to go back to my corner of the world—my home, my family, and Bagirskaya Street. I missed

Tolik, Yulka, Borka, and even the small rascal Sashka, who in spite of being younger than us had become a part of our gang.

Here at camp, every evening I stood at attention in formation with more than three hundred children in the central square, while the commander of my squad marched forward to report our readiness, and then camp's Pioneer Leader-in-charge summed up the day and announced the winners. We competed in everything: sports, best formations, cleanest living quarters, quickest meal cleanups.

After the evening lineup, we had about half an hour to get ready for bed. I rushed through my business in the bathroom, which was drenched in so much chlorine it made my nostrils and eyes burn. When I was done, I sat under the tree outside our barracks, waiting for a bugle to sound taps. It was that magical time of the day when the sun had already disappeared behind the mountains, but the light and the darkness hadn't settled their contest yet.

Other girls gathered under the tree with me. It was the perfect place for our nightly *strashilki* (horror stories). I sat, half listening, distracted with worries about whether my parents would visit me tomorrow as they had promised. It was difficult for them to both leave the apiary.

A girl sitting across from me began in a low voice. "In a dark-dark city, on a dark-dark street, stands a black-black house. In its dark-dark room there's a black-black table." With each new sentence, the timbre of her voice lowered. "On that black-black table sits a black-black coffin. In that black-black coffin lies a black-black skeleton. The black-black skeleton reaches his black-black hands and . . ." The storyteller paused, slowly raising her arms.

"Give me my heart back!" she suddenly shrieked and grabbed the girl sitting next to her.

"Oh, my God," screamed the poor girl, and in panic, we all jumped to our feet. When we realized what had happened, we nervously giggled and nestled back to our seats.

"My grandmother says that if you do something really bad, God will punish you," a girl said.

"Nonsense! How could God punish anybody if he doesn't exist?"

"What if he does?" the girl whispered.

"Shame on you!" It was Rita, an assertive girl who we'd elected the Commander of our Pioneer squad. "What kind of a Pioneer are you if you believe in God? Maybe you go to church with your *babushka*?"

"No, I don't," the girl said softly.

"Girls, girls, listen. I want to tell you a true story," another one yelled. We all shushed each other, ready to listen.

"It happened in a Siberian village where my friend went to visit her grandparents. One day she, her cousin, and two village girls sat under a big apple tree in her grandmother's garden. One of the girls said that God sees and hears everything, and he'd punish anyone who spoke badly about him. My friend's cousin mocked her. 'Let's see what your God can do to me,' he said, and he climbed up the tree. When he got to the very top, he turned his face to the sky and yelled, 'God is a fool,' and then he spat at the sky. As soon as he had done it, lightning struck, and the boy fell from the tree and died."

For a little while, we sat quietly. "I don't believe it," somebody finally said.

"Neither do I," agreed several voices.

"I swear it's a true story," the girl said defiantly. "If you don't believe me, climb this tree and try it." Nobody volunteered. We sat silently until the sounds of the bugle told us that it was time to go to bed.

When I was small and didn't go to school, I thought that God was a bearded old man dressed in a long white robe who sat in the sky, watching us. He punished bad people and rewarded good; he could strike a person dead or revive him. My ideas came from Aunt Nastya's stories and our annual trips to the church.

Every year on October 6, my family went to the Nikolskoye Cemetery, where the majority of the Russian and Armenian earthquake victims were buried in family or communal graves. Here, St. Nicholas Russian Orthodox Church held an all-day mass in memory of the dead.

People came from all over. They brought flowers, artificial wreaths, and bundles with vodka and snacks. We walked with the crowd along the shady alley that led to the church. On each side of our path were rows of hastily constructed grave-sites, sometimes just mounds of earth topped with simple crosses. All the graves had one thing in common—the date of death was October 6, 1948.

Halfway between the gate and the church, we stopped at a blue grille fence. Papa unwound the wire that held the gate closed and let us inside. The small plot inside the fence had been swept clean the day before by one of my aunts.

Each year, we put flowers at the base of a metal pyramid-shaped monument, painted the same light blue color as the grille. Written on its face was a long list of Kondeykins. Papa lit *a papirosa*, and we sat on a small bench next to the grave, waiting for the rest of the family to arrive. When all of them gathered, the women and children went on together to the church, and the men stayed at the grave, talking in hushed voices and honoring the Russian tradition of drinking three shots of vodka in memory of the deceased.

The church was small and always jammed with people. We squeezed inside and bought candles to light under one of the icons. I liked to watch them flicker in the dim light of the church, accompanied by the rich voice of the priest as he prayed. "Lord, give rest to the souls of Thy departed servants in a place of brightness, a place of refreshment, a place of repose, where all sickness, sighing, and sorrow have fled away . . ."

A hunchbacked woman in a long black dress, with a black scarf tied under her chin, removed the bits of burnt wax, making space for people to put new candles in their place. The smell of wax, resin, and something sweet pleasantly tickled my nose and throat. When it was over, the women and children would go back to our dead, where our fathers and uncles were waiting.

We went to the cemetery every October 6, but after I started school and my teachers taught me that God didn't exist, I stopped going to the church. And when I became a Pioneer, our leaders called us to fight against religious prejudices and remnants.

Even in a country that had demolished the churches and declared itself atheist, traditions remained. Expressions as *ne dai Bog* (God forbid), *dai Bog* (God willing), and *radi Boga* (for God's sake) were widely used by the population. Grandparents stealthily took babies to churches to be baptized. When things grew dire, we still turned to the Almighty and begged Him, "*Spasi i sokhrani* (bless and save) my sick child."

My favorite, but most confusing, religious holdover was Easter. Each year on the day before Easter Sunday, Mama and I dyed eggs. There were no commercial dyes then, so we boiled the onion peels that Mama had collected for months. When the water became dark brown, we added a couple dozen eggs and boiled them until they turned golden brown. Then Mama poured the hot water out and allowed me to remove the eggs with a big spoon and place them into cold water, so they would peel easily. When the eggs had chilled, we wiped them with cotton oil so they were shiny.

Later that night, Mama baked *kulichi* (Easter bread), and I would wake to the smell of warm pastry and joy. All day we welcomed visitors—relatives, friends, and neighbors. Papa and I usually went to visit his brothers, carrying the Easter treats Mama had packed for every family.

"*Khristos voskres* (Christ is risen)!" relatives and friends would say to each other.

"*Voistinu voskres* (Truly He is risen)!" was the reply. After that, they kissed three times on the cheeks, and exchanged brown, pink (dyed with lipstick), and green (dyed with antiseptic) eggs, *kuliches*, and sweets.

All the commotion, kissing, and laughter were very festive, but when I became a Pioneer, they told us that Easter was a *religious* holiday, and it was a disgrace for a Pioneer to celebrate it. Our duty, we were told, was to educate our parents. The following Easter, I told Mama that as a Pioneer I objected to celebrating it.

"Christ never existed," I said, "and that's why he couldn't be resurrected." Mama, unfazed, answered that if my Pioneer conscience didn't allow me to take part in preparing and eating Easter eggs and *kulichi*, I should listen to it. But she still had to be ready, because Easter was not so much a religious holiday as it was a Russian tradition. "People will come to our house on Sunday," she said, "and it would be rude to meet them with our table empty."

Mama continued to make her Easter preparations and so did most of my friends' mothers. My Pioneer atheist conscience didn't prevent me from eating their treats for long.

But when I found a tiny effigy of a saint and a baptismal cross on a red string in my parents' wardrobe, my Pioneer alarm bells went off again. "Whose things are these?" I asked Mama.

Mama smiled as she looked at the mementos. "The icon belonged to my mother. It's the only thing I have left from her. And the cross is yours. Before the earthquake, when you were still a baby, your grandmother took you to church and had you baptized. When you got sick with whooping cough, she put the cross on your neck. She believed it would help you to recover. You wore it the night the earthquake happened."

"I'm a Pioneer, Mama. I'm not supposed to have a cross. Let's throw it away."

"It won't hurt you, Milenka," Mama said. I didn't know what to make of her answer, and my cross stayed in her box.

22: About "That"

Something was wrong. My parents had started retreating to their bedroom in the middle of the day to argue, which they had never done before. Papa looked angry, and Mama's eyes were red.

I usually only saw Papa angry when he was drunk. But this was different. He didn't swear or yell. He looked sober.

One weekend morning, I woke to the sounds of yet another argument. "How many times do I have to tell you I didn't take them?" Mama spoke harshly. "You're crazy to suspect me."

"What should I think?" Papa snapped back. "Why else would they disappear?"

My sleepiness disappeared, and I sat up in the bed, trying to hear more.

A few seconds later, my parents' bedroom door opened, and Mama appeared in my doorway.

"Are you awake, Milenka?" she said. "Come with me. Papa and I want to ask you about something."

I followed her into their bedroom with an uneasy feeling. Papa sat on the bed in his black boxers, an unbuttoned shirt thrown over his shoulders. Next to him, on top of the blue bed cover, was *the shoebox.*

For a split second, my heart stopped. I recognized the box. Was this what all of the arguing was about?

"Milenka," Mama said, looking into my eyes. "Have you ever taken this box from our wardrobe?"

My heart sank. "Yes," I mumbled, unable to look at Mama.

"Have you seen what was inside?'

"Yes."

Mama paused. "Have you taken any of them?'

"Yes."

"How many?"

"I don't know. A few."

"Why? What did you do with them?"

"Playing. Yulka and I blew them up, and we also made water balloons." No way would I tell her everything we did with those rubber things.

"When did you first find this box?"

"I don't . . ."

"Stop it. That's enough," Papa said, his face flushing. "Leave her alone."

"No, Vanya. I want *you* to listen. You made me bring her into this, accusing me of using these for *filth* when it was just a child playing." Mama's voice rang with righteous indignation. I shrank from shame.

"Sorry, Milenka." She hugged my shoulders, gently pushed me from the bedroom, and closed the door behind me. We never spoke about it, which was fine with me.

A few weeks before, Yulka and I had found the box when we decided to play theatre. We opened my parents' closet and removed Mama's clothes and shoes. I put on my favorite dress with shoulder pads and a row of small soft ball buttons made of the same fabric, and Mama's blunt-nose high heels that she wore on special occasions. Yulka slipped on Mama's cream-colored blouse with guipure lace collar and cuffs, and a black skirt. She complained that Mama's old brown shoes didn't match her outfit, and she needed different footwear. She reached deeper inside the wardrobe and pulled out a shoebox from under the stack of Papa's sweaters. Instead of shoes, we found a bunch of tiny square packages.

"What're these?" I tried to guess. "Something for our bees?"

Yulka took a package out. "Condom," she read. "I've seen the same things in my parents' nightstand."

"Is it medicine?" I asked.

"I don't know. Mama yelled at me when I asked her what it was. Let's open a package and see," Yulka suggested.

We ripped off the cover and pulled out a small, round, rubber thing.

"I'll ask my cousin Tanya what they are for," said Yuka. Tanya was fourteen and knew everything.

We removed another package and put the shoebox back where it belonged. Forgetting about our intention to play theatre, we made up games with the rubber things. We blew funny-shaped balloons and let them go to spiral across the room. Then we went to our yard and filled the balloons with tap water. We sprayed each other until they both broke, and we threw the bits of rubber down our outhouse hole.

That was before Yulka's cousin Tanya told us, to our horror, that men put that thing on their *pipiska* (peepee) when they *slept* with their wives.

Now we knew what to do. The next time Mama wasn't home, I slipped another paper package into my dress pocket and went to Yulka's house. She blew the thing up until it looked like a huge wrinkled sausage, tied the end of it with a string, and then attached it to her waist so that it hung between her legs. We were going to play grownup. She pretended to be a husband, and I was a wife. Instead of cooking and cleaning, though, we went straight to her parents' bedroom and crawled under the covers. We lay next to each other and closed our eyes, pretending to sleep.

That was the beginning of my chaotic "sex education," which came almost exclusively, piece by piece, from peers who were as ignorant as I was.

None of the adults at school ever talked to us about sex or anything even distantly related to it. The closest we came was when Versanna made an obscure statement that "girls had to keep their honor." She refused to offer any further details or explanations, and her obvious embarrassment made us mortified to ask questions.

In the seventh grade, we had a course in zoology, and when we reached the chapters on animal reproduction, our teacher's voice trembled and she averted her eyes as she told us what pages of the zoology textbook to read at home. Even in the eighth grade, when we studied Anatomy of a Human, there was nothing in our textbook about the structure of male and female sexual organs. The book described a woman's ovum and fertilization, but how a sperm got to an egg would have remained a mystery to us if we didn't have our own network of gossip and half-true stories from friends with older siblings.

Our parents didn't talk about "that" with us, either. Mama could never even bring herself to talk to me about my approaching puberty, and if it was not for my friends, I would have been absolutely unprepared for my first period.

Certainly, no literature or any other information about menstruation existed. There were no sanitary napkins in our pharmacies. Soviet women had to make do with big rolls of cotton. We would take a lump of it and wrap it with gauze to make a pad that was shamefully bulky and inconvenient. When we couldn't get cotton in the pharmacy—it happened often—we used pieces of cloth torn from old bed sheets, towels, or anything else at hand. We washed them after each use and saved them for the next cycle.

Everything related to sex, physical intimacy, or intimate body parts was taboo. Pregnant women hid their pregnancies as long as they could. When it became obvious, everyone was too embarrassed to talk about it. People pretended they didn't notice. Even the word *pregnant* was considered indecent. Instead, people would say "she is in an interesting position."

The word *sex* was never used by ordinary Soviet people. Sex, we thought, was a dirty word that meant prostitution, or the "filthy relationships" of the spoiled capitalist world. There was no decent word or expression to refer to a sexual relationship between two people. When someone wanted to communicate that a woman had sex with a man, they would say "*ona s nim spit*" (she sleeps with him). We, children, simply called it "that."

23: Money, Vodka, and Levak

By twelve, I began to understand more how my family economics worked. Our income depended on how much honey our bees collected the previous season. Each winter, Papa sold the honey, payed off our debts, and we lived on what was left. When the summer harvest was good, we made it through the year. But in bad years, Papa had to borrow money to buy sugar to feed our bees, new barrels for honey, and the wood for building new beehives.

When the money was low, my parents would argue.

"Other people manage to live on their salaries, though they don't earn half of what we made this season," Mama started the conversation.

"I can tell you how others live," Papa said. "They count every single kopeck and save on their stomachs. We eat better, and we dress nicer."

"I know that. But even if we've spent half of it on food and clothes, where has the rest gone?" Mama asked.

"House, electricity, water," Papa counted on his long fingers.

"Come on, Vanya. All of these don't make even the twentieth part of what we had." In the USSR, most of the expenses for public housing were the state's responsibility and so housing costs were among the lowest in the world, typically just 4–5 percent of the family budget.

"Birthdays, holidays, presents, drinks . . ." Papa continued counting.

"Now you're coming closer to the truth. Don't forget all those moochers you feed and water."

"They're not moochers. They're my friends, and they respect me."

Mama shook her head. "They respect your wide-open pockets. The day you don't have money to pay for their drinks, they'll disappear."

"You women are always unhappy. You don't understand what male friendship is," Papa objected.

Mama looked at him incredulously. "Friendship? How many times have your friends picked up the bill in a beer bar?" Without waiting for him to answer, she continued. "None. Or when has one of them invited you to his house? Not even once. Every time you bring them here, I have to feed them, and you put a bottle on the table. That's where the big chunk of our money goes."

"Do we live worse than our neighbors? Are you in need of something?" Papa laid his trump card.

"No," Mama acknowledged, "we're not. But we live from day to day, and we don't have any savings. What if something happens, and you aren't able to work? We have two kids to raise."

"Don't worry. Nothing will happen to me. I'm young and strong, and I'll do anything to keep my family happy."

I heard this conversation in slightly different variations many times throughout my childhood, as friends, acquaintances, and relatives continued coming to our house for holidays, birthdays, and less notable days.

Russian men didn't need much reason to get drunk. Buying anything new was an occasion. "Oh, you bought new shoes? They have to be 'washed' to last longer." No deal could be settled without a bottle of vodka, either. "One can't figure it out without a bottle," Papa would say.

A week before Mama's thirty-fifth birthday, she told Papa that she didn't want a big party. She would be happy just to have a couple of friends and the family over. But Papa insisted that thirty-five was a great number and had to be celebrated well. After some discussion, they agreed on a number of guests. But when people started to arrive with presents and flowers, there were more than she expected.

"You didn't tell me that you invited them," she whispered to Papa in the kitchen.

"Oh, I forgot. I bumped into him in a liquor store this morning and said that I was shopping for your birthday. It was awkward not to invite them."

"I hardly know these people, Vanya."

"Now you'll have an opportunity to know them better."

The party was noisy, with lots of food that Mama had cut, mixed, cooked, and baked for two days, and an abundance of vodka that Papa and his friends would drink to the last drop. Guests sat at the table for hours, talking and drinking, singing and drinking again, dancing and drinking more.

Papa, as host, went around the table filling the glasses, talking, and entertaining guests. Every drink was accompanied by a toast. The first toasts were to Mama, "the best woman in the world," then to her golden hands, next to her family. After that, the men raised their glasses *za zdorovye* (to everyone's health). To love. To our wives. To our children. To our country. To friendship among peoples. To world peace. To socialism. Three hours later, they just said, "*Nu, davai* (Well, let's)," clinked their tumblers, and tipped them off.

Mama scurried around all evening changing plates, adding more food, cleaning the table, and serving dessert. While the women had tea and praised Mama's cake, the men grouped together at the end of the table with their dinner plates and the remaining bottles. The finale was the predictable mix of drunken revelers, unhappy wives, and loud brawls.

When the last guests staggered home afterwards, Papa could barely stand. "What did you tell him in the kitchen?" he questioned Mama, stumbling after her while she cleaned the table and washed dishes. "He looked at you all evening. I saw how you smiled at him."

"Vanya, don't start it again," Mama begged him. "I don't know that guy. Why did you invite him to my birthday? Just calm down and go to bed."

After Papa at last went to the bedroom, bumping into furniture on the way, Mama stayed in the kitchen longer, waiting for him to fall asleep. The day after, he looked guilty, stared at the floor, called himself a fool, and promised Mama he'd stop drinking. This, too, was predictable.

My first clashes with Papa started when I was in the fifth grade. Once, when he came home drunk and began to get after Mama, I rushed to her defense.

"Please, Milenka," Mama begged me, "Don't interfere. You'll only make things worse." But once I started, I couldn't stop myself. Every time I saw him stumble into the house with his eyes glassy, every hair on my body stood straight up and my back stiffened and arched like our cat Murzik's at the sight of a dog.

That was when I started calling him *ty*. According to Russian tradition, I had been taught to address my parents, as well as other adults, respectfully using the formal pronoun *vy* (you). The informal *ty* was used with my peers. But in the heat of my arguments with Papa, *vy* seemed too gentle, and I switched over to *ty*.

"If *ty* raise your hand on Mama again, I'll call the militia," I yelled.

"All my friends see *ty* coming home drunk," I cried another time. "I'm ashamed of *ty*!"

Later, I switched to *ty* with Mama, too, but the reason for that was quite the opposite. The formal *vy* was too impersonal and distanced me from Mama. I wanted her to be my friend, to feel closer to her. In both cases it happened somehow in itself, unconsciously. Mama never objected to the switch.

When it came to the finances, though, Papa was right. There were many people who lived worse than us. It took me some time to understand this. At school, we all wore the same brown school uniforms with black aprons, had the same school bags with notebooks and textbooks, and during our long recess we all ate the small roll with a glass of lukewarm sweet tea that our school provided for us.

If Mama gave me a ruble, I could also buy *pirozhki* stuffed with mashed potatoes, sauerkraut, beef liver, or jam. My friends and I lived in nice houses, with yards where our parents grew grapevines, pomegranates, or apricots. In spring we ate radishes, green onion, parsley and dill from our small vegetable beds. About a dozen chickens cackled in each yard, and the roosters' *koo-ka-rey-koo* woke me up early in the morning before school.

But I noticed that many of the kids at school never bought an extra treat. Borka's sweaters were old and had patches on elbows. Tolyan, our squatters' son, grew out of his short trousers and jacket, which he wore to the very holes. Neither of them had a bike like Sashka or me, and we never were invited to Borka's yard or house to play.

The differences became even more obvious one afternoon, when I ventured into Gazha to pay a visit to a girl from my class. Asya had broken her leg and couldn't come to school for a whole month. Versanna encouraged us all to visit her and help her with homework so she wouldn't lag behind. When it was my turn to go, Asya's next door neighbor, Kolka Malov, offered to accompany me to her house.

After school, I gathered Asya's homework, a roll from our school lunch, and an apple Mama had put into my school bag that morning. I followed Kolka down Engels Street, along Startsev garden, and then up the narrow and steep Gazha streets.

Asya's shack, with its tiny windows and small, dark rooms, could hardly be called a house. Without knocking, Kolka led me into a poorly lit kitchen. Half-rotten onions and sprouting potatoes lay in the corner next to a rough, cross-legged table. The remnants of yesterday's supper or that morning's breakfast—half-eaten, shriveled pickles on chipped plates, sauerkraut in a glass jar, crumbs of stale bread, and turbid liquid in ribbed-glass tumblers—looked as if everyone had left the table in a hurry. Only empty bottles of cheap, fortified Turkmen wine, called Chemen, suggested that the meal had not been abandoned.

Next to the kitchen was a room with three metal beds. Sleeping in a nook behind a half-drawn curtain was a fully dressed man wearing only one shoe. His mouth was wide open, and bubbling sounds came out of it at every exhalation.

"Who's that?" I asked Kolka, hesitating.

"He's Asya's father. Don't pay attention; he's drunk. He and my father both work fifteen-day shifts at the borehole in the desert. They just came back yesterday. They'll drink until the money is gone."

"Where's her mother?" I whispered.

"She's at work. Don't be scared. Just follow me."

Kolka pushed another door open, and we found Asya reclining on a shabby divan with a book in her hands. She looked paler than usual, and her leg in the heavy cast seemed too big for her skinny body. Her only window was so dirty that the light could hardly penetrate inside. I handed her the homework, roll, and apple. She thanked me and put everything aside.

I liked Asya. She was a timid girl, not the best student in our class, but she liked to read. I often lent her my books. But now I felt awkward, and as soon as I dropped off the homework, I left the house and Gazha district.

Levak

Yulka and Sashka still lived in the duplex owned by the education department. Since both sets of their parents worked most of the day, we spent most of our free time playing in their shared yard. The duplex was surrounded by a tall fence, and the yard was just big enough for an outhouse and a storage building, each divided into two parts—one for each family.

The door of Sashka's storage shed was always open, and we often played in there, hiding among the old furniture, boxes, and construction materials. Yulka's side of the storage, though, was always closed, and her parents told her not to play or touch anything there. Sometimes, when nobody saw us, she and I would go inside.

In one corner, we found Aunt Vera's collection of German fashion magazines called *Burda Moden.* Those magazines were rare, and we often took them outside and sat under the grapevine arbor and examined the pictures.

The rest of the storage room was occupied by old files. There had to be hundreds or even thousands of them in there, stacked along the walls in big piles. They all looked similar, full of drawings with some kind of technical descriptions, and the word "Thesis" on the front page. One day, Yulka and I were sitting in her yard when Yulka's father came outside, opened his storage, and started to rummage through the folders. He sat there for a long time, opening one folder after another, looking through them, putting them back in the stack and choosing others.

That night, Yulka told me, Uncle Yevgeny sat in his study, which was also Yulka's bedroom, drawing on paper that he placed on a big slab of glass between two chairs with a lamp shining underneath. He was copying something from the old file he had found in his storage.

The next night, he told Yulka that she couldn't sleep in her bedroom, so we had a sleepover in their yard. We thought it was great. Nobody told us it was time to go to bed, and we sat under their grapevine arbor, telling stories and giggling until at least midnight. The light in Yulka's room was still on when we finally fell asleep.

In the morning, I woke when somebody knocked on their gate. Still half asleep, I saw Uncle Yevgeny unlock the gate and let in a young Turkmen man.

After a short conversation, Yulka's father went inside the house, and immediately reappeared again with a folder in his hands. Through the slits of my half-opened eyes, I saw him hand the folder to the man. In exchange, Uncle Yevgeny received a small packet wrapped in a newspaper.

"He just got money for his *levak*," Yulka whispered after her father stepped inside the house.

"What's *levak*?"

"I don't know. They just call it that. Papa copies old theses and sells them to his corresponding students. Mama said that he hit a pot of gold when he found this *levak*. They'll kill me if they find out that I've told you."

Yulka's father was the head of a department at the local Polytechnic school. Unlike my Papa, he drank booze alone, sitting in his kitchen. When Uncle Yevgeniy was drunk, he turned from a gloomy, intimidating person into a pleasant and talkative man. Yulka told me she wished her father was always drunk, and I said I preferred if mine was always sober.

Yulka's parents liked to party, but they always invited the same couple or two—happy looking, well-dressed people who didn't have kids of their own. When the guests came, she was set free until the party was over. She would show up at our house just on time for supper. "Yulka's nose can smell food a kilometer off," Mama used to joke.

When her parents were not home, we would go inside the house and she would show off their new divan, which she called by the fashionable foreign word *sofa*, and a beautiful vase or a figurine her mother had recently acquired from somebody for "big money." Yulka's house was full of expensive things: the furniture on which she wasn't allowed to sit, fancy dishes she was forbidden to use, and pricy doodads she was not allowed to touch. Everything in their house had been *acquired* from special people, not bought in our Univermag or another Ashkhabad store. The walls in their guest room were painted in different colors, and one of them was completely black. It was very different than our whitewashed simplicity. Yulka called it *stilno* (stylish), imitating her mother.

Aunt Vera was in awe of everything Western. Uncle Yevgeniy drank cognac with his guests, not vodka like my Papa. Aunt Vera's hands were white and soft. She was the only woman I knew who hired a cleaning lady to help her around the house.

Yulka's parents lived *stilno*. The only thing in their household that didn't match their way of life was Yulka herself.

After several years of beekeeping, and with Andrusha and I both in school, my parents decided that we needed an additional source of income. They agreed that Mama would continue to take care of the apiary in the summer, while Papa found a job in Ashkhabad. He worked in a few different places before he found a job as a taxi driver.

Now, like all of my friends' parents, he went to a job at a certain time every day and got paid on the first and fifteenth of each month. "It's not money," he would say, handing Mama his earnings. "It's cat's tears. How can anybody live on a salary? If the government paid people better, nobody would have to look for the ways to make more money."

By then, I understood what Yulka had meant when she talked about *levak*, the illegal profit that Soviet citizens made by using public equipment, tools, or time for personal gain.

Before long, Papa was coming home after his shift with pockets full of crumpled ruble bills. He would sit at the table, smoothing them out and stacking them together by color. He gave part of the pile to Mama, and the other he put back into his pant pockets. This was his *levak*, the cash he didn't include when he submitted the day's revenue to the taxi park cashier after his shift.

As a taxi driver, Papa shared his car, a Volga GAZ-21, with another driver, alternating day and night shifts. It wasn't a new vehicle, but it was reliable. And before long, Papa's partner introduced him to the finesse of the profession.

During a shift, every taxi driver was expected to make a certain amount of money. At the end of their shift, the driver submitted the cash they'd received to the taxi park cashier, along with the speedometer and taximeter readings from their car.

"Of course, once I have made my quota I can keep working until the end of my shift and submit the whole profit to the cashier," Papa explained to Mama. "If I'm really good, at the end of the year I'll be awarded a Certificate of Honor by the taxi park administration, and my photo will be placed on the Board of Honor. But I'll still bring home the same miserable salary. Or I have another option—I can hand in the daily norm *and* keep whatever cash is left over for my own pocket. Some of it I'll need for bribing a mechanic to speed up repairs if the car breaks, the shift manager if I don't want to work odd hours, and the garage chief if I want a new car. But the rest is mine."

Papa, of course, chose the second option. For a part of every shift, he worked with his taximeter on, making the daily profit for his taxi park. Then he disconnected the meters, and the remaining day's gain went into his own pocket.

The legality or morality of *levak* was too complicated for me at twelve. Yulka's father selling old theses to his students, Sashka's mother giving private piano lessons from her home, and Papa's taxi bonanza were just the ways our parents earned additional cash. Those who wanted to live better, to eat white bread and meat instead of dark bread and cheap liver sausage, to teach their children music, to dress well, to have a TV and nice furniture and sometimes take their families on vacation, meant that families had to increase their income.

But even without *levak*, nobody in Khrushchev's USSR starved, and everybody seemed to be content. Our future was secure—our education, jobs, healthcare, and housing was all taken care of by our government. During the XXI Congress of the Communist Party in January 1959, Nikita Khrushchev declared the complete and final victory of Socialism in our country. We entered a new phase in our development—the period of extensive building of Communism.

24: Bagirskaya Street

Bagirskaya Street was green and unpaved, lined with acacia, mulberry, and ailanthus trees along the narrow *aryks*. Here, we played *vybivalk*i, with a ball flying back and forth between two groups targeting the runners in the middle, and *chizhik,* where we hit a small piece of wood with a long stick, competing for who could send it farthest from the starting line.

Our most popular game was *voinushka* (war game). Though my peers and I had not experienced The Great Patriotic War ourselves, it was in our blood. We had sucked it in with our mothers' milk and our fathers' stories. The war was the focus of our favorite movies and books. We inherited the pride of our victor fathers, and we valued strength, honored endurance, and worshipped heroism. Our only regret was that we had been born too late and were deprived of a real war.

When we were young, our games were noisy but harmless. We split participants into two groups, which was difficult because nobody wanted to be "Germans." For weapons we used sticks, and when the "enemy" was located, we pointed our "rifle" at him and shouted "ta-ta-ta."

By the time we turned thirteen, our games had become more violent. We "fought" furiously until cut and bruised. "The Gestapo" beat us, gagged us, twisted our arms, and tied our wrists. But even under threat of death, "Russians" did not give up.

One of the games almost ended my musical career. Hiding from my pursuers in Yulka's yard, I climbed her fence in order to sneak behind the enemy and attack them from the rear. When I jumped to the ground, I lost my balance and landed on all fours. My left hand hit a rusty metal rod left behind by construction workers, piercing the middle of my palm. When I pulled my hand free, a fountain of blood sprang from the gash, leaving a crimson path as I ran to the gate, calling for an urgent armistice. Sashka tore a long strip from a bed sheet hanging on a line in the yard and bandaged my hand, while someone ran to the phone booth to call an ambulance.

The emergency room doctor stopped the bleeding, cleaned and bandaged my palm, and checked how my fingers moved.

"You're lucky," he said. "It's a miracle the rod went through your palm without seriously damaging nerves or tendons."

With my hand hanging in a sling in front of my chest, I looked like a wounded soldier. The respect in my friends' eyes made me feel like a hero.

In April, Mama left with the apiary, and I stayed home with Papa until the end of the school year. He was rarely around, either at work driving the taxi or off to the fields to help Mama move the apiary or extract honey. I was free to come and go whenever I chose.

A couple of days a week, Aunt Nastya came to cook something for us. When two of the squatter families in our yard received government apartments, Papa demolished their shacks and built a small home for her.

My aunt thought children were raised like flowers—you water them on time and watch them grow. I was free to come and go as I pleased. Aunt Nastya never asked if I attended school or why

I came home so late, and I was happy to keep it that way. Papa stopped by only to have a meal and stuff the fridge.

The older I grew, the more I wrangled and quarreled with my father. We did not agree on anything—the popular music I enjoyed was just irritating noise to him; he called our dances "jerking;" and my generation's youth were "disrespectful youngsters." The sugar had been sweeter, the sea saltier, and the sun had shone brighter in *his days*.

Our arguments grew into serious conflicts. If I objected to something or had my own opinion, Papa would say, "You're too young to teach me," or "eggs don't teach the hen." Infuriated, I usually left the house in a huff. In fact, I spent as little time there as possible.

When I wasn't at school or piano lessons, I horsed around with Tolik, Borka, Yulka, and Sashka. Smarter and shrewder than his peers, Sashka preferred to hang out with us, the older children. He was strong, fearless, and competitive, and we liked having him on our side. There was no shade of shyness in him. If we needed to negotiate something with the adults, like permission to go to the swimming pool or the movies, we sent him to treaties, and he'd set out with a winning smile. The word "no" didn't exist for him—he got whatever he wanted one way or another.

He was like a younger brother—annoying, often embarrassing, but impossible to get rid of. He followed me, spied on me, and showed up in the least appropriate places and at the worst possible times. Once, I promised to beat him up if he didn't stop chasing me. Instead, to my embarrassment, he announced publicly that he would marry me when he grew up.

At eleven, he was almost my height. His curls were bleached by the chlorine of the swimming pool, where he practiced every day. He travelled with his swim team around the country during school vacations and came back with medals and certificates, which he hung on the wall in his room. I felt proud of him, as I would of my own brother.

When her parents were out and Sashka was not around, Yulka and I would escape to our secret headquarters in the attic of her duplex, which we kept secret from everyone. We dragged a long ladder to her front porch and climbed inside through the small window above her door awning. We called our headquarters SHKIM, for the Headquarters of Kondeykina and Mayorova, and painted it in huge letters on the beam supporting the roof. We cleaned and dusted our space and furnished it with an old chair, a wooden box that served as a table, and someone's old briefcase, where we kept our "military log" and other top-secret documents.

In that log, among important entries about our fights, victories, and war secrets, there was one that read, "Followed a spy. Prevented a terrorist act."

There was a popular Pioneer song at the time called "A Brown Button," about a Young Pioneer, Aleshka, who found a small brown button with unfamiliar letters written on it. He reported the finding, and for four days and nights the Soviet border guards galloped on horsebacks, without food or sleep, in search of the stranger who lost the button. On the fifth day, they found a man "with a missing button and a map of the fortifications of the Soviet border in his pocket."

Should we ever have an opportunity to catch a spy, Yulka and I dreamed, we wouldn't miss it.

One afternoon, coming back from musical school, Yulka and I noticed a stranger on the corner of the First of May and Gogol Streets. He was pointing his Leica camera at the Hotel Turkmenistan. The man wore a black raincoat, even though it was sunny outside, and had a black briefcase. He was clearly a stranger in our city.

"See that? He looks suspicious. What if he is a spy?" I said. "First, he takes pictures of the hotel, and then he'll blow it up. We have to stop him!"

"How?" Yulka looked as if the hotel was going to explode in front of our eyes.

"Let's follow him and see where he goes," I suggested.

The stranger took another shot, hung the camera over his shoulder, and headed in the direction of the Russian Bazaar. Definitely a spy, we decided. Like two hounds following game, we trotted behind him.

We did everything we'd learned from Soviet spy movies to disguise ourselves—we kept a distance, and when the man paused to see where he was going we stopped "to tie a shoe" or gazed into shop windows.

Our spy crossed a street and headed to a bus stop, the same stop Yulka and I used to go home. This day, we watched our bus leave without us—we were on a mission. We blended into the crowd of people and waited. When a new bus arrived, the man boarded with a dozen others. Yulka and I hid behind an elderly Turkmen woman with two huge milk cans and climbed on. We didn't have any idea where the bus was heading or how long it would take us to find our way home. But none of that mattered to us.

The bus was packed with people, sitting and standing in the aisle, and we could not see our suspect. At every stop, we watched who got off, ready to spring out at any moment. We passed most of the city and the streets looked unfamiliar, but our spy still sat at the back, looking out the window.

The bus turned and started jolting on an unpaved road, going farther into an area that looked more like a Turkmen village than the Ashkhabad we knew. A foul smell started to penetrate the bus.

Soon it turned into a terrible stench. Yulka wrinkled her nose with disgust. I covered mine in a cup of my hand.

After several more minutes of shaking and rattling, the bus stopped and the driver declared, "Meat Processing and Packing Factory. The last stop. The bus goes to the park." The door opened and the three of us, the only people left on the bus, got off.

The street was empty. The long concrete wall of the Meat Processing Factory occupied the whole block. Our spy never even looked at us as he crossed the road and stopped at the factory gate. He rummaged in his briefcase, took out a paper, and disappeared behind the doors of the checkpoint.

We lingered a little while on the sidewalk before walking back to the bus stop to wait for another bus to take us home.

The next day, we didn't find any information about spy activities in the local newspaper, and Hotel Turkmenistan still stood in its usual place. If it wasn't for our vigilance, we decided, the man would have done something terrible. He saw us following him, and it scared him off.

25: The Decisions

By the spring of seventh grade, my classmates had all started to look and act differently. The girls gathered in small groups, whispering and casting glances at boys. The boys smoked behind the outhouse during breaks, bickered with teachers at lessons, and often missed classes. Sometimes, at the end of a school day, I could detect the familiar smell of alcohol on some of the Gazha boys' breath.

All of us were thinking about the future. We had one more year in what was called our incomplete secondary school. After that, we would have to choose whether to go to the ninth grade and complete the eleven-year secondary education, or to enter one of the vocational or technical schools and learn a profession. We would also have the option to work and complete our mandatory secondary education at evening school.

I was still clinging to my childhood fantasy of serving in the Soviet Army. Without telling Mama, I wrote letters to the commanders of the Suvorov Military School in Moscow and to the Nakhimov Naval School in Leningrad, the two most prominent schools of a kind in the Soviet Union. I explained that although I knew the schools accepted only boys, I hoped they could make an exception for me. I told them how much I wanted to serve my country and asked them to make an exception and let me take the entrance exams.

I don't know if my desire to serve was based on my patriotism, my pride for our victorious army and my family's service in the Great Patriotic War, or my youthful aspiration for a more exciting life of risk and adventure. Probably all of that was true. I was thirteen, and nothing seemed impossible.

Two months later, I received an official-looking envelope, addressed to me. "Dear Ludmila Kondeykina," it said. "The administration of the Moscow Suvorov Military School has received your application. We are sorry to inform you that our school is strictly male, with no exceptions for girls." The Nakhimov Naval School remained silent.

At the end of May, I took my piano exam at the musical school. I passed with an excellent grade and the examination committee recommended me for admission to the musical college. "Come to my house on Saturday to get your summer task, and we'll talk more about it," my teacher said. "And don't forget to bring all the music you have."

Deep inside, I had doubts about a career in music. Tamara Mikhailovna used to say that if Yulka had my head and fingers, or if I had Yulka's musicality, one of us would make a great pianist. But I didn't have Yulka's sensitivity to music and suspected that it wasn't something I could learn.

But with my piano teacher encouraging me to consider the musical college, I pushed away my doubts. Maybe Tamara is right, I thought. And it would make Mama happy. She often told me how proud she'd be if I were a piano teacher.

When we returned to school that fall, the surge of adolescent hormones pushed everything else—Pioneer activities, academics, and sports—aside. Boys started to make *friendship proposals* left and right. Usually it came as a note—"I like you. Let's be friends." If the sender of the note received a rejection, he would send a similar message to another girl. During recess, the girls stood in a circle, discussing the latest developments.

I didn't get any proposals at first, but I didn't pay much attention. I was busy getting ready for musical college, and Tamara Mikhailovna insisted that I practice three hours a day. Now that she was home from the apiary, Mama wouldn't get off my back if I didn't do exactly what I was told.

To free my evenings, I adjusted my schedule to wake at five forty-five and practice from six to nine before school. I finished the hardest part of my daily work just as my friends were starting their day. After breakfast, I reluctantly started working on my homework. Whatever work I couldn't finish, I would copy from my friend Natasha's notebook during a school recess. Her notebook and her heart were always wide open for every student of our class.

Mama stopped pressing me about my academics, and most of my grades slid down to a three, or satisfactory. Only PE remained a subject in which I excelled without effort. I was strong and athletic. My picture hung at the very top of the School's Best Athletes board. But Mama was not impressed. "Quick legs feed only a wolf, and you need a profession," she would say when I bragged about my athletic achievements.

Still, I continued to dream. That spring, the news came like a thunderstorm on a clear summer day, in the form of a TASS (Telegraph Agency of the Soviet Union) radio announcement. "On April 12, 1961, in the Soviet Union, the world's first satellite spaceship Vostok, with a man on board, has been launched into orbit around the Earth. The pilot of the Vostok is Major of the Air Force Yuri Alekseyevich Gagarin, a citizen of the Union of Soviet Socialist Republics."

I laughed and yelled with other people on the street and hugged a stranger. The first man was in cosmos—and not just a man, but a *Soviet* man. We had beaten the USA. Once again, our country had proved the advantage of our socialist society over the capitalist system.

Within a day, Gagarin, a twenty-seven-year-old from an ordinary Russian peasant family, became an international hero. The next morning, his beaming, boyish face looked at us from every newspaper. *That's it*, I thought. *I want to be the first woman to go to space. If he did it, why can't I?*

Wanting to follow Gagarin's footsteps, I decided to join a flight club, where I could learn how to jump with a parachute and how to fly a plane. Then, like him, I would go to a flight school.

On a bright Sunday morning in May, Yulka accompanied me on the bus to the outskirts of Ashkhabad, where the aero club of *DOSAAF* (All-Union Voluntary Society for Assistance to the Army, Air Force, and Navy) was located. Yulka said that she wouldn't try a parachute jump for a million rubles, but she would keep me company. We found ourselves on a huge field, with some light construction along one side. A crowd of young men waited in front of its entrance. There were just two other girls. As I listened to the conversation around me, I realized I wasn't the only person dreaming of becoming a cosmonaut. It felt as if they were all stealing my dream.

About an hour later, a short man with a brown, weather-beaten face came outside with a stack of paper. "Everyone who wants to join the club has to fill out this form," he said. He looked around the crowd and stopped his eyes at our girls' group.

"How old are you?" He pointed at me.

"Fourteen," I mumbled, embarrassed by his attention.

"Want to become the first woman cosmonaut?" he asked, grinning. I felt like I had just swallowed my own tongue.

"She wants to learn how to parachute," Yulka yelled coming to my rescue.

"Good. Come back when you turn sixteen and get your passport, and we'll find something for you to do here." He handed out the forms to the rest of the group, and Yulka and I trampled across the field to the bus stop.

I remained one of only three or four girls in my class who didn't have a boyfriend. Yulka and I both expressed our contempt for boys and their stupid proposals, and we vowed that if we ever got one, we'd never accept it, anyway. Deep inside, though, I felt hurt and puzzled. What was wrong with me?

Once, when nobody was home, I entered my parents' bedroom, removed my clothes, and stood in front of Mama's mirror scrutinizing my figure—narrow hips, thin strong legs, a wasp waist, and straight shoulders. I looked as lean as a whippet.

I wished I had the rounded thighs and busts that my female classmates had been showing off, like new dresses, since last fall. In winter, I had worn two layers of warm underwear every day to make my hips look a little wider, but now in spring, I had "lost" even that little shape. I looked like one of our boys. No wonder they didn't pay attention to me.

Although Yulka and I tried to convince ourselves that we already had lots of boyfriends on Bagirskaya Street, we both understood that it was different. Even Sashka, who imagined himself to be my boyfriend, was just a friend.

Then, during the last days of the school year, the friendship proposals started raining down. The first note came from Mishka Shishlovskiy, a dark-haired boy with big brown eyes, who, because of his shyness, wasn't popular among the girls.

"I like you. Let's be friends," read Mishka's note. My heart jumped. I couldn't wait to share my news with Yulka.

"We vowed not to accept any propositions from boys, remember?" she told me, looking hurt.

"Of course I do," I said, feeling sorry for Mishka's broken heart.

"No," I wrote back to him the next day. Two days later, he made another proposal to a girl from my class, and she accepted it. But Mishka's quick consolation didn't frustrate me very much. I already had a victory in my pocket, and it was enough to pump up my damaged pride.

School was over and only three exams separated us from finishing the eighth grade when Vovka Nosik, a harmless class joker and tough Gazha errand boy, came up to me with an oral message.

"Kolka offers you his friendship," he said. I was stunned. Kolka Malov, a suntanned and fair-haired athletic teenager, was one of the most popular boys in our school. Many girls had tried unsuccessfully to get his attention.

This time I did not seek Yulka's advice. I said yes.

That evening, Kolka came to my house to take me to *Molodezhny*, our neighborhood outdoor movie theatre. The night was pure magic. As I walked next to him, a light breeze caressed my legs under my short cotton skirt and light sandals. One strap of my white blouse slipped, stripping my shoulder, and as I talked and laughed at his jokes, I pretended not to notice it. When Kolka's shoulder touched mine, it made my head spin.

26: The Fire

At the end of July 1961, my family was coming back from a three-week vacation trip to Leningrad and Moscow, where my parents took Andrusha, who was going to the first grade in September, and me after I successfully passed the entrance exams in the musical college. After three weeks of visiting museums and memorials, creeping in a multi-hour line to see embalmed, yellowish bodies of Lenin and Stalin in the Mausoleum on Red Square, and days of exhausting shopping in Moscow stores, we were resting in a compartment carriage of the high-speed train that would take us home.

It was a long ride. We crossed the Volga River, and the Russian landscape of birch forests, green meadows, and white-washed villages gave way to the steppes of Kazakhstan—flat and empty land, with rare railway sidings of two or three huts. Then came two days of dull and empty space—the boundless Aral steppes and flats of Uzbekistan with little signs of life. Closer to Tashkent, the train passed cotton plantations and melon fields, where Uzbek women in colorful dresses worked under the scorching July sun, their heads and faces wrapped in white veils. When we woke up on the third morning, Mama said that we were already in Turkmenistan. Our train was crossing the Kara-Kum Desert, and our trip was coming to an end.

After breakfast, our car stewards, two Turkmen men, went around collecting the linen and tea glasses. An announcement over the intercom said that our train had entered the border zone, and passengers were asked to stay in their compartments and prepare for the passport check in Kaahka, our last stop before Ashkhabad.

In our compartment, Mama packed our bags, and I folded the mattresses for Papa to lift to the narrow shelves below the ceiling. When we were done, he said that he needed to shave before our arrival and left the compartment. Andrusha, for lack of space inside, stood in the deserted passageway outside our compartment, looking at the blue ridge of the Kopet Dag Mountains on the left side of the train.

The closer we were to home, the more my excitement grew. I had so many stories to share with my friends. *Coming back, coming back, coming back,* I heard the train wheels, tapping on the tracks, say.

"Mama, the dust is coming out from the next-door compartment," Andrusha said, sticking his head inside.

"It's fine," Mama said. "The car steward hasn't swept the floors today." Andrusha's head disappeared.

In a minute he was back. "Mama, come and look at it. There's more dust now." If Andrusha got something in his small head, he'd never quit asking until he got what he wanted.

"I'll be back," Mama told me, putting aside the bag she was stuffing with the leftovers of our food.

A moment later, I heard her knocking on the neighbor's door. "Is anybody there? Open the door! There's smoke coming out of your compartment!"

I stopped wrestling with the suitcase and went out to see what was going on. Mama stood in front of the closed door of the compartment on our right. Andrusha squatted, watching thin white wisps coming out through the ventilation holes at the bottom of the door. I grabbed the door handle and tried to slide it open, but it didn't yield.

"Comrade, open up! There's smoke coming out of your compartment!" Mama shouted now, banging on the door. Nobody answered. I pressed my ear against the smooth surface and listened. There were faint rustling sounds inside, like dry autumn leaves driven by the wind.

"Hey," I yelled. "Wake up! You're on fire!" The door was locked from inside, but nobody answered.

"Run and tell our stewards," Mama said.

I ran down the car and pulled the door of the service compartment where our linen and extra mattresses were stored. It was locked. The next compartment, where our stewards slept in turns when off shift, was empty. No one was in the front vestibule, either. The long passageway, with eight or nine four-berth compartments, was deserted. All of the doors were closed. The passengers were getting ready for their arrival.

Smoke drifted across the floor, floated up, and stirred in a crazy dance with the air streaming from the open windows. Mama and Andrusha stood where I left them.

"They're not there," I said. "I can run through the train and find them."

"No, go back to our compartment and stay there," Mama said. Her eyes were tense, and the creases between her eyebrows became more pronounced. "I will run to the front car and tell the steward there. They may need to stop the train. I'll be right back."

She hurried down the aisle. I knew that the only way to stop the train was to pull a s*top-kran* (emergency brake) located in the front and rear vestibules of each car. Could the train go off the rails if it had to stop at such a high speed? I grabbed Andrusha's hand and pulled him back to our compartment.

"Sit here and hold tight to the handrail," I told him. "I'll go and tell other passengers that we're on fire." Andrusha nodded. His dark eyes were huge and serious. “Hold on tightly,” I repeated. He grabbed the railing with both hands, and I rushed into the passageway again.

The smoke seemed darker and thicker now, and it was quickly filling the aisle. Some of it was now also coming from the service compartment door.

I ran to the back of the car, knocking on every door and warning the passengers about the fire. They stuck their heads out, saw the smoke, and shouted orders to their spouses and kids. On my way back to my compartment, I faced them running toward me with suitcases, bags, and boxes. Jostling against the current, I worried about Andrusha. Why had I had so stupidly left him behind at the front of the car?

“Where're you going, girl? Can't you see all that smoke? Run the other way,” a man growled, trying to stop me.

“My brother!” I yelled. “I have to get my brother!”

When I reached our compartment, it was full of smoke. Andrusha was where I left him, still clinging to the handrail. I could barely unclench his small hands.

“Let's go!” I pulled him down the aisle.

“Where's Mama?” he cried, coughing. “Where's my Mama?”

“Run!” I yelled, dragging him to the rear of the car. “You'll see her soon.” The train was slowing down. I heard the grinding of its wheels against the rails and the silence.

“Where's Papa?” Andrusha asked.

Papa? I stopped.

I hadn't seen our father since the fire started. Could he still be in the bathroom? But which one? The bathroom at the head of the car was out of reach now. I knocked on the bathroom door in the rear vestibule.

“Papa! Papa!” I called. “Are you there?” The door opened, and Papa stuck his head out, wiping soap from his face.

“Is it already Kaahka?” he asked.

We were the last three people to leave the burning car. I jumped down onto the railway embankment first, and Papa handed me Andrusha, then followed. Passengers were leaping out of other cars to see what happened. I saw Mama running in our direction from the front. Catching her breath and brushing away tears, she hugged Andrusha and me.

"I was so scared for you. I couldn't get back to our car." While Mama described the events to Papa, she didn't let go of our hands. The passengers of our car stood around us with their luggage and listened to Mama's story. Everyone's eyes were glued on the burning car. The puzzle of the locked compartment was on everyone's tongue.

"I know a man from that compartment," Papa said. "I smoked in the vestibule with him. He is an army officer, coming back from his father's funeral."

Is he still there? Was he drunk? Did he fall asleep smoking and cause the fire? People guessed.

Somebody picked up a rock and threw it into the compartment's window. There was a popping sound of breaking glass, and a huge tongue of flame soared out and began licking the roof of the car. I felt a blast of heat on my face, and more sharp sounds of popping windows came. The whole car was enveloped in flames.

"If he was there, he is dead now," somebody said.

"Nobody is dead. It's my compartment," a man's voice behind me said.

I turned around. The man wore green Soviet Army trousers and slippers on his bare feet. In his hand, he held a toothbrush; traces of toothpaste were smeared on his chin. In a different situation, he would have been quite comical.

"Why didn't you say so? We all worried about him, and he is standing here alive and not saying a thing," a woman blurted out. Just a minute ago she was terrified of the idea that somebody could be still in the car, and now she yelled at him because he wasn't.

"I was in the bathroom when I smelled smoke," the man explained. "I ran out and wanted to go back to my compartment. My *partbilet* (Party membership card) is there, in my jacket pocket. As a Communist, I have no right to lose it under any circumstances. I wanted to get it, but it was too late. The door was jammed."

"Officer, you could easily have died in that fire. Your Party will forgive you for losing your *partbilet*," Papa said.

In the turmoil, I had left our compartment barefoot, and now the scorching desert sand burned the soles of my feet. Seeing me hopping around on the ground, Papa took off his enormous sandals and gave them to me. Then, barefoot, he rushed to help uncouple our car from the rest of the train. The back of the car in front of ours was already smoldering, and if nothing was done, soon the whole train would catch fire.

When a fire truck arrived from Kaahka, everything was over. It took about ten minutes for our bright green car to turn into a charred skeleton, but thanks to the heroic efforts of Papa and the other passengers, the other cars were all saved.

The locomotive made a long whistle, and passengers began climbing back to their cars. The fire victims trudged, loaded with their bags and suitcases. Only my family and the officer trailed behind empty-handed—he in his green galife pants and slippers, barefoot Papa in his new striped pajama pants and sleeveless T-shirt, and Mama holding Andrusha's hand. I shuffled behind them all in Papa's huge sandals.

We rode for the rest of the trip in the dining car. Mama told the story of how it all began and how she pulled the *stop-kran*. The waitresses gasped and bustled around us, serving lemonade and chocolate candy in colorful wrappers. Papa drank vodka with the director of the restaurant.

It was late afternoon when our train pulled into the Ashkhabad station. As soon as we were home, without changing out of my reeking-of-smoke-and-soot dress, I ran outside to see my friends. I was eager to tell them about our adventure, but I had lost my voice. My story, told in a hoarse whisper, sounded even more dramatic.

Ever since my earliest Pioneer years, I had dreamed of being a hero, to save a drowning person or pull a child from a burning house. I wanted to have my picture printed in a newspaper and be awarded with a medal.

Now, although there were no medals or newspaper articles, and nobody even thanked us on that day, I was satisfied. I was proud of my family, and especially of Mama, who pulled the emergency brake and stopped the train.

All our belongings, money, and documents had vanished in the fire. Three big suitcases with new clothes, various boxes with canned food, Moscow delicatessen and confectionary treats, a heavy box with sheet music for my college, and even two Uzbek melons Papa bought in Tashkent were all gone. My parents didn't fret about it. "We're all alive and in good health, which is all that matters. The rest we can buy," Papa said.

The investigation took several months, and the trial took place the following spring. The cause of the fire was determined to be a cigarette butt that had flown into the open window of the service car, where mattresses and linen were stored. The steward on duty who had abandoned his working place was convicted of criminal negligence and sentenced to a monetary restitution for the damages to the Soviet property. The State paid us a nominal amount for the loss of our belongings.

Andrusha, who was the first person to discover the fire, was summoned to be a witness. He surprised everybody with his detailed description of the accident.

27: If You Are Young

On Saturday evening, when the loudspeakers in the Molodezhny movie theatre came to life, Yulka and I hurried in the direction of the music, full of the anticipation of meeting our boyfriends. Yulka had accepted a friendship proposal from a Gazha boy named Lopuh not long after I said yes to Kolka.

There was still almost an hour before the movie began. The ticket booth was dark, but the theatre's double doors were open, and I could see a woman sprinkling water on the dirt aisles between blue wooden benches. The familiar smell of wet dust tickled my nose.

Across the street from the theatre, a group of Gazha guys squatted under a big mulberry tree, smoking. I knew most of them from our school. Kolka and Lopuh were there, and when they saw us, they got up and walked in our direction. Kolka, whom I had not seen since I left for Moscow a month ago, looked taller. His face and arms were more tanned, probably from spending too much time at the swimming pool. He grinned at me.

The four of us discussed our plans for the evening. Kolka offered to go to the movie theatre to watch a new Russian comedy called *A Striped Voyage*. The movie had just come out, but he had already watched it twice and wanted us to see it too. I was up for anything. No matter where we went or what we did, I enjoyed it—going to a park, wandering the Ashkhabad streets, watching movies, or just sitting on a bench and listening to the boys' stories. I was fourteen, and life was wonderful.

While we were waiting for the ticket booth to open, Kolka described scenes from the movie, depicting its characters, gesturing, and laughing so loudly that people began to turn around. By the time the door to the theatre opened, we already knew all funny moments and jokes from the movie.

We moved slowly with the stream of people to the entrance, and Kolka handed our tickets to the attendant and then stepped back for Yulka and me to go first. But the woman suddenly blocked our way with her chubby body.

"What is on your head?" she asked, pointing her short sausage-finger at Yulka.

"Where?" Yulka asked, turning her head left and right. "What?"

"On your head. Your hairdo," the woman demanded.

"This? It's just a ponytail," Yulka said, making the innocent face that she always used when she sensed trouble. Ponytails were just coming into fashion in the Soviet Union. I had seen plenty of young women with their long hair tied to the back of the head in Moscow and Leningrad, but here in Ashkhabad it was still rare. Yulka's long blond hair tied at her nape with a black ribbon, as well as the bangs that covered her forehead down to eyebrows, attracted attention. People openly stared at her; some pointed and laughed. The ticket-taker's question wasn't completely a surprise.

"A *horse* tail? I won't allow you to enter the theatre with that thing on your head."

"Why? It's just a hairdo," I said, rushing to the aid of my friend. A crowd of people with tickets in their hands started gathering behind us.

"Because," she snapped, "you're too young to question me. If I said no, it means no. If your girlfriend wants to watch the movie, tell her to undo her tail." She turned away from us.

"Show us where it's written that she cannot enter the theatre with a ponytail," Lopuh demanded.

"You talk more, *soplyak* (sissy), and I'll call the militia," the woman yelled at him. "Move aside and don't hold up our customers."

"Let the girl in," a young baritone from the crowd called out.

"You pass by, comrade. It's none of your business. If I allow her to go inside with her horse tail, tomorrow she'll come here naked. What will you say then?"

"He'll probably like it," a woman's voice behind us shouted. The crowd burst into laughter.

"Don't let her in," another one said. "These young people are terrible nowadays. No decency."

"You're right," the ticket-taker agreed. "What's wrong with a Russian braid? Neat and beautiful. Much prettier than this ugly horse tail. It's all the influence of the West. Today they come to the cinema with a tail, and tomorrow they'll betray their motherland."

Her words made my blood boil. "Who gave you the right to judge?" I yelled. "If you wear this old-fashioned bump on your head, you think it makes you a patriot of our country?" I had never dared to talk to an adult like this before.

"You see how insolent this modern youth has become. No respect for elders at all," the ticket-taker blasted, looking around for support. "If you don't leave right now, I'm going to call the militia." She put a whistle, which hung on a dirty string between her huge breasts, into her mouth and looked at me with a challenge.

"Call anyone you like," I shouted, but Kolka grabbed my arm and dragged me away from the scene. I was shaking. My mouth was dry. "Let her call the militia," I raged, trying to pull away from him. "How dare she call us traitors?"

Our evening was ruined. Yulka was crying, and we all felt humiliated. Kicking stones in frustration, we trudged into the darkening pathways of the park.

"I hate the adults," Yulka said. "Why do they think they have to tell us what hairdo is right for us, or what we should wear?"

"Yes, why?" I fumed. "No bangs at school, no nylon stockings! In the sixth grade somebody said I curled my hair, so our teacher took me to the bathroom and dampened my head to check if my curls were natural."

"*Nel'zya* (not allowed) this and *nel'zya* that," Lopuh echoed. Anything new is not allowed. Ask them why, and they tell you, 'Just *nel'zya* and that's all.'"

Eventually, we quieted down. "Now what?" Kolka asked.

"Let's go somewhere else," I offered. "Does anybody want ice cream?"

"I don't want to go anywhere," Yulka said. "Let's sit here in the park."

It was getting darker, and the overgrown paths were dimly lit. Most of the lights were burned out or broken. We found a bench hidden in the bushes. Two boards of the seat were missing, so we climbed on top and sat on its back rest. The boys lit a cigarette and passed it back and forth. Yulka and I silently watched its glowing tip.

"I got my salary today. Let's buy a bottle of wine and *obmoyem* (wash down) my first pay," Kolka suggested.

It sounded so grownup after all the frustration of the evening. Why not? Adults washed down all kinds of purchases and events.

"They won't sell you wine. You're not sixteen yet," Yulka said.

"Nonsense. I've been buying wine for my dad since I was twelve, and nobody asks me about my age," Lopuh said.

"Where will we drink?" I asked.

"Right here. On this bench."

"Without glasses?"

Kolka flicked the cigarette butt. It made an arch, sending tiny fireflies into the darkness before disappearing in the bushes.

"We can steal a glass from the soda-water machines around the corner," he said, getting up. In Ashkhabad, carbonated drinks were dispensed from machines into communal glasses, rather than individual-serving bottles.

"Don't worry. Lopuh and I will run to a *Vino-Vodka* store, and you girls go and get a glass at the soda stall. Wait for us at the entrance. We'll be back in ten minutes," Kolka said.

At the soda-water machines, several people were drinking water from cut-glass tumblers. Yulka and I waited for our turn. A man in front of me finished drinking and handed me his glass. I put it upside down into the washing recess and pressed on the bottom of the glass to activate the water fountain underneath. When it was clean, I moved it under the dispenser and inserted one kopek into the slot. With a metallic gurgle, the machine swallowed my coin and I heard the familiar sound of fizzy water pouring into the glass.

Yulka and I sipped it in turns, waiting for the right moment. When nobody was around, I poured the remaining water out, put the glass into a pocket of my skirt, and we hurried back to the entrance of the park. I had never done anything like that before, and my hands were trembling.

Our boyfriends showed up a few minutes later, smiling triumphantly. Lopuh carried a bottle wrapped in brown paper. "We've bought *Ter-Bash*," Kolka announced. "It's the best lady's wine."

Back in our secluded corner, the boys opened the bottle, and we passed the glass from one to another. For Yulka and me, this was our first wine. I took small, cautious gulps of the sweet liquid, which left a burning trail inside my chest. A minute later, I felt a light fog in my head, and the bench started slowly rising and floating in the air. The frustrations of the evening went away, and everything seemed terribly funny now—Yulka's silly smile, Kolka's jokes, and Lopuh's freckled face and red hair. We mocked that stupid ticket-taker, calling her different names and laughing at our own wit.

It was about eleven o'clock when the movie ended. Talking and laughing people flooded the pathways, and it was time for us to go home. When I stood up, I realized that my legs felt as if they were made of cotton, and I had to concentrate to steer myself down the alley.

Twenty minutes later, we approached Bagirskaya Street. Aunt Vera stood on the corner, holding her husband's belt.

"Oh, I'm late," Yulka sang. "I'm going to get a scolding." Only then did I notice how drunk my friend was.

"Do you know what time it is?" Aunt Vera asked, her voice promising nothing good.

"Ne-ah," Yulka said, without a hint of worrying. In a normal state, she would have been terrified.

"Go home now," Aunt Vera demanded. "Your father is waiting for you."

After that, our mood wilted. Lopuh left, and Kolka took me to the gate of my house and was gone, too. Papa wasn't home. I undressed and went to bed, thinking about Yulka. Her father could be nasty even without a reason. If he found out that Yulka was drunk, he'd beat her.

I thought how lucky I was that my parents weren't home. But even if Papa was there, he probably wouldn't have detected the smell of alcohol on my breath anyway, because usually he was soused by that time of day himself. And even if he had, he would never touch me. He waved his fists and crashed windows when he was drunk, but he had never raised his hand to me or Andrusha. Mama's stern look and dry voice would have been far worse.

The next morning, I had to attend a meeting for new students in the musical college. On my way to the bus station, I stopped by Yulka's house. She stepped out onto the street giggling, one hand on her forehead as if she was having a bad headache.

"What happened?" I asked. "Did he hurt you?"

"No. *He* was asleep when she dragged me home. It's *her*."

"Did Aunt Vera hurt you? Show me," I demanded, expecting to see a big bump or a bruise on her head.

Still giggling, Yulka lifted her hand. Her forehead, which the night before was covered with even bangs, now was empty. Short, uneven stubs of unruly hair bristled in all directions.

"What's that?" My jaw dropped in disbelief.

"She cut it off last night. Just grabbed my bangs and *cheeeck*," Yulka made a scissor-like movement with two fingers. I couldn't help laughing.

"Why?" I asked at last, wiping my tears.

"So I would sit at home and go nowhere. Can you believe it?"

"She was right. You cannot show up anywhere like that," I said.

Yulka rolled her eyes. "I cannot sit here by myself all the time looking like a clown."

And she did not. By the time I got back in the afternoon, Yulka already had a new, impressive fringe that began in the middle of her head and went over the bits of her former bangs, covering the damage completely.

"Now she'll definitely kill me," she said with a grin.

"Well, at least you'll die looking nice."

28: The Piano Teacher

Ashkhabad's musical college, named after Turkmen composer Dangatar Ovezov, was located in a long, one-story building in the heart of the city. From the outside, it looked like hundreds of other structures built after the earthquake—a long barrack built in a hurry, with low, barred windows and peeling, whitewashed walls.

The barrack was not big enough to accommodate all of the students, so several other structures had been added in the courtyard: a concert hall with a stage and rows of benches, a musical literature library, classrooms for brass instrumentalists, and the outhouse.

I was a student of the piano department, one of the most prestigious sections in the college. I was one of only eight first-year piano students—two boys and six girls. Our mornings were filled with individual and group lessons: piano, which we called the specialty class; elementary music theory; solfeggio, which taught us pitch, sight singing, musical dictation, and hearing analysis; musical literature and history; and accompaniment.

In the afternoons, we had classes in typical school subjects. This way, our musical school diplomas would not only give us the right to work as music teachers and accompanists, but also would allow us to continue our education in music or any other field if we wished. All of the school's attention, though, was directed towards our future musical specialty, and neither the students nor the teachers took general education seriously. In four years of study, I don't remember doing any homework in the afternoon subjects I studied.

My specialty teacher that year was Cheper Atayevna, a small, olive-skinned Turkmen woman about Mama's age. During our first lesson, she told me how lucky I was to get into her class, because she was the first Turkmen woman to graduate from the prestigious Moscow Conservatory. When she played an excerpt from Beethoven's Appassionata (Sonata No. 23 in F minor) for me, I thought that I had never seen anyone play the piano with such vigor. She attacked the keyboard with all her energy, jumping up and down on every chord and furiously tapping the pedal with her right foot.

The program she chose for me to learn that year was ambitious, but after just a couple of lessons, she told me I had a bright future in front of me. When she met my parents and informed them what a rising star they had, Mama was in seventh heaven.

Cheper Atayevna became a frequent guest in our house. No party or family gathering took place without her, and she appeared to enjoy my parents' hospitality. Every holiday, Mama sent her a present, and Papa gave her three-liter jars of honey for her son, Chary, who often had colds and needed better nutrition.

My teacher didn't hesitate to ask for favors. More than once, she left Chary with us for a couple of days at a time. She asked Papa to lend her money, which she forgot to repay. She fed my parents' generosity by constantly reminding them about my talent and promising to assist in my admission to the Moscow Conservatory.

My piano lessons with Cheper Atayevna were unusually stress-free. Tamara Mikhailovna had always paid lots of attention to my piano technique, sound quality, and expressiveness. She demanded I play three or four hours daily, and she missed nothing. Playing a note with the wrong finger equated to a crime and was punishable by long confinement at the piano. My sheet music was heavily marked with her scribbling—fat circles around false notes; curved lines showing where I had to play *legato*, claws of *crescendo* or *diminuendo*; and lattices of sharps and flats that I had missed. Holes in the page showed the places where my teacher's irritation with my mistake pushed her pencil all the way through the paper. When the time for an exam came, I knew my program so well that I could perform it with my eyes closed from beginning to end.

Lessons with Cheper Atayevna, on the other hand, were easy and relaxed. Most of her instructions were basic—"learn this part by heart," "play the left hand softer," "slow down at the end." My music sheets looked as if they had just left the shelf of a store. I didn't need to slave at the piano at home to please this teacher. One or two hours a day seemed to do.

At the beginning of November, I became a member of the *VLKSM*, The All Union Leninist Communist League of Youth. This was the political organization of Soviet young people between the ages of fourteen and twenty-eight, and the next step after we outgrew the Young Pioneer Organization. I saw becoming a Komsomol as another step into adulthood.

While Young Pioneers collected scrap metal, grew silkworms, and ran errands for disabled veterans, Komsomols hammered away at All-Union Komsomol Shock Constructions in Siberia, developed the virgin lands in Kazakhstan, and explored and conquered the cosmos. I had watched them enviously and longed to join their ranks, but when my time at last arrived, it was nothing like what I expected.

At the beginning of December, our group of Komsomols was sent to sort potatoes. Turkmenistan didn't grow potatoes of its own, so every fall, freight trains of them arrived from Russia and

Ukraine. After long travel through freezing weather and long waits on railway sidings, the potatoes arrived in Ashkhabad looking tired. After a few more days in our warm climate, they began to rot. Fearing that the citizens of Ashkhabad wouldn't have any potatoes left to put into their borscht, the City Council and City Committee of the Communist Party instructed the local Komsomol and Party leaders to organize student brigades for a potato rescue mission. *When the Party says, 'You must!' The Komsomol replies, 'We'll do!'*

All of the classes at the musical college were cancelled, and the students went to the Vegetable Base in the Hitrovka district to sort potatoes.

When we arrived at nine o'clock in the morning, an employee took us to the place where we would work. Before I even saw the potato mountain tower, I could smell it. For eight hours we sat, hunchbacked on bricks, and sorted potatoes covered with Russian black earth, putting good ones into a wooden crate and throwing soft and slimy ones into a pile.

When nobody watched us, we started potato fights. The pianists threw potatoes at the stringers, the winders at the singers, and *teoretiki* (theory of music students) at the percussionists and folk instrumentalists. Our cheering filled the base when a sticky bomb reached its target. Bit by bit, the heap shrank along with our cheerful mood. Our backs hurt and our hand, covered with a black crust of dirt and rot, ached. The black gunk under my nails wouldn't wash out, lingering until my nails grew and I trimmed it away.

When we finished, the potatoes were delivered to city vegetable shops, where people purchased sacks of them for the approaching winter. Mama kept ours in the cellar, spread on a big piece of cardboard. She used them frugally, trying to stretch our supply as long as possible. That year's potatoes appeared frostbitten. We could eat them, but they tasted unpleasantly sweet. By the end of February, most of our reserve was gone. The remaining pieces shrank, began to sprout, and were difficult to peel.

After the winter session, I got my first student *stipendiya* (stipend) of fourteen rubles a month. Getting a stipend in the USSR was not difficult—everyone who passed their exams with good grades was eligible. Honor students received a little more money, and if a student only got a three (satisfactory) grade in one or more subjects or failed an exam, the *stipendiya* was denied until the next successful session.

Fourteen rubles per month wasn't much—the minimum wage of a janitor or a salesperson was about sixty rubles per month at the time—but for me, it was a fortune. I had never earned money of my own before. I put the money into my coin purse, snapped its tiny ball clasp, stuck it in my sheet music tote, and headed to the bus stop.

When I got home, my coin purse was gone. I took all of my books out my tote and shook every one of them as if I was looking for a needle. It wasn't there. Devastated, I told Mama about my loss.

"Probably it was stolen in the bus," she said. As soon as she said it, I remembered a young man who had decided to leave the bus at the last moment. He pushed me aside and yelled for me to let him go, even though the bus wasn't crowded, and I seemed to be out of his way. I knew what had happened to my *stipendiya.*

"I've told you to be careful on buses," Mama said. "Those guys are looking for a scatterbrain like you. Don't cry. It'll be a good lesson for you in the future."

In late spring, our physical education teacher, Vano Alikovich, dug a jumping pit, drew a line with a piece of a stick, and said that we were going to do long jumps. He gave a tape-line to two girls who, embarrassed and blushing, had told him that they couldn't do any athletics that day, and he told them to measure. The rest of us lined up for a running start and, one after another, jumped into the pit. He wrote down our results in his tattered notebook.

"One meter, eighty centimeters," announced the girl at the end of the measuring tape. "Two meters, fifty centimeters . . . two meters, ten . . . four meters, five . . ."

"That's not right. Measure again," Vano Alikovich said without looking up.

"Four meters, four," the girl said after re-measuring. I stood near where I had landed, far past the other girls.

"Have you stepped over the line, Kondeykina?" he said. "Go and make another try."

I went back to the starting line, ran up as fast as I could, and took off. This time I landed a little farther. He measured it himself.

"Not bad for a pianist. Where did you learn to jump like this?"

"At school," I said.

"I don't know how good a musician you are," he told me. "But you'd certainly make a good athlete."

The next week, Vano Alikovich gave me a piece of paper with a name written on it. "This man is a track and field coach," he said. "I've told him about you, and he'd like to see you. He coaches at Locomotive Stadium every day from five to seven in the evening."

Serafim Feodorovich turned out to be a tall, heavy man with a big stomach and a booming voice that could be heard at either end of the stadium without a loudspeaker. He was the head track-and-field coach of the Youth National Team of Turkmenistan. I didn't know what Vano Alikovich had told him about me, but the first time I met Serafim Feodorovich, he invited me to join the team the next fall, after he and his athletes returned from their summer recreation camp and the national competitions in Russia.

While I was excited about the unexpected opportunity to compete with the Turkmen national team, that spring was weighed down by a bigger challenge. My first college year was coming to an end, and my first specialty exam was approaching. The closer I got, the more I realized how utterly unprepared I was. Every piece of music I needed to perform in front of the examination committee was still raw and unpolished. One place in the concerto, I realized as I practiced in the concert hall just days before the exam, sounded especially bad.

"Don't worry," Cheper Atayevna said, seeing my frustration. I was practicing Beethoven's Concerto for Piano and Orchestra, which was arranged for two pianos, and my teacher would play the other part during the exam. "Play that place softer, and I'll play the part of the orchestra louder. Nobody will notice your mistakes."

That was my teacher's solution? I was in panic.

The night before the exam I had a nightmare. I'm sitting at the grand piano on stage. My hands are on the keyboard, but I've forgotten how to play. The audience is waiting. It's so quiet that I can hear my own heartbeat. I'm frantically trying to remember at least something, but I cannot. The silence around me becomes tangible. It looks at me with hundreds of eyes. *It envelops me with its soft hairy body and squeezes my chest. I cannot breathe. I panic.*

That dream became a recurring nightmare that tortured me for years. Eventually, it started visiting me less often, but it never vanished. Even now, so many decades later, it still wakes me up with my heart racing. I'm scared of those silent people, waiting for me to perform.

Cheper Atayevna's last words before I went up on stage were, "Just play the whole program without stopping. If you forget something, skip it and continue from any place you can." She didn't say a word about paying attention to the sound, phrasing, dynamics, or pedaling.

I finished my program and got a four-minus, barely enough to keep my stipend, but I felt miserable. I was just a mediocre student of a mediocre teacher who had been milking my parents all year with tales about my nonexistent talents.

My maternal grandparents, Matryona Yakovlevna and Andrey Kondratievich Ilyukhin, Russia, 1916

Grandfather Andrey shortly before he was arrested

Grandpa Andrey with his sons, Yevgeny (14) and Boris (18) in the forced settlement in Shchelyayur, Russia, 1936

Uncle Yevgeny in Technical School of River Navigation, Shchelyayur 1936

My big Kondeykin family gathered for a photoshoot on the occasion of Peotr, Papa's eldest brother, coming home for leave after being wounded in WWII. (Grandfather Mikhail and Grandmother Praskovya in the middle of the first row; their sons Peotr (in uniform), Mikhail Jr. and Nikolai standing next to their wives and two sisters). My father is not in the picture. He is fighting the fascists at the front. Ashkhabad, 1943.

My father, Ivan Kondeykin (19), at Flight School, a year before the German invasion of the USSR, 1940

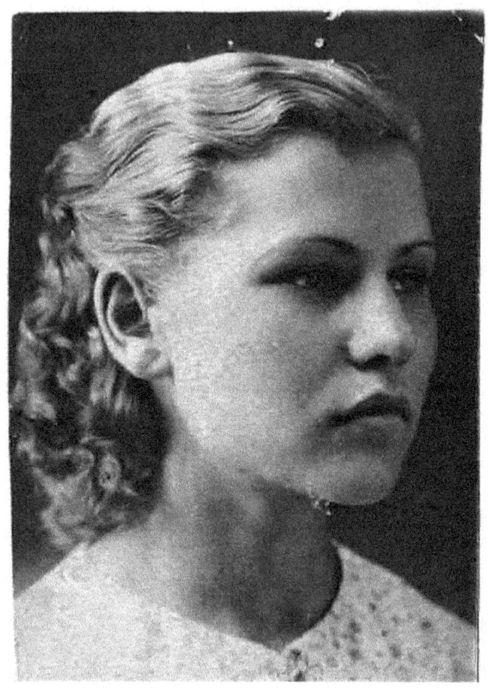

Valentina (17), my mother, the year her mother died

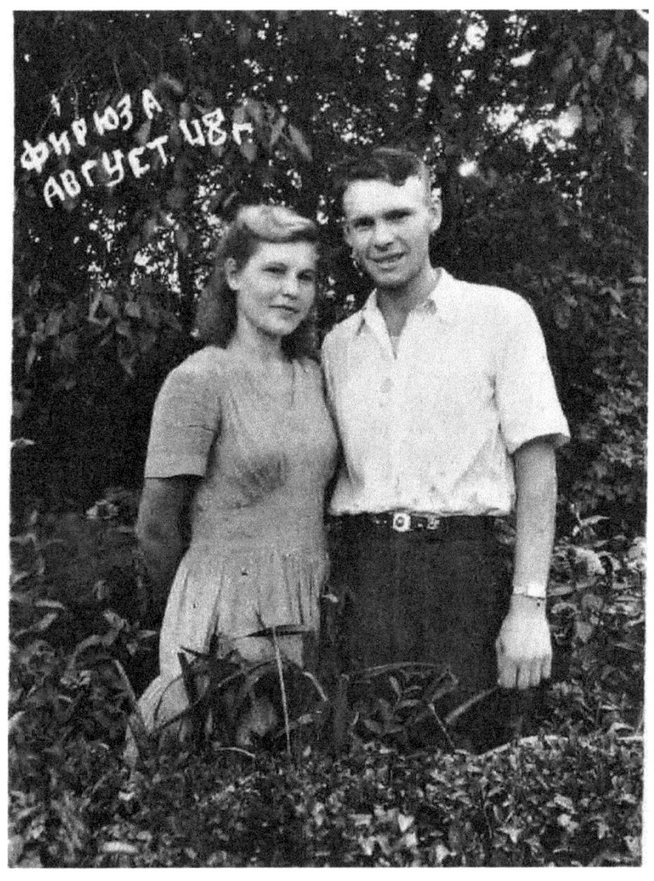

My parents in August 1948, two months before the deadly Ashkhabad earthquake

Mama and three-month-old me

Papa and I in Firuza mountain resort near Ashkhabad, August 1948

Ashkhabad on the first days after the earthquake

Burial of Ashkhabad earthquake victims in mass graves at Nikolskoye Cemetery, October 1948

My cousins Kolka, Tanya and Lida. The girls, my Aunt Pasha's daughters killed in the earthquake.

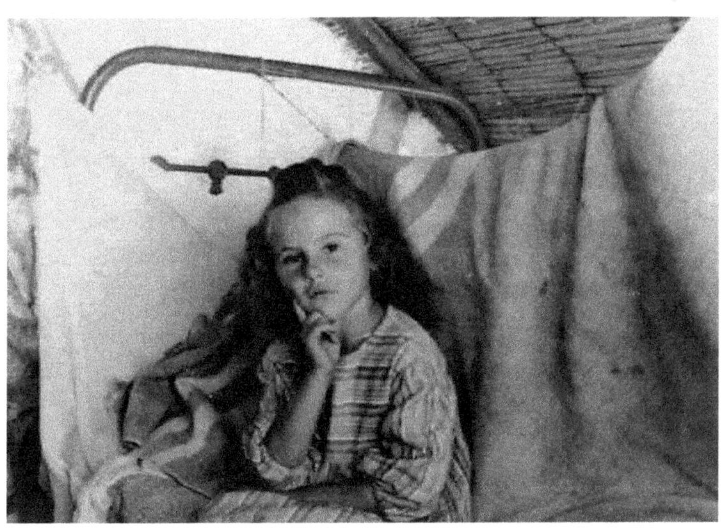

My nomadic childhood. I am at age 4 at one of the apiary sites.

The beekeepers pose beneath a huge bee swarm. The black mass above our heads is a colony of about 50 thousand bees that escaped from their hive.

At the summer Pioneer Camp. I am in the center of the upper row.

My best friend Yulka and I are 12

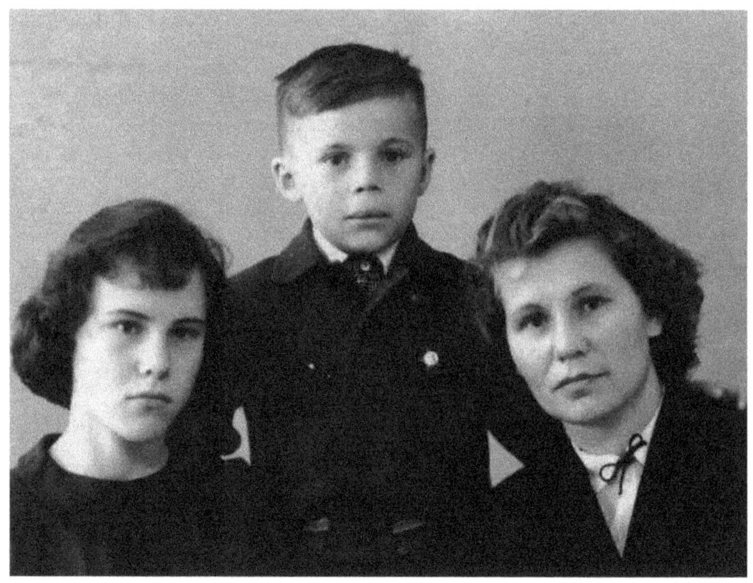

My brother, Andrey (7), is a first grader. A picture made on his becoming an "Oktyabrenok"—a child of October Revolution. He has a red star with a portrait of Lenin on his chest.

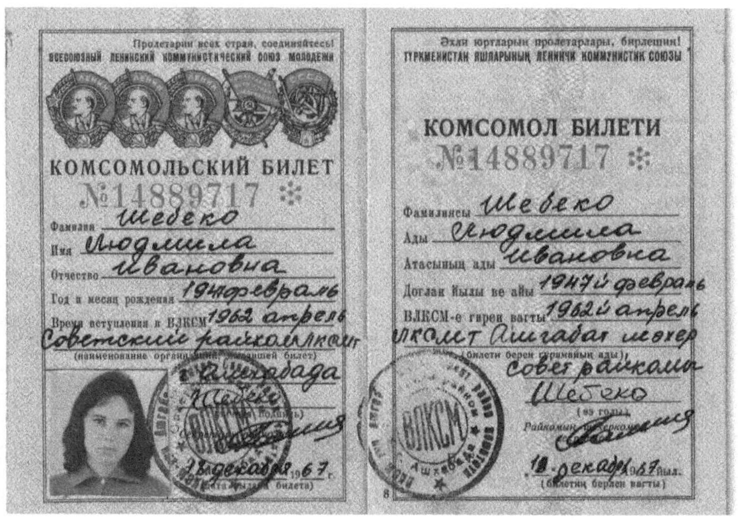

Пролетарии всех стран, соединяйтесь!
ВСЕСОЮЗНЫЙ ЛЕНИНСКИЙ КОММУНИСТИЧЕСКИЙ СОЮЗ МОЛОДЕЖИ

КОМСОМОЛЬСКИЙ БИЛЕТ
№14889717

Фамилия Шебеко
Имя Людмила
Отчество Ивановна
Год и месяц рождения 1947 февраль
Время вступления в ВЛКСМ 1962 апрель
Советский райком ЛКСМТ
(наименование организации, выдавшей билет)

18 декабря 1967 г.
(дата выдачи билета)

Әхли юртларың пролетарлары, бирлешиң!
ТҮРКМЕНИСТАН ЯШЛАРЫНЫҢ ЛЕНИНЧИ КОММУНИСТИК СОЮЗЫ

КОМСОМОЛ БИЛЕТИ
№14889717

Фамилиясы Шебеко
Ады Людмила
Атасының ады Ивановна
Доглан йылы ве айы 1947 й февраль
ВЛКСМ-е гирен вагты 1962 й апрель
(билети берен гурамының ады)
Шебеко
(өз голы)
Райкомың
18 декабря 1967 йыл.
(билетиң берлен вагты)

My Komsomol Membership Ticket

My Bagirskaya Street gang

Sashka and I with our newborn son, Dima

The day before Sashka was drafted into the Soviet army

Piano lesson with my student, Natasha G.

Mama with my son, Dima

My father and I

My 4th grade class at Ashkhabad school #44

My son (14) and I in June, 1981

29: On the Warpath

That summer I was fifteen, and life became so exciting that it was difficult to keep all my emotions inside. Every night, I sat in bed with my gray leatherette-covered diary and described the events of the day. I hid it under a pillow in my bedroom.

One night, Papa came home from work early. I heard him take off his shoes and step into the corridor. I was about to leave my room when my door burst open, and he barged in.

"You could have knocked before entering," I snapped. "I've just finished changing."

"Where were you last night?" he asked sharply, ignoring my words. His speech wasn't slurred, but in his eyes I could see he was drunk and angry—a bad combination. I cringed.

"Yesterday? On Bagirskaya Street with Yulka and the boys. Why?"

"After I went to bed," he demanded.

"I was at home reading until twelve and then fell asleep."

"Really?" he asked with a sly smile on his lips. "That's not what you wrote here."

Only then did I see my diary in his hand.

"You! You've read my diary! How could you? That's disgusting!" I was choking with indignation.

I couldn't believe I was so stupid to leave it under my pillow. He had probably got it when he came home for lunch and read it.

The previous night, I had left the house after my father fell asleep. It wasn't the first time I had done it. As before, Kolka waited for me at the end of our driveway. His bike stood next to him, leaning against the neighbor's fence. "Let's go," he whispered. I sat on the frame in front of him, and we rode along the dark, deserted streets of Ashkhabad. The warm air ruffled my hair, and I felt Kolka's hot breath on my back and neck. Strange languor filled my chest, and I wished our ride would never end.

Neither of us talked. From Sokolovskogo Street, he turned left to Maksim Gorkiy and rode past the Summer Pioneer Day Camp, Middle School #3, and Bunina Banya. We stopped at the City Park, and Kolka bought us a glass of water at the soda machine. We sat on the bench, talking and listening to the frogs' trilling somewhere in the depth of the park. At midnight, Kolka pedaled me home.

"What did you do with that guy in the middle of the night?" Papa yelled. His angry face came closer to mine. "You're a little slut!"

He raised his hand and slapped me on the cheek.

I gasped at the insult more than the blow. Kolka and I had never even kissed. He'd tried a couple of times, but I became so furious that he never made another attempt.

When other girls talked about their first kisses, I almost gagged. Their stories and dreamy eyes took me back to a time I tried to forget.

I was twelve. My friends and I were playing one of our noisy war games on Bagirskaya Street—chasing, ambushing, and "shooting" at each other. It was the time of the evening when we were afraid that our mothers would start calling us home. That always happened in the heat of the game, as if they waited for that moment to spoil our evening.

Zhenka was sitting on the neighbors' bench, watching our game. He was the son of a widowed neighbor and was much older than my friends and me. Mama said he had to be at least nineteen, because he was born before the war. But he had never attended school or worked. Behind his back, everybody called him Zhenka-*Durak* (the fool). He had a large body with a fleshy, pimply face and big, slobbering lips. He looked like a grownup man, but he mostly acted as harmless as a child.

That day, I noticed that he intensely watched me hiding behind a tree with a "gun" in my hands, but I was caught up in my game and didn't see when he got up. Suddenly, he grabbed me and wrapped his huge, sweaty body around me. I heard his heavy breathing, and before I could understand anything, I felt something wet on my face.

He started kissing me on the mouth. He smelled of onions, pickled herring, and something repulsive that came from the depths of his bowels. Like a fly on sticky tape, I struggled in his arms, trying with all my might to free myself, dodging his kisses.

"Milenka," I'd heard Mama's voice from our yard. "Come home. Supper is ready."

Moments before, I had been afraid that she'd call me, but now her voice came like a lifeline to a drowning person. Zhenka released his grip, and for a second I stood with my back against the tree, dizzy and unable to move.

After I fled home, I vomited in our bathroom, unable to stop the spasms. Mama said I probably had stomach flu and put me to bed without supper.

Now, when my own father called me a slut, I felt as if the whole world had turned against me.

"I hate you," I hissed into his face. "If you ever again step into my room or raise your hand on me, I'll kill you." I snapped my diary from his hand and rushed out the door.

Yulka and I burnt my diary in her yard, and I promised that it was the last time I would reveal my soul to paper.

Instead, I threw myself even deeper into horsing around with Yulka and our Gazha boyfriends. Their free spirits and adventurousness suited my rebellious mood. We rollicked in the public pool, played cards in the stands, or sat in the shade listening to *blatnyie* (thief) songs to the accompaniment of a guitar.

Those *blatnyie* songs described hard prison life, longing for freedom and lost love, and old mothers waiting for their sons to come home. The mournful melodies and simple, unpretentious words touched my heart and brought tears to my eyes.

That summer, I also learned how to smoke. A pack of BelomorKanal *papirosa*s (Russian cigarettes with hollow ends) was always sitting on our veranda table next to Papa's ashtray. He never caught me stealing from it.

We all knew that "nicotine is a poison" and that "a drop of nicotine could kill a horse." But in spite of posters and multiple warnings about the adverse effect of smoking, few Russians really paid attention. "Whoever doesn't smoke or drink will die healthy," they joked.

To prove that Yulka and I were not faking it, we had to pass a test.

"Light up a cigarette," one of our Gazha friends instructed us. "Take a long, deep draw. Now hold the puff and say, 'Mama built a fire—smoke is coming out' and then exhale."

To their cheers, I produced a long stream of blue smoke into the air.

30: Facing Reality

In September of my second year at the musical college, I bumped into a former classmate, Luda Borovkova, at a bus stop. While waiting for our bus to arrive, we talked about our summer vacation, her school where she was in the tenth grade, and my life at the musical college.

Standing next to her, I couldn't understand what had changed since I saw her last—Luda had the same tall, slim figure, dark eyes, and round face. She had cut off her braids and wore a Komsomol badge pinned to her black school apron. But there was something about her that I couldn't figure out. Finally, just as the bus appeared, I realized that it wasn't her; it was me who had changed. Luda had always been the tallest girl in our class, but now I didn't have to raise my head when I talked to her. Her eyes looked straight at mine, not down, as it was just a year ago.

I had grown.

When Yulka entered the musical college, we decided that instead of taking general education classes in the afternoon, as I had done in my first year, we would go to *Vecherka,*[8] the Evening School for

---

[8] Slang, a derivative from the Russian word *Vecher* (evening)

Working Youth. Many of our Gazha friends attended *Vecherka* four evenings a week, and it sounded like more fun.

Despite my new smoking habit, I began to practice track and field with the team at the Locomotive Stadium. Serafim Feodorovich, my coach, was happy with my achievements, and he pushed me hard to get me ready for competitions. My long jumps exceeded our republic's record, and he told me that I could compete in the All Union School Olympic games the following summer in Volgograd.

That fall, Sashka and I bonded over our athletic efforts. He was also getting ready to go to the School Olympics as a member of Turkmenistan National Youth Swimming Team. He had been to Volgograd once before, when it was still called Stalingrad, and he promised to show me around. We dreamed about all the things we would do in our free time.

The pesky little boy who had bothered me so much as a child was now my good friend.

In February I turned sixteen and received my first Soviet passport. Now I could find a job if I wanted to, buy alcoholic beverages and cigarettes, and go to movies to which children were not allowed. Most importantly to me, that summer I could start my parachute jump training, a dream I had not given up since Yuri Gagarin's flight into space.

As I entered this new season of adulthood, my clashes with Papa continued. We fought not only when he was drunk, but when he was sober, too. I couldn't stand the way he criticized and expressed cynicism about the Soviet way of life.

"You steal, as well," I snapped once during supper, when he said that all Communists were liars and thieves. "How do you make that *levak* of yours?"

"Don't be stupid," Papa retorted. "I do it for *you*. My salary is eighty-five rubles a month. Do you want to know how much a pair of good import boots cost? One hundred and twenty rubles! You don't want to wear a pair of boots made at Ashkhabad *Udarnik Factory*, do you?"

"Can the two of you ever eat in peace?" Mama asked. "I'm getting tired of your arguments."

"What do you know about life?" Papa pressed, ignoring her. His eyes fixed on mine. "You can judge me only when you start working and living on your own. For now, just look around and pay attention."

"Look at what? According to you, everything in the Soviet Union is done through bribes or pull," I persisted.

"Pretty much so. Do you think you would have entered your musical college without a bribe?" Papa pointed a sharp index finger at my face.

"Ivan, stop it!" Mama abruptly rose and began gathering dishes from the table.

"What do you mean?" I felt small hammers pounding in my temples as my father's words raised the first shadows of my doubt.

"I mean you can't do anything here without *blat* (favors) or bribes. I paid to get you in the musical college."

"No, you didn't! I earned it myself. Right, Mama?"

She stacked the empty plates and carried them to the kitchen without saying a word, and then I knew.

My motto, "The bitter truth is better than a beautiful lie," decorated the front page of every note or address book I had. Nothing upset me more than insincerity and hypocrisy. And now I realized that I'd been living a lie.

"Who asked you to do it?" I yelled, anger rising inside me. "If I wasn't accepted, I'd go back to school and enter the university after graduation."

"Then I'd have to pay ten times more for the university," Papa said, throwing up his hands.

"I don't need your *help*. That's it! I'm done with music!" I stormed out the door without acknowledging Mama's "Milenka!" behind me.

She was waiting for me when I came back home later that night. "Mila, don't be mad at Papa. He just wanted to help you," she said. "You did play well and would have entered the college all by yourself, but he wanted to secure it, just in case."

"In case of what?" I asked, still angry. "In case I didn't play well enough to get in?"

"No, quite the opposite. In case somebody who played worse than you took your place because they paid a bribe."

"Did you know about it?" I asked.

"Yes," she said.

"How can anything be right in this country if people cheat?" I asked.

Mama sat silently, examining her hands as if she saw them for the first time.

A few days later, my heart sank when Mama said, "Here comes your father. Look at him!"

I glanced out our veranda window. Papa was stumbling up our walkway, struggling to stay within its borders. His hat had slipped down to the side of his head, and his jacket, pants, and shoes were stained with a thick layer of mortar.

"Oh, God," Mama said. "He must have walked through the construction site on the First of May Street and fell into a mortar box."

Earlier that morning, Papa put on his two-piece navy suit and a fedora and said he was going to a meeting with a friend from the Ministry of Inner Affairs who had promised to help him get border crossing passes. It was the end of March, and my parents were getting ready to take our apiary to the Kopet Dag Mountains.

"Vanya, please don't drink. Come home early. We have so much work to do," Mama had told him.

"I'll be back in a couple of hours," he promised.

"Let a goat in the garden, he will devour all cabbage," Mama mumbled as he had disappeared behind the door.

Eight hours later, there he was in all his glory—soaked and dirty like a pig. He looked so ridiculous that Mama, Andrusha, and I burst out laughing. We were still giggling when he barged into the house.

Even in his drunken oblivion, he apparently wasn't numb enough not to feel the embarrassment of the situation, and our laughter was the drop that overflowed the vessel of his vanity. His bloodshot eyes froze on us, and then, without a word, he grabbed a stool and began smashing the veranda windows. Shards of glass flew in all directions. Broken pieces crunched under his feet as he turned to Mama.

I had never seen a fat lip or a black eye on Mama's face, but on the windowsill of their bedroom, she always kept a small jar of grayish powder. Once, I asked her what it was and why it always sat there. "It's *badyaga*," she said. "It helps to get rid of bruises faster." I didn't ask more questions, and she didn't volunteer to continue.

Now, scared that he would hit her, I grabbed his shirt and pulled him away. He staggered, trying to keep his balance, but dropped the stool, stumbled over it, and fell to the floor.

"Valya, I'll kill you!" he bellowed, trying to get up. His bloodshed eyes cast lightning.

All three of us piled on top of him like Lilliputians on Gulliver, grabbing his swinging hands, pressing him down with our knees, and pulling his head down by his hair so he wouldn't get up. Mama and I held him down while Andrey pulled Papa's belt from his pants, and we managed to bind his wrists behind his back. If he wasn't so drunk, we would have never overpowered him; at least for once the alcohol in his body was our ally.

Shouting obscenities, demanding that we untie his hands, and threatening to settle with Mama later, he lay on the floor in his black satin underwear, his pants twisted around his ankles. His legs looked pale and skinny.

Sweaty and panting, I couldn't subdue my rage. All the humiliation, fear, and resentment that had accumulated inside me over the years of his drinking now spilled out into an uncontrollable, animalistic fury. I started kicking him in his back, chest, legs—wherever my feet and my ire landed. "I hate you," I yelled. "I hate you! You've spoiled my life! I wish you were dead!"

"Milenka, calm down! Please, please . . ." Mama begged me, sobbing and pulling me away from him.

That night I couldn't sleep. My anger was replaced by remorse. What had come over me? How could I raise my hand—rather my foot—to my own father who I loved so much when I was small?

I remembered how happy I had been when he used to take me to the Victory Parade or October Demonstration. I'd walked next to him, holding his strong warm hand and thinking how lucky I was to have the best father in the world. Tall and handsome, he stood out in the crowd. It seemed like half of the city was his friends. "*Privet, Ivan. Kak dela?*" (Hi. How are you?) He smiled his wide smile and talked to everyone. He was the most generous person I knew. He never said no to anything my family needed. I thought he could pluck a star from the sky for me if I asked for it. *How could it be,* I thought, *that he, who provided all that security for us, made me feel so insecure in my own home?*

Normally, after a drunken debauch, Papa would claim he had been too drunk to remember anything. But the day after I lost myself, Mama pulled me aside and told me he remembered me kicking him when he was down on the floor.

"We had a long discussion," she said. "I have never seen him so miserable."

In the following days, Papa averted his eyes at the sight of me, and I tried to avoid him. He stopped drinking. He came straight home after work and helped Mama secure frames in beehives or worked in his shop, tightening hoops on the barrels. My parents laughed and teased each other, and Mama's eyes shone with happiness.

It was the longest stretch of peace and quiet in our house that I could recall.

He resumed his drinking a month later, but he stopped fighting with Mama, at least when Andrusha and I were around.

31: Bald

On a warm, spring day in April of 1963, Yulka and I sat on the old metal bed in her yard, discussing what to do with her hair. When I had arrived half an hour earlier, Aunt Vera had been hanging laundry on the line and scolding her daughter.

"Look at your friend's head," she told me. "How many times have I warned her not to sleep all night with those metal curlers on her head? She never listens to me."

"Beauty requires sacrifice," Yulka chuckled sadly.

"Good. Don't complain then," Aunt Vera hissed. "Milka, see for yourself. This fool doesn't believe me that she's getting bald."

Yulka let me examine her head. The top looked fine, but the hair on her temples seemed thin, and I noticed several red, finger-length scabs with no growth on them.

"So, how does it look? Is it really that bad?" Yulka kept asking impatiently.

"You know, your mother is right," I said after my inspection. "You *are* getting bald." She responded like a patient who had just been told that she had only a week to live.

Yulka's hair was her pride and her curse. Every day, she sculpted and groomed it into an intricate bouffant, which our older neighbors called a "lice hut." In sunny weather, her hair stayed puffed and curly almost all day. But in the damp spring air, her hair flattened and hung like overcooked noodles. No matter how much I tried to convince her that she looked great without the bouffant and curls, she refused to go out without them.

"What am I supposed to do now?" she moaned.

"Stop using curlers," Aunt Vera said with irritation, "and let your head heal."

Yulka twisted her lips and looked at me.

"They say if you shave your head, the new hair grows healthier and thicker." I offered her another option.

Yulka looked at me as if I had just fallen from the moon. "Are you crazy? What will I do while it grows back? Just sit home?"

"No, you'll wear something on your head. Just for a short time until your hair grows a little." Yulka sat silently for a few minutes pondering.

"Let's shave together," she said at last.

I laughed. "Why? I don't have any problem with my hair."

"Because you're my friend, and friends have to support each other."

"Oh, stop blabbing!" Aunt Vera said. "You'll never have the guts to do it." She hung the last piece of clothing on the rope and disappeared inside the house.

It was probably the worst thing she could have said to us. Yulka and I gave full rein to our imagination. We fantasized what it would be like to go to the First of May demonstration dressed like boys, with our short hair and no makeup. We would have even more fun in summer, we decided, when we went on vacation with Yulka's parents. Everyone would think that we were twin brothers. We even came up with names—she would be Sergey and I chose to be Sasha.

When I was younger, I had wished I was born a boy. Now, shaving my head was a little like my childhood dream coming true. "Let's go and see if my Mama can help us," I suggested.

In our yard, Mama was squatting in her vegetable garden, tending to the radishes. "Are you hungry, girls?" she asked before we could say anything. "There's borscht on the stove."

Whenever I came home, alone or with a friend, Mama's first question was always whether I wanted to eat. She had starved so often when she was young that now she could not bear the thought that someone might be hungry.

"No thanks," I said. "Mama, Yulka and I decided to shave our heads." I explained the problem with Yulka's hair.

"Does your mother know about it?" Mama asked Yulka.

"Yes," Yulka confirmed.

"What about you? Your hair looks fine," Mama asked me.

"Mine will also grow thicker and healthier. Please, Mama. Can you shave us?"

She contemplated us both for a long minute. "Are you both *sure* you want to do it?"

"Yes," Yulka and I answered in unison.

"Fine then. I'll go to borrow Uncle Pavel's hair clipper, and you girls get yourselves ready." She washed her hands and headed toward the gate. Halfway there, she turned around. "Are you *really* sure you won't regret it?"

We said we were.

When Mama left, Yulka and I grew silent. I started to feel a prick of doubt, but backing away now would mean breaking a promise and showing my weakness. We waited until Mama returned, carrying a manual hair clipper that our neighbor used to shave his grandchildren every summer. She carried a chair onto the tile floor in the corridor and asked, "Well, who will be the first?"

Yulka and I looked at each other, but neither of us volunteered.

"Let's draw a token then," Mama proposed.

I kept wishing she would talk us out of our crazy idea, but she didn't. She just took two matches, broke one in half, and hid them in her fist with the two intact ends showing. "Whoever pulls the broken one will be the first," she said.

Yulka drew the half match. Obediently, she sat down on the chair. Mama put a kitchen towel on her shoulders and brought the clippers to Yulka's forehead. She progressed slowly right over the top of Yulka's head and then down to her neck. A big tuft of light hair cascaded down to the floor, leaving a shiny lane in the middle of Yulka's former bouffant. Her face reminded me of a clown's, with tufts of hair sticking out at the sides. The whole thing suddenly felt insane, and a hysterical laugh choked me.

Mama stepped back to observe the results of her work, and I saw the confusion in her eyes. Yulka went to the mirror hanging on the wall, and her face contorted in panic.

"It's your turn," Mama said to me, pointing to the chair. When I sat, she repeated the same procedure, shearing the middle strip on my head. Yulka stayed at the mirror, messing with her hair. She lifted a long strand from the side of her head, backcombed it, put it over the sheared part, and secured it with a hair pin. It hid her cropped streak almost completely.

"You know," Yulka said, "I've changed my mind. Let's leave our hair as it is."

I went to the mirror and tried to arrange my hair in the same way, but it was too short to hide the damage. I looked like our music theory teacher, who had long slick hair on one side of his head that he combed over his bald crown. He looked ridiculous, and the whole college, even teachers, made fun of him.

"Look girls, just half an hour ago you begged me to shave your heads. I've asked you if you were sure you wanted to do it, and you both said 'yes.' Be the masters of your word now, and let me finish my job," Mama said.

She sheared us both like sheep until we were bald. Yulka and I laughed through the process, snorting and wiping tears from our eyes. Mama laughed with us, but her eyes looked strained and guilty.

After Yulka left, I took a shower, covered my head with a scarf, and sat down to practice my piano. All kinds of questions swarmed inside my head while I played. *How can I go to college, evening school, and track practice? What will people say?*

The sudden popping sound of broken glass startled me to my feet. I ran to the window and pulled back the curtain to find long cracks spreading from a hole in the center of the window. There were muffled voices in the darkness outside, and then our gate slammed shut.

Mama came in from the yard, shaking her head. "It was Sashka," Mama said. "What a crazy little bastard! He saw Yulka, and she told him about your hair. He fired his air gun at the widow to express his outrage. He's lucky your father isn't home."

That night I slept with my head under the blanket, and I dreamt that Sashka was trying to rip off my covers and see my bald head. I woke at dawn, terrified of the coming day.

Yulka came back in the morning, loaded with her mother's stuff—colorful scarves, a pair of hats, and even an ancient hairpiece. Everything we tried looked ridiculous. In the end, we decided the best option was to put on our normal winter coats and fur hats. We pulled the hats over our foreheads, raised the collars up, and left the house.

The apricot trees in our yard were in full bloom, and the midday temperature was twenty degrees Celsius (about sixty-eight degrees Fahrenheit). People blatantly ogled. I could feel their grins on my overheated skin.

At the musical college, the students just glanced and whispered at our odd hats, but evening school was certain to be harder. On

Monday, three days after our haircut, I gathered my folder and my courage and walked nervously to evening school with Yulka by my side. We both wore headscarves with the free ends tied at the nape, and we arrived after the first lesson had started. Our Gazha friends gawked in silence as we marched to a vacant desk and sat down, side by side. Kolka was sitting a couple desks ahead of us, and he, too, turned around and stared.

When the lesson ended and the teacher left the room, someone yelled, "Hey, they are both bald! Let's see their heads!"

The boys leaped from their seats and formed a circle around us. Several hands reached to my handkerchief. Horrified, I looked for Kolka to rescue me, but he was still in his seat, watching. I dropped my face on the desk, clutching the scarf with my both hands in a deadly grip. Next to me, Yulka squealed.

The commotion around us died suddenly, and I heard the principal's booming voice. "Stop it! Leave them alone!" He said something else, but I didn't hear him. I grabbed my folder and stormed out of the classroom door. Yulka followed at my heels.

We never went back to *Vecherka*, and neither Kolka or Yulka's Lopuh showed up at Bagirskaya Street again.

32: May Day

On May 1 every year, the Soviet Union celebrated International Workers' Day with a parade. This was a very important day for us all. People gathered in the morning near their schools and workplaces. Women dressed up in new summer dresses and perms. Men, with their fresh haircuts and perfect shaves, wore neatly ironed white shirts and polished shoes.

Party officials distributed flags and portraits of Lenin, Khrushchev, and other prominent Party leaders as they checked attendance. Every large organization and school was required to provide a column of demonstrators. For Party and Komsomol members, participation was mandatory, and for the rest of us it was what was called *dobrovol'no-prinuditel'no* (voluntary-coercive). Either we came on our own, or the administration found ways to punish us for not showing up.

There was a popular joke in Turkmenistan at the time about this. Once, they said, Churchill and Roosevelt asked Stalin why Soviet farmers joined collective farms and worked so hard without being paid. "Neither British nor American farmers would ever work for free," they said.

"My people work voluntarily-compulsorily," said Stalin.

"How does that work?" Churchill asked.

Stalin pointed to a cat that happened to be in the same room and asked, "Can you make this cat eat the mustard that is sitting on the table?"

Churchill poked the cat's snout into the mustard, beat her, and pulled her tail, but accomplished nothing. Roosevelt stroked the cat and scratched behind her ears, but the cat didn't eat the mustard.

"You see, gentlemen," Stalin said. "Neither voluntarily nor forcibly can you make her eat it. Now see how my voluntary-compulsory method works." He lifted the cat's tail and smeared mustard under it. She screamed and immediately began licking her butt.

"Brilliant!" Churchill and Roosevelt cheered.

May Day of 1963 was glorious, with a warm breeze and plenty of sun. No wonder the Soviet press called this day the Holiday of Spring and Labor. The trees and bushes, washed by spring rains, glistened. Red flags fluttered in the breeze, and a huge red banner stretched across the street proclaiming, *People and The Party are United!* Loudspeakers on poles spread across the city broadcast the event.

I wished I was out there, celebrating with everyone else, as I had done every year since I joined the Pioneers. But this year, Yulka and I had to stay home. Over the past few weeks, the world had been divided into *them*, the people who had hair, and *us*, two outcasts with bald heads and injured self-esteem. Not even *dobrovol'no-prinuditel'no* could force us to show our faces, or our heads, to the crowds that would gather that morning.

Yulka's parents went to the parade with their colleagues and students. Afterwards, they told us, they were going to a party with friends.

Disappointed and lonely, Yulka and I decided to have the celebration of our own. We counted our cash and went shopping.

The streets were deserted; the parade had already started. In the liquor store, we bought our favorite Turkmen wine, *Ter-Bash,* and a pack of Bulgarian cigarettes. We set the coffee table in Yulka's guest room with the leftovers from her fridge—a chunk of dried sausage, a half-eaten can of sprats in oil, several pickled cucumbers, and a quarter of a loaf of bread from Yulka's bread bin. We opened our bottles—half a liter of fortified, sweet wine per person. Then we toasted all the workers in the world and gulped our first glass. Pleasant warmth slowly spread all over my body and made me slightly dizzy. I felt great.

When our bottles were half empty, we turned on Yulka's tape recorder and danced the Charleston, an old dance I loved. Normally, I danced it well. When we were at the public dance floors and the Charleston played, people would step aside to give me room and watch me dance. But that night, my arms and feet acted like they had never met before, and I could hardly keep up with the rapid rhythm of the melody. Yulka jerked next to me, swaying her arms and kicking her legs in all directions.

We drank more and laughed hysterically at each other's jokes, smearing drunken tears mixed with mascara on our cheeks until Yulka felt sick and rushed outside. Several minutes later, I heard her shuffle to her room and collapse onto the bed.

I busied myself with hiding the evidence of our celebration—discarding empty bottles, washing dishes, and cleaning Yulka's mess. I was just finishing up when I heard the knock on the door.

To my relief it was Sashka. I hadn't talked to him since he shot at my window three weeks ago. But I had heard from him often. The Shebekos had a big collection of vinyl records of popular Soviet singers in their house, and Sashka loved to play them. Whenever I was at Yulka's place during those lonely days of our self-inflicted seclusion, somehow Sashka knew. He would put a record on and, by manipulating the dial of his record player from the loudest to inaudible, sent me his messages.

I remember one of the songs, called "I Love You, Life." It was performed by a famous Soviet singer, Mark Bernes, and, all I heard was "I love you . . . I love you . . . I keep falling for you over and over . . . I love you . . . and I hope it is mutual . . . ."

Sashka's "wooing" didn't irritate me anymore. In fact, after the betrayal of my actual boyfriend, I was touched by his stubborn loyalty.

Still, that night I felt uneasy to see him standing in the doorway. But he just came up to me, touched my head, and laughed. I began laughing with him, grateful that I didn't have to explain for the umpteenth time why I had done it.

Sashka brought several records and put one on Yulka's record player. We listened for a while, sitting side by side on Yulka's sofa.

"Let's dance," he said when a new song began, and reached for my hand. Hesitantly, I gave it to him, and he pulled me from the sofa. It was a love song called "*Pchelka i Babochka* (A Honey Bee and a Butterfly)." We danced, slowly shifting our weight from one foot to the other. Sashka held me by my waist, and his curly hair touched my cheek. The music was languid and sentimental, the room was half-lit by the setting sun, and the air became too warm to breathe. My heart was skipping beats. My head was spinning from the wine. When the song was over, Sashka, still holding one hand on my waist, reached out and moved the needle back. "Once the bee on a warm spring day . . ." the singer started again.

It was the third or fourth time we danced to the same song, when Yulka walked into the room and turned on the lights.

"*Salute* (the fireworks) starts in five minutes," she mumbled.

It was already dark, and the street was full of adults and kids, heads thrown back as they waited for the sound of thunder and the flashes in the sky. Every blast was followed by a loud chorus of children shouting, "Hooray!"

When it was over, Yulka, Sashka, and I sat outside smoking in the darkness, listening to bursts of laughter, discordant singing, somebody's screaming, and a woman's cry. The holiday was over, and tipsy people were returning home after the long day of celebration.

When Yulka's parents showed up late at night, Sashka was gone, and Yulka and I were sleeping on the metal bed under the grapevine arbor in their yard.

33: Unfulfilled Dreams

After two days of the May holidays, I returned to my track and field practice at Locomotive Stadium on a gray Friday afternoon. When I arrived, I found Serafim Feodorovich sitting alone in the stands.

"No one else showed up," he said. "Apparently, they decided to stretch the holiday until Monday. You can go home if you wish, or we can work on the hitch-kick technique."

"Let's work a little," I said.

During our last practice he had started to teach me a new long jump technique called "scissors." It was a complicated series of movements, and I had made very little progress so far. Today, I was determined to get it right.

After a warm up stroll around the stadium, we went to the long jump pit. I sprinted and jumped over and over again, trying to follow my coach's instructions. My run-ups and take-offs were fine, but I just couldn't get the running-in-air part right. On top of all, it started raining.

"That'll do, Milka. It's enough for today. Let's go home," the coach said. "We'll continue on Monday. Don't worry. You'll get it." He picked up his blazer from the grass, turned around, and headed to the stands.

I did worry. In two months I would fly to the All Union School Olympics, but instead of improving, my long jump was getting worse. *I'll jump one more time while he isn't watching,* I decided. *And this time, I'll do it right.*

I made my approach, trying to gain as much speed as I could, bounced, and took off. My legs came in; I pulled my body forward and tried "separate leg action" as he had taught me. But in midair I already knew that it didn't work again. *Damn it,* I had time to think. *What are my legs doing?* My feet went far apart, and when my heels hit the sand, I heard a popping sound—my left knee gave out from under me. I screamed.

I was writhing in pain when Serafim Feodorovich reached me. "Don't move. Let me check your knee." He examined my leg. Nothing seemed broken. My knee was in place. But when he helped me stand, I couldn't put any weight on my left leg.

He picked me up and carried me across the square to the nearby train station's medical room. A nurse in a white medical gown checked my knee, secured it with a bandage, and gave me a painkiller. Serafim Feodorovich helped me jump on one leg to the station square, where he caught a taxi and took me home.

Later that evening, the pain increased, and my knee became swollen and hot. The painkiller didn't give me any relief. My parents called an ambulance, and the paramedics came and gave me a shot of strong pain killer. All night, I drifted in and out of hazy slumber. Every time I opened my eyes, I saw Mama sitting in a chair beside my bed.

On Monday, I was admitted to the Sports Clinic, a small building on top of a hilly area in the southeastern corner of Ashkhabad's huge medical complex. The Clinic had only two wards—a men's and a women's—with several beds in each. It was quiet that spring—the only patients were two noisy football players, both with leg injuries, a petite female gymnast with a sore back who was discharged not long after I arrived, and me, hobbling around on my crutches. We were cared for by a nurse, a physical therapist, an on-call doctor from the orthopedic department, and a nursing aide. Our procedures and treatments were all conducted in the morning. In the afternoon, the staff locked most of the doors, and the clinic looked deserted.

The first doctor who examined me said that I had a pinched meniscus. "The recovery will be easy," he promised. "Ultrasound therapy, warm paraffin treatments, and rest." I spent a week in the clinic, taking procedures, resting in my bed, and reading on a bench outside the clinic.

Three times a day, the hospital kitchen staff brought our meals from the kitchen. I ate the bland hospital food for breakfast and dinner, but every day at lunchtime, Mama came to visit me. Out of breath from walking fast, she would sit next to me on the bed, pull a package out of her bag, and peel away a bath towel, then a newspaper, and at last a kitchen towel wrapped around a small pot. It was always still hot, and when she lifted the lid, the pungent aroma of Mama's cooking filled the room.

In the evenings, I went outside to read on the bench in front of the clinic and wait for Sashka. He came every night after his swim practice. First, I would see the light of his cigarette dancing in the air as he rode his bicycle up the hill. Then I heard the squeaking of the wheels, and eventually his dark silhouette would appear in the clearings between the trees.

He was panting from the steep climb. His curly hair was disheveled by the wind, and his unbuttoned shirt exposed his smooth, muscular chest. The nurse called him "your pretty boyfriend." Although I didn't think of Sashka as my boyfriend, her words didn't irritate me, either.

Sashka was an excellent storyteller. Whatever he talked about—the latest book he was reading or movie he had watched—sounded amusing, and I would sit and listen to him for hours. We sat on the bench until the night nurse declared that she was going to lock the door, and I had to go inside. While I hobbled on my crutches along the corridor to my room, Sashka circled the building and waited for me outside a lattice window in my room. We would continue to talk in hushed tones until I heard the irritated voice of the nurse say, "Turn off the light and tell your boyfriend that it's time for him to go home."

I jumped into bed, but Sashka didn't move. He continued whispering, his hands holding the bars of the lattice and his forehead pressed against the metal grill.

"Go away," I begged him. "Please, Sashka. It's awkward."

"It's awkward sleeping on the ceiling. The blanket falls down," he would jest, but didn't move. Only when my chamber door opened and the nurse showed up in the doorway, would he at last disappear.

A week passed, but I still couldn't walk. The doctor was called again, and he said my meniscus had probably gotten caught in the joint between my knee bones. He wanted me to have a procedure where they would release it. That afternoon, a nurse took me to the procedure room and gave me a shot of morphine. I sat on a high table with my feet dangling while the nurse hugged me around my waist to hold me in place. Two heavyset women hung on my injured leg, pulling it down. I don't know what they expected to happen—a pop or a crack—but at the end of the procedure they said that they were not strong enough to do the job. "We should have brought a couple of strong men," I remember one of them saying.

Through his acquaintances, Papa found a specialist in Turkmen orthopedics who agreed to see me. After he listened to my story about the accident and examined my knee, he declared that I had a torn anterior cruciate ligament and probably more damage to other structures in my knee.

"She is lucky they didn't find those strong men in the Sports Clinic," he told Mama. "They would have completely ripped her knee off."

I left the Sports Clinic in a full-leg cast, which the doctor told me to wear for ten weeks. I should come back in the middle of August, after he returned from his summer vacation at the Black Sea resort.

I was devastated. My dreams for the Olympics in July and the parachute jumping class that spring were lost.

Due to my injury, I was excused from musical college classes and transferred to the third year without exams. When Mama went to my evening school, to my surprise they gave her my report card saying that I had also completed the ninth grade. My summer vacation had started early, but it didn't look like a lot of fun to me.

Then there was the final blow. On June 16, 1963, the first woman-cosmonaut, Valentina Tereshkova, went into space. She robbed me of my dream of becoming the first woman-cosmonaut. I blamed my stupid knee for everything I couldn't accomplish that summer, but nothing could prevent me from being young and happy.

That summer, the American western movie *The Magnificent Seven* swept Ashkhabad. Inspired by Brit, one of the movie characters, my friends and I put aside our BB guns and started competing in knife-throwing. Our mothers complained that knives began disappearing from their kitchens.

Sashka installed a large wooden board with a target drawn in the middle in his yard, and we spent hours honing our technique. I eventually got bored, but Sashka's fascination with knives grew into obsession. He spent lots of time making *finka* (Finnish knives)[9]—searching for steel plates, sharpening them into blades, hardening them in fire, and assembling handles from multiple bone or plastic rings.

By August, the cast on my leg was dirty and loose from ten weeks of violent wear and tear. I couldn't wait to get rid of that piece of junk. But when the day finally came to go to the hospital to cut it off, I was terrified. My leg looked like a gnawed chicken bone with no meat left. My knee was so weak and wobbly that at first I couldn't walk. But the worst thing was that my left leg was hairy. I cried as I looked at what had become of my strong, muscular leg.

"Don't be so frustrated," Mama tried to calm me. "Have you noticed that piglets, when they're young, are always thin and hairy? But as they grow older, they fatten, shed their hair, and their skin becomes nice and smooth."

"Thanks for the encouragement, Mama," I said through the tears. "I'll wait until I become a fat pig."

"No, really, Milenka. I also had hairy legs when I was young. See? It's all gone now."

---

9 The *finka* (Finnish knife) was popular in the criminal underworld in the Soviet Union. It had been banned in the USSR since the 1930s because of its criminal association.

34: White Gold

On the first of September, young people throughout the Soviet Union returned to their schools after their summer vacation. I was sixteen and starting my third year in musical college. I had not seen my fellow students since April. And now, with my knee healed and my sassy short haircut, I felt especially happy to be back.

But when I joined the group of my fellow students, instead of happy greetings they met me with surprising news. "We're going to cotton fields!"

Every fall, at the directive of the Party and the Komsomol, students of colleges, technical schools, and universities all over the Soviet Union were dispatched to collective farms to help harvest crops. In Russia, Ukraine, and Belarus they had to dig potatoes, beets, or gather cabbage; in Moldovia and the Caucasian Republics students picked grapes; and in Turkmenistan and other Central Asian Republics, we picked cotton. Classes were postponed, and students stayed in the fields until the Republic fulfilled that year's harvesting plan, typically in the middle of November. Everyone had to go, with the rare exceptions of serious illness or a death in the family. Those few who refused to participate faced tough administrative measures, including expulsion from school.

Until that fall of 1963, though, the musical college students had been spared from cotton-harvesting duty. Probably someone at the top considered puny musicians unfit for physical labor. But now our director informed us that we were not only going *na khlopok* (to cotton), but we had been ordered to go to the collective farm "*Communizm Yoly*" (The Path to Communism) in the Kunya-Urgench district of the Tashauz region, the coldest and harshest area of Turkmenistan.

We had three days to prepare for the trip—collecting food, light clothes for warm days, warm clothes for colder weather, essentials, and bedding—before we were all to gather at the train station, packed and ready for departure. The collective farm would provide us with one meal a day, he said, but we had to stock up with enough food and money for at least two or three weeks, until the college could organize the delivery of food parcels from our parents.

"Be ready to stay there at least two months," he warned.

Our classes were cancelled, and we were sent home. Mama had come home from the apiary at the end of August to prepare Andrusha and I for school, and as soon as I told her, she sprang into action. She briskly sent Papa in search of a *telogreika* (wadded cotton jacket) and tarpaulin military boots. I was assigned the duty of buying bread, canned meat stew, condensed milk, and other basics like soap, tooth powder, and Vaseline. Mama wrote everything down in her distinctive handwriting, with the wrong slope to the left.

Overnight, the whole city looked as if it was anticipating a disaster. People ran frantically from store to store in search of necessary products. Bread was in short supply. I had to stand in a long and angry line to buy a couple of bricks of brown bread. I managed to buy everything but the canned stew, which ran out just before I reached the counter. They said more would be delivered from the warehouse the next day.

Mama spent hours boiling tins of condensed milk in a big pot of water, cutting bread into tiny cubes and toasting them in the oven, and mixing honey with butter. By the end of the third day, I was outfitted with a dark-green *telogreika*, quilted military pants, tarpaulin boots, and a cap with ear-flaps that Papa bought from a sergeant who was a manager of the military warehouse. In a separate heap lay a mattress, a blanket, a pillow, an aluminum cup and a bowl, a spoon, and a jack knife.

Papa tried to teach me how to wrap long strips of *portyanki* (cloth footwraps) around my feet to wear under the boots, insisting that it would be easier and more comfortable than wearing socks.

"Believe me," he said. "They are warmer and better protect your feet from rubbing. I went through the whole Great Patriotic War in those babies." He spread the cloth on the floor, put his big foot on one end of it, and started wrapping the *portyanka* in an intricate pattern. The whole procedure seemed too complicated for me, and to Papa's dismay, I refused to take the footcloths with me. He looked hurt.

By evening, everything was packed and strapped together between the folding parts of my camp cot. I was excited and a little nervous, as I always was before something new began.

The next morning, the train station buzzed like our beehives. Hundreds of students and their parents, weighed down with supplies like mine, scurried around the platform in search of the correct train cars. Mama and I squeezed through the crowd to read a big message board with a list of colleges and their cars. The musical college was assigned to the end of the train. Somebody told us that our cars would be detached at one of the stations and then latched on to another train, which would take us to Kunya-Urgench.

While we waited, Mama gave me her last instructions. "Drink only boiled water. Do not sit on the wet ground. Do not catch a cold. Dress warmly. Don't jump. Remember what they told you at the hospital? Be careful. Try to protect your knee."

I pretended to listen to her while scanning the crowd for my friends, shouting their names and waving as they arrived. At last the locomotive shrieked, and train conductors opened vestibule doors. We all rushed into the car to claim seats. At last, the train jerked and began slowly picking up speed. I looked out the window at the half-empty platform. Mama stood among other parents, waving. I read her lips. "God save you."

The train took us north toward the border of the Republic of Uzbekistan and arrived at Kunya-Urgench late at night. The collective farm workers who met us loaded us and all our belongings onto flatbed trucks—girls and boys separately—and off we went. We had been agitated and excited earlier, laughing and talking throughout the ride, but now we sat silently, overwhelmed by the infinite darkness. The dust thrown up by the leading trucks suffocated us. It penetrated my nose, rasped on my teeth, and filled my lungs. I pulled a handkerchief and pressed it against my face. With my other hand, I gripped the side of the flatbed as it jumped; the girls screamed and grabbed each other, trying to stay inside.

Finally, our truck stopped and the engine went quiet. At first, I only heard ringing in my ears, but soon I started recognizing sounds—chirping crickets, singing frogs, and other familiar noises from my childhood in the desert.

Vano Allikovich, our physical education teacher, the head of our cotton campaign, came up to our truck. "Girls, you can unload. You'll be staying here." Other trucks continued on to different locations.

Thirty teenage girls jumped out, along with two teachers. One was a young woman, just nineteen, who had graduated from our college last summer. She stood among us, not knowing what to do next. The night air felt cooler than in Ashkhabad, and I shivered.

"*Mamochki* (dear mama)," a girl squeaked in a tiny voice. "Where're we?"

"On the edge of geography," someone answered.

The truck lights lit the silhouette of a mud wall in front of us. Vano Allikovich explained that we would stay in a *koshara*, a barn built for sheep. With his flashlight, he showed us the way through the wide door and into a huge adobe room with a low ceiling and a mud floor. The distinctive ovine smell hit my nose.

"Unpack and place yourselves for the night," Vano Allikovich said. "If you want to go out for your needs, take a friend with you."

"Where's our bathroom?" the young teacher, Larissa Alexandrovna, asked.

"You're in the field. There is a growth of trees outside. For now, you can go there. Tomorrow I'll think of something to make it more private," Vano said before leaving.

"*Mamochki*," the small voice said again. "I'm scared."

With flashlights, we untied our cots and pulled out our mattresses and blankets. The girls who didn't have cots spread their mattresses directly on the mud floor. When we finished, there was only a narrow path separating one solid row of beds from another.

The next morning, we woke up to the sound of banging on the door.

"Get up, girls," Vano yelled. "You have an hour to get dressed and have your breakfast. Today I woke you up two hours later, but starting tomorrow, you'll get up at six. Your working day will start at seven in the morning and end at five in the afternoon. Hurry up."

I opened my eyes, frantically trying to recall where I was. Through a gap under the roof and cracks in the door there was a little light to make out the windowless room. The girls around me began rising, moaning. We had slept in our clothes. Gingerly, trying not to step on anyone's bedding, I went outside into the bright September sun. Our barn, I saw, was roughly put together with clay bricks. Threads of pale yellow straw stuck out of it like hairs on a mangy dog. We were surrounded by cotton fields, spreading to the horizon. There was a narrow irrigation ditch and a single dusty road.

We trudged to the thickets, where someone had dug a hole in the ground and tied two bed sheets between saplings. After the toilet, we rinsed our faces in semi-turbid water from a canister that stood against the wall of our barn, and then gathered around a big zinc tank with boiling water. We drank slightly sweetened tea that smelled of smoke and ate our home supplies—toast, condensed milk, and whatever else our parents had stuffed in our bags. I passed around my half-liter jar of honey mixed with butter, and it came back with only a tiny smidge left at the bottom.

Before we finished eating, a tractor with a long trailer rumbled up. It took us to a *harman,* a dirt area between the fields where the collected cotton was accumulated and sorted. In one corner, two local men sat cross-legged on a gray felt rug, drinking tea and smoking. The older man appeared to be a foreman. He greeted us and explained that every morning we would come to the *harman* and be assigned to a cotton field. Mostly, he said, we would work *na podborke*, which meant that we would gather remnants of cotton on fields that had been harvested by machines—anything left hanging from bushes or laying on the ground. "Never mind if it's mixed with dry leaves or dirt," he said. "Just take all white stuff you can find."

Each of us received a huge linen sack and an apron, and he explained how to use them. With that, the future professional musicians and singers of Turkmenistan became cotton pickers.

Our aprons were big pieces of cloth that we tied around the waist, then folded the bottom part of it on top and knotted its ends behind our back again, forming large pockets on our bellies. This kept both our hands free as we moved between rows, picking cotton and stuffing it inside our apron. When full, it held about six kilograms (thirteen pounds) of fluffy fiber. We unloaded the apron into our linen sacks, which from time to time we dragged to a new location as we progressed.

At the end of the day, we lugged our cotton to the *harman*, helping each other lift the sacks onto our backs. The second young Turkmen we'd seen there was our accountant and weigh-man. His primitive scale consisted of a stick tied to the middle of a tripod. On one side of the stick hung a metal bowl where he put weights, and on the other was a hook for our sack.

Our daily quota per person was forty kilograms (eighty-eight pounds). Cotton was bulky, but it didn't weigh much. After almost ten hours of slouching between rows on that first day, I gathered only nineteen kilograms. Others didn't do much better. My back and my knee hurt, and that night I could hardly turn in my bed. Girls moaned in their sleep. Somebody cried.

As days passed, other problems surfaced. Without running water, sewer, or a place where we could wash ourselves, girls started complaining of stomach pains and diarrhea. The only way to wash ourselves was with leftover water from the supper tea, which we collected in metal mugs and bottles. We were not bathing as much as "smearing dirt on our bodies," as Mama would have said.

The girls who reported being sick were allowed to stay home from the field, but they had to clean our "toilets" and the area around our living quarters. Many preferred to go to the field, fill their sacks with a little cotton, spread it somewhere between bushes, and lay down on top. At the end of the day, we would all chip in some cotton to help our sick friend.

The seriously ill were taken to the local Turkmen village to see a doctor, whose remedy for every ailment was a dose of *Phthalazol*, a medicine usually prescribed for treating stomach problems.

When a girl had a headache, Vano Allikovich gave her a tablet of aspirin and sent her back to work. Headaches were common, probably caused in part from sun and dehydration. But I later learned that there was another, more serious reason for our headaches.

To facilitate machine harvesting, the Turkmen cotton fields were dusted with highly toxic defoliants similar to Agent Orange. This caused the cotton plants to lose their leaves and accelerated the opening of mature bolls. Once the mechanical cotton harvesters had finished their work, students and local schoolchildren were sent to the same polluted fields to pick the remnants that the machines had been unable to remove from the bushes. Nobody measured the amount of chemicals sprayed on the fields. I don't know if anybody at that time even knew about the harm such chemicals could cause to a human being.

The cotton pickers were all women, students, and local children. I never saw men, except those operating machinery, weighing and supervising. The Turkmen schoolchildren were small and skinny, and some looked younger than Andrusha, who turned ten while I was away.

Once a day, we had a hot meal of thin soup with potatoes or macaroni and canned meat. Twice a day, in the morning and after we came back from work, we had tea and a piece of brown bread. The food we brought from home was soon gone, we were always hungry and looking for something else to eat.

At the end of September, a truck came from Ashkhabad with food parcels from our parents. We ate everything we received within days and started counting the weeks until the next truck would arrive.

The money we brought from home was also gone, but we wouldn't get paid until the end of the campaign, back in Ashkhabad. They told us we would receive four kopeks per kilogram, because we gathered Egyptian cotton, which was the cheapest kind grown in Turkmenistan. Long-staple cotton was the highest quality and paid ten kopeks per kilogram, but it was picked only by hand by collective farmers.

By mid-October, the days became chilly. Unopened cotton bolls burst with the onset of cold weather and rain. The burrs holding the cotton had sharp edges, and when we pulled out the fibers, they scratched and cut our stiff fingers. Our musical hands became rough, our faces sunburnt and weather-beaten, and our unwashed hair dull. Our backs, though, stopped aching and our stomachs got used to bad water, poor nutrition, and the monotonous diet.

Still, we were sick and tired of cotton. We worked seven days a week from dawn to dusk, with only an hour off for lunch. There was not much cotton left, but our supervisors still demanded we make the daily forty kilograms, promising us all sorts of trouble for poor performance.

To make our life a little easier, we would put a big stone or a melon in the bag of cotton. After it had been weighed at the *harman*, we threw the extra load away and piled our sack in the heap with others.

"Why not?" we asked each other. "They cheat us by making us do the worst job for the least money, so we cheat them."

Only once during the whole time did I manage to fulfill the daily quota, but it was also my last day as a cotton picker.

On a bright and crisp day, my friend Larissa and I sneaked into a faraway field that had not been harvested. It was a beautiful spread of dry cotton bushes pregnant with white locks of fluff. No one was around. We feverishly picked cotton with both hands. By the end of the day, our bags were so packed and heavy that we couldn't carry them back to the *harman*.

At the road not far from our field, I noticed an ass tied up to a mulberry tree. I decided to use him for his intended purpose, as a beast of burden, and then bring him back. Gingerly, I untied the rope and started leading him toward our sacks. At first, he cooperated, but when we were almost there, he suddenly stopped. No matter how hard I pulled the rope or Larissa hit him, he stood rooted.

Then he started hee-hawing, over and over again. In response to his cry, somewhere from afar came a callback, long and urgent. At the sound, our ass became very agitated, and the black thing on his belly started growing before our eyes, almost reaching the ground. He suddenly jerked around and started pulling me toward the sound of the other ass.

Trying to stop him, I dug my heels into the ground and pulled the rope with all my strength. I felt a sharp pain and a familiar popping sound in my left knee. I let the rope go and sat on the ground, defeated and in pain.

Larissa ran to find help. She came back with two young men from our college, who shouldered our cotton sacks as Larissa helped me to get to the *harman*.

The next morning, Vano Allikovich checked my swollen knee to make sure that I wasn't just trying to skip work. He took me to the doctor, but there was nothing he could do.

I was transferred to kitchen duty. All day, I sat outside on an empty wooden crate and peeled potatoes while Chornyi, our cook, fussed next to me, opening cans, cleaning the huge, soot-covered pot, or kindling the fire. He filled the time by telling me anecdotes about his service in the army or asking me about my stories. For some reason he called me *Pishik,* which in Turkmen means a kitten. I liked the way he talked to me.

"Where did you come from, *Pishik*?" he asked me once.

"Ashkhabad."

"Where did you family come from," he asked.

"Russia."

"*Kulaks*?"

"What do you mean?" His question surprised me. "They were not *kulaks*. They came to Turkmenistan because of the famine in Russia."

"That could be, too," he said. "But most Russians came to Turkmenistan in the 1930s because they had been expelled from Russia by Stalin."

"*Kulaks* were the people's enemies. My grandparents were not *kulaks*," I argued. I knew from all of my history classes that kulaks had been fierce enemies of socialism.

"Don't be silly, *Pishik*. Most of the *kulaks* were not enemies. They were good farmers who lived better than others because they worked hard. That's not a crime. My grandfather was sent to a labor camp for ten years because he refused to give his ten sheep and a camel to the collective farm. He got a year for each sheep."

I didn't know what to say. I had never heard anybody talk like this except Papa, but he always made me mad with his skepticism and distrust of the Communist Party. All our conversations usually ended with shouting. What Chornyi told me echoed Papa's words, but somehow it didn't make me as angry. Instead of conviction, I heard notes of sympathy in Chornyi's voice.

That night, I thought about what he said. I knew almost nothing about my grandparents. They existed only on a couple of old, yellowed photographs and in the vague answers my parents offered to my rare questions. I don't even know their full names. My brother was named after my mother's father, Andrey. But whatever happened to Grandpa Andrey? It was strange that I knew so little.

I thought about how Mama left the room when I read stories about bloodsucker *kulaks* from my history book. Was she concealing the fact that my grandparents were *kulaks*? What if Chornyi was right? Were they good people wrongly accused by the Soviets? Or were they bloodsuckers forced off their land by Stalin?

Tears dripped onto my pillow, but I didn't know for whom I was crying—me, Mama, or my long-vanished grandparents.

With my bad knee, I couldn't return to work in the fields. When the truck with food parcels from our parents arrived at the end of October, I was sent home. I left my camp cot, tarpaulin boots, and *telogreika* to the girls who needed them and said goodbye to the cotton fields.

Two weeks later, the rest of the students came back. Classes did not start for another week because the musicians all needed to treat our cracked fingers and voices.

When we went to the college cashier to get the money we had earned as cotton pickers, I discovered that I had not earned anything. In fact, I had to pay most of my eighteen-ruble stipend for the food the collective farm provided for me.

At the end of November, Turkmenistan officially declared the successful implementation of that year's plan for harvesting the "white gold."

35: The Truth

"Was your father a *kulak*?" I asked Mama the morning after my return from the cotton fields.

We had just finished our breakfast, and she had already sent my brother out the door with her usual, "Andrusha, be careful when you cross the road." Now she sat at the table, sipping her tea while I told her my cotton stories. I sprung the question on her to see how she would respond.

Mama's hand froze in midair. She stared at me for a long second as if she didn't understand.

"No," she said finally, slowly lowering her cup back to the table. "My father was an honest and hardworking man, and everything we had was earned by his own hands and wits. We were not wealthy enough to hire farm help or lease our agricultural machinery. We were not rich peasants, so-called *kulaks*. But our family lived probably better than the majority."

"What happened to Grandpa Andrey?" I asked. "How come you never told me anything about him?"

Mama sat silently, tilting her cup on the table from side to side and watching the golden liquid swirl. Then she lifted her head and looked straight at me.

"During Stalin's collectivization[10] in 1930, he was wrongfully *raskulachen* (dispossessed); our land, house, and everything we owned was taken away, and we all were sent to exile."

"But why? You said he wasn't a *kulak*," I asked.

"No, he wasn't. But everybody lived so wretchedly then that by those standards we were rich. We had a bigger house, a horse with a colt, two cows, and some chickens and geese. During the NEP[11] years, my father worked in the city as a clerk for a wealthy *nepman*.[12] He saw how much better city people lived, and he learned from them and tried to introduce those innovations in our life—an iron roof, wood floors, a bicycle, a gramophone, and lots of books and magazines. But his fellow villagers didn't understand such luxuries and condemned him for it. 'Why does he need all

---

10 After seizing power in 1917, the Bolsheviks began widespread nationalization of all private enterprises. The collectivization of agriculture (1923-1933) moved all land into sole possession of the state. Peasants were forced to give up their individual farms and join large farms. Although they were called collective, the Soviet government controlled everything.

11 The New Economic Policy (NEP) was an economic policy proposed by Vladimir Lenin in 1921 to revive the Russian economy, which was almost ruined after the devastating effects of the First World War, the Revolution, and the Civil War years. It was a step back from the Leninist policy, a temporary concession to capitalism in order to gain strength for transitioning to socialism. During the NEP time, peasants were permitted to sell some of their produce for profit and small traders were allowed to run businesses. As a result, some of them became quite rich, the economy picked up, and people were much happier. NEP was abandoned in 1928 when Joseph Stalin became a leader of the USSR after Lenin's death.

12 A shopkeeper or a small business owner who profited from the NEP.

those books and magazines?' they asked. My father dreamed that my three brothers and I would get an education and have a better future. But that's not a crime, right?"

I saw how badly Mama wanted me to understand. She was afraid of my judgment.

"When you were three years old," she continued, "I took you to Bestuzhevka, my home village. I wanted to see the place where I was born and to visit Aunt Polya, my mother's sister, and other relatives who still lived there. On our first day in the village I went to see our former house. I was small when they kicked us out, but my memory kept the image of a beautiful fairytale palace. Instead, I saw an ordinary old house with a rickety porch and peeling paint, much smaller than this house where we live now. It's amazing how deceptive our childhood memories are." Mama sat silently; her gaze fixed somewhere in her past.

"What happened to Grandpa Andrey after he was *raskulachen*?" I asked.

"They took us all to the train station and shoved us into cattle cars packed with other people—men, women, children, and babies. The train moved very slowly, with lots of stops in a bare field. Nobody knew where we were going. On the eighth day, the women with children—including my mother and my brothers and me—were unloaded at a small station somewhere near Vologda city. Our father continued further to the north with the other men.

"We were driven to a beautiful red brick church with golden domes on the edge of a village. Inside, there were four tiers of roughly built bunks, one for each family. Our family got the top one. On the third day, my toddler brother, Misha, fell from our bunk. He was ailing for a while but thank God he recovered.

"It was cold and overcrowded inside the church. We starved. Soon, small children started getting sick and dying. We would all have died there, but the local authorities took pity on us and allowed to write to relatives to come and take the children. Uncle

Syoma, my Aunt Polya's husband, came and took my three brothers and me back to Bestuzhevka. We lived with them for two years, until our mother came back from the labor settlement. I was young and don't remember those years well, but I know that after she returned home, my mother worked in a collective farm in our village."

Mama spoke softly. Her intertwined fingers lay motionless on the table in front of her, her tea forgotten. I listened, holding my breath and praying that no one came to interrupt her story.

"For three years, we didn't know anything about our father," she continued. "But one day in 1933, Uncle Syoma received a letter from him, in which he wrote that he had been in exile in the Komi Republic, working as a logger on the banks of the Pechora River. For his good work, he wrote, he had been transferred to the free settlement and got a job at a ship repair workshop called Shchelyayur. He wanted to know what had happened to his wife and children.

"Uncle Syoma wrote him back that we were all alive and living in his house. In the next letter, my father said that he had bought an old hut and wanted us to come. He was not allowed to leave the settlement, but he sent us money via telegraph. Our mother quickly packed our few belongings, and we went by horse from our village to the Kuzovatovo station, then by train to Moscow, and by another train to Arkhangelsk. After that we travelled by sea to Naryan-Mar. It was an exhausting trip with endless standing in line at ticket offices and sleeping on the floor at stations and ports. It took us more than three weeks to get to Naryan-Mar. I was seven then, but I remember the trip well."

Mama got up and went to the big map of the Soviet Union that hung on our wall. She placed her finger on the northern edge, and I saw a small dot at the mouth of the Pechora River.

"This is Naryan-Mar," she said. "When we finally got there, our father was waiting for us at the pier. I didn't recognize him at first. Instead of the dark-haired, handsome man with a thick, well-groomed mustache that I remembered, in front of me stood an old, white-haired man with deep wrinkles on his emaciated face, and heavy, worn hands. Only the eyes, soft and attentive, were our father's."

I didn't know what to say, so I silently waited.

"From Naryan-Mar, we traveled by boat up the river to Shchelyayur." Mama moved her finger, showing the route her family took. "We lived there until the next summer. My youngest brother, Misha, stayed at home with our mother, and Yevgeniy and I went to the local school. Boris, who was already sixteen, entered the River Navigation School. It prepared mechanics, machinists, and skippers. Later, Yevgeniy would enter the same school.

"Our father was happy to have us with him, but one thing constantly nagged him—his unfair conviction. He always talked about it. In the summer of 1934, he decided to take our mother and the two younger kids, Misha and me, to Bestuzhevka for a visit. He acquired the necessary documents for travel. I think he wanted to prove to the villagers that he was wrongly convicted, and that now his children went to school, and we all lived in our own house again. In July, we headed home. Father said we would visit, have a look, and then come back in time for us to start the school year.

Mama closed her eyes, as she often did when she tried to remember something. "It never happened," she said at last. "Almost as soon as we arrived, during the first week, the local NKVD came and arrested him. No one knew why. Our mother took the two of us and fled to Ashkhabad, where Uncle Syoma had an old friend he'd met in World War I. Yevgeniy and Boris, my older brothers, had to abandon their River Navigation School. They ran away to escape arrest just for being part of our family, and they joined us in Ashkhabad.

"We received word through my uncle that my father was sentenced to five years in a labor camp at the Rybinsk Reservoir, then later that he had escaped, was caught, and convicted again. On the 25th of December 1936, my eleventh birthday, we received a letter written by the wife of one of the prisoners at Dmitrovsky Correctional Labor Camp, so called Dmitrovlag, where hundreds of thousands of political prisoners worked on the construction of the Moscow-Volga Canal. She informed us that our father had died, but she offered no details. It wasn't safe to write about those things back then. We never received any official notification about his death."

Tears rolled down Mama's cheeks, and she brushed them off with the back of her fingers. The door to her past had opened so completely, I didn't know what to think, but her story was not over. After the long pause, she continued.

"My poor mother fled Russia from the brutal Stalin's regime. She thought we were safer here, in Ashkhabad, but she was wrong. I was in the seventh grade, when your Uncle Boris was arrested in Ashkhabad. He was nineteen at that time. They came at night, two men and our *domouprav* (house manager). Those two ransacked our room searching for something: every mattress was turned over, every drawer opened and shaken out in a big pile, every book thrown on the floor. We stood half-dressed, watching them in terror. Having found nothing, they left, taking Boris with them in a Black Raven.[13] I can still hear my mother's cry."

There was another pause. Then Mama started speaking again.

"Do you know what his fault was? He and six other young men from the Ashkhabad Silk-Spinning Factory, where Boris worked at that time, had organized a photo group. After work they gathered in an old projection room of the factory's club and printed photos. Someone reported their 'suspicious activity' to the authorities. All

---

13 Special vehicles of the 1930s and 1940s, called Black Raven, were used for the transport of detainees, convicts, and prisoners. The nickname came from their black color and the purpose.

of them were arrested. They were forced to confess to conspiracy. When Boris's friend, Alesha Nagibin, couldn't withstand the torture and died, the others pleaded guilty. Boris was sentenced to a ten-year imprisonment in a strict-regime labor camp."

"Why haven't you told me about all this before?" I asked.

"You were too young to understand, and I didn't want you to feel bad about your grandparents and Uncle. Now you're old enough to know that it's not a good topic to talk about with others. Many here have the same fate, but nobody wants to stir up their past. They never talk about where they came from, or why they ended up in Ashkhabad. It's better to put your past aside and go on."

"When you have a huge political task, such as liquidating the whole class of rich landowners," our history teacher had told us once, "mistakes are inevitable. *Derevo rubyat—schepki letyat* (When wood is chopped, woodchips will fly)."

Now I realize that those chips were real people—men, women, and children, the innocent victims of the big class struggle and among them were two of my grandfathers, Grandpa Andrey and Grandpa Michael, with their families. But back then, Mama's experience did not shake my belief in the overall goodness of the Soviet system. I felt deeply saddened by the injustice that had happened to my grandfather, for my Mama's unhappy childhood and all the misery my grandmother must have suffered, but I was convinced it had all been an unfortunate mistake.

36: My First Job

The week after I came back from the cotton fields, I found a job. Several of my classmates had been working at various musical clubs since last spring, and before we'd been sent to pick cotton, I mentioned my desire to work to Sashka. "I'll tell my mother to help you," he said. Tamara not only taught piano at the musical school, but she was also the best accompanist in the city. She was a familiar face in the Ashkhabad musical scene.

Through Sashka, she sent me a message to go to the Republican Musical School. They had a piano teaching position open, and she had recommended me.

The next morning, I took a trolleybus to the university district. The school was located a couple of blocks past the Turkmen State University in a handsome, two-story brick building. My heart began to race as I stepped into a spacious hallway and plunged into familiar sounds—a cacophony of musical instruments, children's singing, and the sonorous voices of teachers.

As I turned at the end of the corridor, the school noises died away, and instead I heard the machine-gun sound of a typewriter. I followed it to the door of the administrative office. The secretary paid no attention to me as I hesitated in front of her.

At last, she stopped, zipped the document from the roller, and peered at me above her glasses. "I'm listening to you," she said without a smile.

"I've heard you have a part-time position for a piano teacher," I said, trying to suppress my nervousness.

"Who told you about it?" she asked.

"Tamara Mikhailovna Shebeko, my former teacher," I said.

"Oh, well. You're Mila, then. She told me that you were coming." Her expression changed from indifferent to curious. "Do you have a passport? Are you over sixteen?"

"Yes, I do. I'll turn seventeen in three months." I nodded with too much enthusiasm.

She pulled two pieces of plain paper from her desk and handed them to me. "Here. Take a seat and write an employment application."

I didn't have any idea how to compose an application. Noticing my confusion, she pointed at a sample she kept under the glass on her desk. I carefully copied it, signed my name, dated it, and gave it back to her. She skimmed it and stuck it in a thin folder.

"Good," she said, putting the folder aside. "If Comrade Annamuradov approves, you'll have to bring me your passport and a *spravka* (affirmation) from the management of the musical college that you're permitted to work. Now go upstairs to meet with Violetta Sergeyevna, the Head of the Piano Department."

I knew Violetta. She had been a graduate student when I was a freshman.

"Ah, Mila," she greeted me warmly when I knocked on the door of her classroom. Violetta asked me questions about the college and our teachers. We talked about cotton picking and how bad it was for students to lose so much time from college. We didn't talk at all about work or my teaching experience, of which I had none.

"Can you start on Monday?" she asked at last. "The students have been loafing for two weeks. We're getting complaints from the parents."

"I guess so," I said. Everything had happened so fast that I didn't have time to be nervous.

"Good. I'll let the parents know. I don't have a classroom available for you, so you'll have to work in whatever empty room has a piano. Stop by my class at noon, and I'll give you the list of your students."

On Monday, I met my first students. A new musical school teacher usually "inherited" the unpromising kids established teachers wanted to give away—those with bad academics, lack of musical inclinations, brawly parents, or all of the above. My first class of six students was no different. But it was a big step for me. Now, two afternoons a week, I was a piano teacher. Schoolchildren and staff addressed me respectfully by my patronymic name, Ludmila Ivanovna. It seemed strange at first, but I got used to it.

I jumped at the opportunity to teach my students everything I knew about proper hand and body positions, different techniques of drawing sound, and tempo and phrasing. I corrected their mistakes, going through the same process over and over again until they could play every note with the right finger; articulate every portamento, legato and staccato; and express every nuance.

Like Tamara Mikhailovna, I was strict and demanding, but when my students worked hard, I spared no words of praise. When I did, their eyes sparkled, and they ran home swinging their musical folders just as I had when I was their age. The looks of distrust and doubt on the parents' faces (*What can this teenager teach my daughter*?) gradually changed to respect. Once, somebody's mother told me how much her daughter wanted to be a piano teacher like Ludmila Ivanovna.

37: The Thaw

The best years of my youth fell in the late 1950s and the first half of the 1960s, which also happened to be the most lenient and exciting period of Soviet history, what would later be labeled as *Khruschevskaya Ottepel'* (Khrushchev's Thaw).

Khrushchev denounced Stalin's policies, eased repressions, and released millions of prisoners from labor camps. More than that, he tore off the planks from our boarded-up windows into the outside world, letting in a wave of fresh air from the West. There were foreign exhibitions, sport competitions, and scientific conferences in Moscow and Leningrad that attracted millions of people from all over the world. The stories and images made their way to even our remote Soviet republics, although sometimes with considerable delay.

Until 1957, when the International Festival of Youth and Students was held in Moscow, ordinary Soviet people had seen foreigners only in the movies or on the pages of *Krokodil* (Crocodile), a popular illustrated satirical journal that Mama subscribed to for years. *Krokodil* aimed its humor at the flaws hindering the building of socialism. It mocked drunkenness, loafing, negligence, tardiness, minor bureaucracy, and religious prejudices—safe topics that would not offend anyone in charge. It was full of political cartoons and caricatures ridiculing the capitalist West. Americans were portrayed either as unemployed poor men—gaunt, unshaven, and in rags—or fat-bellied bourgeois in tails and top hats, thick cigars in their mouths. There was a third category, too—the poor, oppressed *negr*, the victim of the Ku Klux Klan and that fat American in the topper.

To everyone's surprise, the foreign guests didn't look like those cartoons at all. They had friendly faces and wore clothes that looked comfortable and casual. They stood out in a Soviet crowd that was always dressed up as if for a holiday. Even to go to movies, visit our friends and relatives, or attend classes at college, we'd spruce up as if we were going to the Bolshoi Theatre or an official reception in the Kremlin—a two-piece suit, a tie, polished loafers, high-heel pumps, a shiny dress, jewelry, coiffed hair. It took too much effort to get our good clothes for us to simply let them hang in wardrobes.

Never before had the Soviets shaken the hand of a foreigner, touched or even eyed a black person, sipped Pepsi Cola, or worn jeans and sneakers. Western clothing, hairstyles, music, and even chewing gum became objects of our desire. *Zhvachka* (gum) became a cultural shock. Children chewed it in turns, passing it around from one to another.

But our freedom was relative.

Around this same time, the so-called *bardy* (bards)—Soviet lyric poets who sang and accompanied themselves on the guitar—became popular. Like any new trend, their appearance was met with resistance from the authorities, who accused the *bardy* of being empty and alien to our Soviet ideology. Radio, television, and recording studios shut their doors to them. The fuss around them only aroused more interest among the youth. We learned about them via illegal amateur recordings made by their friends and fans in cafes and small private, often improvised concerts.

In the summer 1965, Sashka came home from his swim camp in Russia with a guitar. He knew just three basic chords, but that was enough to sing "April Duty," "The Little Orchestra of Hope Conducted by Love," and "A Komsomol Goddess."

"Whose songs are they?" I asked when he stopped.

"Bulat Okudzhava's," he said. "All of Moscow is crazy about him."

Soon I would learn new names—Alexander Galich, Yuriy Visbor, Yuliy Kim, and, several years later, the king of them all, Vladimir Vysotskiy. They became part of our youth and part of our lives.

Sashka also brought home *ryobra* (ribs) from his travels. "Music on ribs" or "jazz on bones" was what we called black-market records of foreign contemporary musicians who were banned from broadcast in the USSR. Music and songs were recorded onto used, flexible medical x-ray films obtained from hospitals or clinics. Looking at them, I could often still see pictures of someone's lungs, tibia, or ribs. On the reverse side of the film, in clumsy letters, was scribbled the word "Beatles."

Sashka put the film on his record player and lowered the needle. At first, I heard only hissing sounds, and then a young voice singing in English. We didn't know what he was saying, but I had never heard anything that simple, warm, and frank.

The quality of the record was terrible, but we listened to it over and over, until Tamara Mikhailovna told us that she couldn't stand it anymore. Soon Sashka had more ribs with Beatles songs, and Sashka, Borka, Tolik, Yulka, and I would pile into his room and listen in silence.[14]

---

14 In 1967, the album *Musical Kaleidoscope* was released in the USSR. One of the songs listed on its label was "Girl - Folk music and lyrics - Quartet Beatles." Later I'd find out that the song was actually written by John Lennon and Paul McCartney.

The 1960s was the time of a happy universal delusion. The ice had only melted a little, but we believed that spring had come, and summer would follow. Still, many things were regulated and controlled by local authorities, even the length of our skirts and the width of young men's pants. Militia and Komsomol activists patrolled the streets of Ashkhabad looking for troublemakers. Someone with the wrong outfit or hairstyle—young men with long hair and cropped Beatles pants, or women with flowing hair, ponytails, short cuts, or "Babette" hairstyles—could be detained, warned, and humiliated.

After Nikita Khrushchev was removed as First Secretary of the Central Committee of the CPSU and replaced with Leonid Brezhnev in 1964, the policy of openness and democratization began to wind down. The *Thaw* era and my country's good fortune was over.

PART III

38: Sashka

I was seventeen when I met a guy at my cousin's birthday party. Vadim was tall, well-built, and attractive. He was a couple of years older than me, a winner of the City Tennis Championship, and a biker—the combination impressed me. We danced and talked the whole evening, and he took me home on his motorcycle. I felt triumphant when he offered to teach me how to play tennis.

The following Sunday, I met Vadim at the court. We were having a good time when suddenly Sashka materialized behind the mesh fence. He stayed and watched us with a smirk on his face, smoking one cigarette after another.

After our second session, Vadim suddenly disappeared. I was heartbroken. It wasn't until a month later that I learned from my cousin that Sashka and two other guys had waylaid Vadim. They warned him that they'd break his ribs if he didn't leave me alone. I was furious.

Sashka turned sixteen. His curls were darker, and his body was muscular. His face had lost its youthful softness, and his gray-blue eyes acquired an ironic twinkle. I thought he looked like the Greek God Apollo. When he was annoyed, his gaze became icy and his mouth twitched in contempt, but he still looked at me with the same devotion.

Sashka had a naturally beautiful voice, and he constantly replenished his musical repertoire with new songs by Soviet bards. He was often the center of attention. Young women cast admiring glances at him, but he seemed not to notice anybody around him. He always sang only for me, looking straight into my eyes.

Ты у меня одна,	You are my only one,
Словно в ночи луна,	Like the moon in the night,
Словно в году весна,	Like the spring in the year's cycle,
Словно в степи сосна.	Like the pine in the open.
Нету другой такой	There has never been
Ни за какой рекой,	Your like across any river,
Нет за туманами,	Nor beyond fogs,
Дальними странами.	Or in any distant world.[15]

Even though I was angry with him about chasing away Vadim, I still felt a weird satisfaction: this handsome, unruly guy, who was not afraid of anything or anybody, belonged to me. He'd do whatever I wished.

His parents had divorced a few years before, and Tamara Mikhailovna spent her days and evenings either at work—college, concerts, playing on TV—or socializing, so he had his house and small, skinny yard all to himself. Borka, Tolik, Yulka, Sashka, and I were left alone with our crazy ideas, and Sashka always ran the show.

---

15 "You're My Only One," a song by Soviet bard Yuriy Vizbor. Translation by Caroline Kraabel.

With Sashka everything was on full throttle—games, drinks, fights, competition, even books. He started smoking when he was eight or nine, and drinking at twelve. Later, I'd learn that at fifteen he had an affair with his mother's best friend, who was also a musician and a college teacher. Somehow Tamara found out, and the woman disappeared from their lives.

Sashka was always the initiator and instigator of our mischief. He was an inexhaustible fibber, and he drew lots of his ideas from books by Mark Twain, James Fenimore Cooper, Jack London, and Arthur Conan Doyle. Later, he proceeded to Stefan Zweig, Erich Maria Remarque, Thomas and Heinrich Mann, Émile Zola, and Guy de Maupassant. Oddly, it was Sashka, not my teachers or my parents, who instilled in me my love of foreign literature.

Confessions of Felix Krull, *Three Friends*, and *Bel Ami* were his favorites. He did not just read them; he learned from them. He mimicked their heroes' behaviors and built his image accordingly. A life of adventure and drinking, love and friendship, courage and recklessness, resourcefulness and lies—he had it all figured out and adapted, some from books, some from his mother, and mostly from his own restless nature.

One summer, the boys were obsessed with making explosives. They prepared magnesium shavings from old brake pads and mixed them with crystals of *margantsovka*[16] (potassium permanganate) from their medicine chests. A long piece of a clothesline soaked in kerosene served as a fuse. The sound of explosions terrified Sashka's neighbors, and they complained to his mother. The boys disappeared, but Sashka continued his experiments.

---

16 *Margantsovka* was considered to be a good antiseptic. Our mothers used to add crystals of it in the water for bathing new babies; treated our wounds, cuts, and chickenpox sores with it; used it as an emetic for food poisoning. Our fathers made wood stain for toning furniture and used it for purifying *samagon* (moonshine).

I happened to walk through his gate moments after he planted a bomb in a small dip near his kitchen window and lit the fuse.

"Duck and cover," he yelled. I barely had time to run around the corner before the explosion boomed. It was so strong that I could feel the earth tremble under my feet. When we came out of our hiding places, a big chunk of the corner of the house was gone. I could see the kitchen table through a hole in the wall.

"Oh *chyort* (devil). I planted it too close," he said, admiring the opening. "See how powerful it is? If I added a little more, the whole house would have blown up."

The damage was significant, and all of Sashka's attempts to camouflage it failed.

"Idiot!" Tamara yelled at him when she came back from work. "Stop destroying the house. Soon we will have nowhere to live!"

I could not say exactly when my mood toward Sashka started changing. Was it when I started noticing that my college girlfriends were flirting with him? Or did it happen when he went away for the summer, and I realized how dull my life was without him?

The night Sashka came back from his long trip, Mama was still at the apiary and I was sleeping at Yulka's house. It was stifling hot, and Yulka's parents slept inside with all the doors and windows open. Yulka and I dragged our mattresses and pillows outside and settled in the yard under the grape arbor. Lying on our stomachs, we whispered and giggled until my eyelids felt heavy and my mind drifted away.

I woke with a start, realizing that someone was crouching over me. I couldn't see in the dark, but I already knew who it was. The smell of tobacco mixed with a grassy scent of grape tendrils belonged only to Sashka. He had a habit of chewing grape leaves, thinking that it would conceal the odor of cigarettes from his mother.

Gently, without making any noise, he sat down on the edge of my bed. I didn't move, pretending to be asleep. If we started talking, I thought, Yulka's parents would hear us and see him on my bed. He leaned closer, and I felt a slight touch of his lips on my cheek. Then another. My heart raced so hard that I was sure he would find out that I was awake. I could hardly breathe.

He slowly rose and walked away into the darkness. Neither of us mentioned his visit the next day.

The following night, I couldn't sleep, because I was wondering if Sashka would come again. I was afraid, and at the same time I hoped he would. He returned when all of the sound and movement around me had hushed, and everyone else was asleep. This time I "woke up" and told him to go away. He said he wouldn't leave unless I let him kiss me.

I agreed "just to get rid of you." He kissed me, and then he kissed me more. His lips were full and warm, and I felt dizzy.

After that, when we met with our friends, Sashka's arm stayed over my shoulder, as if he wanted the whole world to know that I belonged to him. During the past decade everyone had gotten so accustomed to seeing us next to each other that they probably took this shift in our relationship as a natural course of events. But not Mama.

When she returned from the apiary in October, our romance was already in full bloom. More than once, I caught her alarmed gaze fixed on Sashka and me. She didn't like him. She thought he was spoiled, high-handed, and rampant. So far, she had put up with our friendship only because he was my teacher's son, but now Mama looked worried.

That fall I started a full-time job at the musical school where I'd been teaching. I'd graduated from musical college, and Mama's dream of seeing me as a piano teacher came true, but I was still not convinced that being a musical teacher was my calling. I wanted to do something real and important, something that would make me feel good about myself.

Sashka didn't return to school that fall, either. He told me he was going to find a job and start attending evening school. Instead, he stayed home and read books, composed songs, and faithfully pumped up his already bulging muscles. He mostly gave up swimming, although a couple of times he took part in competitions and once won the finals. (His record in the breaststroke would remain unbroken for many years.)

Our Bagirskaya gang had fallen apart: Tolik was in Russia, studying in the Sasovo Flight School of Civil Aviation; Boris had a job and a girlfriend, and we only saw him rarely; Yulka was busy with her final year in musical college and was dating a new boyfriend. With nobody else to pal around with, Sashka and I were left alone.

By the beginning of winter, our innocent hand holding and kisses had become more intimate. Sashka's demands grew intense and impatient. I started feeling vulnerable. When I tried to stop his advances, he became bitter and sarcastic.

"How long are you planning to remain a virgin?" he asked me when I stopped his hand from trying to unbutton my blouse. Just minutes before, I'd melted in his arms as he kissed me and swore his love. "It's ridiculous." He laughed his curt-as-a-cough angry laugh. "You're going to be nineteen."

His sarcasm, like a cold shower, brought me back to reality. I got up from his sofa and started gathering my things.

"Don't worry about me, Sashka. I'll be fine," I said. "And you know what? Find yourself a younger girl and stop chasing me. I'm getting tired of you, anyway."

That night Sashka got himself drunk. He was so rowdy that Tamara sent Boris to fetch me. It had happened before—Sashka would act up because he wanted my attention. I'd come. He'd yield, apologize, and we'd reconcile.

This time I refused to go.

39: Spoiled

On a December afternoon, I was working with my student, Vova Pepko, to polish the pieces he would play at a mid-winter exam. Vova was the pupil every music teacher dreamed of. He had talent, charisma, and personality. The progress he made and his hunger for music were absolutely astonishing.

He had just finished playing the etude when the door of my room opened a crack, and the school secretary, Vera Ivanovna, appeared in the opening.

"Ludmila Ivanovna," she said politely. "Could I have a word with you outside?"

Vera Ivanovna's appearance at your door was always a sign of trouble. I didn't like her. She knew all the school news and gossip: who came late and who left five minutes early, and whose student left the classroom before the bell rang. She reported every small violation to the deputy or the director.

"Could it wait until the end of the lesson?" I asked, searching my memory for a possible reason for her visit.

"No," she said. "It's very important."

I asked Vova to play the prelude at a slow pace, emphasizing downbeats. I listened to the beginning of the piece to be sure that he had understood the task, and then left the room. Vera Ivanovna's face was alarmed and unusually soft.

"Ludmila Ivanovna," she started, "a few minutes ago I received a call from a man. He said that Aleksander Shebeko has been hit by a car. He is seriously injured. I'm very sorry." I could see that she really was sorry. Tamara Mikhailovna had been a teacher here for years, and everybody had known Sashka since he was a small boy.

"Where is he now?" I asked, startled.

"I don't know. The man said only that you have to go to their house immediately."

Pictures of Sashka lying in a pool of blood flashed in front of my eyes. Shouldn't he be in the emergency room or a hospital? I had to call his mother.

"The man asked that you not call Tamara Mikhailovna," the secretary said, as if she'd read my thoughts. "She has already been notified."

"What about my students?" I asked, already reaching for my coat.

"Don't worry. Let Pepko go, and I'll put a note on your door that all classes are cancelled for today."

While I rushed down the stairs and through the long corridor, putting my scarf on and trying to button my winter coat with trembling fingers, the secretary was already in the courtyard talking to a taxi driver who had just delivered somebody to school.

"He'll take you," she said. "Let us know if Tamara Mikhailovna needs any help."

"Thank you." I slumped onto the back seat and slammed the door.

"To the corner of Bagirskaya and Maxim Gorky Streets," I instructed the taxi driver.

I agonized all through the drive to Sashka's house. This was all my fault.

The day after I refused to return to Sashka's house, Tamara had come to our house. I was at work, so she talked to my mother. When I came home, Mama looked stern.

"What happened?" I asked.

"Tamara Mikhailovna came this afternoon to talk to your father and me about you and Sashka," she said. I felt a twinge inside.

"What did she want?"

"To ask your father for your hand," Mama said. "Isn't it a little too early for the two of you to start thinking about marriage?"

That was the last thing I expected her to say. "I'm not thinking about marrying anybody! I cannot believe she could even bring this up," I assured Mama.

"She told me that you and Sashka are madly in love, and he insisted she come and talk to us. I can't believe she is seriously considering her son's marriage. He's only sixteen, for God's sake! What is she thinking?"

It sounded so crazy that I couldn't find anything to say.

"No education, no work," Mama continued. "I asked her what you were going to live on. You know what she said? 'You have money, and you'll help at first. I'll do whatever I can, too.'" Mama looked me in the eye. "Mila, have you two been talking about marriage?"

"No. I've already *told* you. You know he's talked about marrying me since he was nine."

"Yes, I know. But you were just kids, and it was funny. But not anymore. What if your father was home when she came?" Mama's eyes were intense.

"Don't worry. I'm not going to marry him or anyone else for a while," I assured her.

"You certainly have your own head on your shoulders," she said with a sigh. "But I'd think well before connecting your life with such a troublemaker as your Sashka."

Two days after, I bumped into Tamara herself on my way to work.

"Sashka's on the verge of a nervous breakdown." she told me. "You know he's in love with you. You're purposely hurting him. If something happens to him, it'll be your fault."

Her words spun in my head as I sat in the taxi on my way to the Shebeko's house. Was she right? Is whatever happened to Sashka my fault? If I had gone to his house and reconciled with him the night he was upset, he'd probably be safe and sound now. Why, why didn't I go? Yes, he hurt me. But hadn't I been rude to him many times, ordering him around and pushing him away?

The car slowed down to turn to Maxim Gorky Street. My heart started pumping harder in anticipation of what terrible news I was going to learn. When the taxi stopped, I sprang out of it and rushed across the road towards Sashka's house. The driver's shouts stopped me.

"*Devushka* (teen-age girl), you forgot to pay me!"

I ran back, grabbed a bill from my purse and shoved it into his extended hand.

"Take your change!" I heard him calling after me.

The gate leading to Sashka's yard was locked, but even before I started banging, it swung open. I stepped over the threshold. The gate slammed shut behind me. I turned around and saw Sashka. He looked fine.

"What the hell?" was all I could say before he shoved me inside their narrow passageway and turned the key in the lock. Struggling to stay on my feet, I lost my balance and my head hit the corner of the house. Not allowing me to get my balance, he grabbed me from behind and wrapped his left arm around my throat. With his right hand, he put something sharp to my neck. From the corner of my eye, I saw his fist gripping a red-and-black composite handle.

I recognized the knife. I had admired it last summer when he finished it. "It's the most beautiful and dangerous-looking knife you've ever made," I told him then. Now its sharp end pierced my skin as he pushed me toward the porch of his house.

None of my pleas or threats or tears helped. Sashka was drunk. He looked like a wild beast running amuck, and for the first time in my life, I could not tame him. He forced me inside the house, along the corridor, and into his mother's bedroom.

I was still in my coat. My girdle, stockings, and panties were scattered all over the floor around Tamara's bed. Crying silently, I got up and started gathering my belongings. He was watching me from the bed, his knife still at his side.

"You are my wife now," he said.

I did not answer. I felt empty, drained of all emotion and dry inside. The shame, fear, disgust, and hate came later.

I did not hate him as much as I hated myself: for being trapped, for provoking him, for letting him touch and kiss me. How could I be so stupid as to fall in love with this crazy teenager who had been my embarrassment for so long?

That night I lay in my bed, motionless, staring into the darkness of my room. The heavy load weighed down my chest with such force that I could hardly breathe. I didn't want to see the sun rise. I was afraid to hear Mama's voice in the morning and to look into her eyes. I wanted to die, to forget everything that had happened to me.

I remembered how, when I was in grade school, I overheard a neighbor telling Mama about one of her students. "She was such a lovely girl. This scoundrel spoiled and abandoned her. Who will marry her now? She has to live with this stain all her life."

How anyone could spoil a person, I wondered at the time. In the first grade, when Versanna allowed me to write with a pen for the first time, I accidentally doused ink on my white school apron and Mama said it was spoiled and I couldn't wear it anymore. Soup could be also spoiled if you forgot to put it in the fridge. That was clear. But when I tried to imagine a girl who had been spoiled, I couldn't.

When I asked Mama about it, all she said was, "This was an adult conversation, and you were not supposed to listen to it. When you grow up, you'll learn what it means."

Later, I heard the half-whispers at school about a girl who had been raped or seduced—it was never clear which, nor did it matter to anyone doing the gossiping. Some people, usually women, felt sorry for the girl. But there were always others who'd say, "She is to blame herself. She shouldn't have shaken her ass in front of him." Someone else, usually a man, would assent. "Right. The Russian saying is correct. *Suchka ne zakhochet, kabel ne vskochet* (If a bitch doesn't want, a male dog wouldn't hop up)."

I heard the same phrase from my own family when my cousin, Yurka, was accused of seducing or raping (again, it didn't really matter which) his girlfriend, Tomka.

She complained to the Komsomol Committee of the college where they were both students. The Committee announced an urgent all-college Komsomol meeting to address "The Immoral Behavior of Komsomol Member Yuriy Kondeykin." He was given an ultimatum—either marry her or the Committee would expel him from the college and send the case to the militia. Yurka said no and was kicked out of college. Frightened that the militia would get involved, his parents forced him to marry her. "You can divorce later," they told him. I remembered the Kondeykins calling her a slut and blaming her for ruining Yurka's life.

No matter what, the blame and disgrace always fell on the woman. Now it was my turn.

When the first rays of light started diluting the darkness, I knew that I'd never tell anybody about what had happened to me. I dressed, put on a thick turtleneck sweater to cover my cuts and bruises, and left my room.

It was Saturday. Mama was in the kitchen, and the house smelled of pastry. The sweet aroma reminded me of things I used to enjoy that didn't make sense now. I couldn't bear the thought of having to keep breathing, moving, talking, or even seeing my own mother.

Somehow, I made it through the day. On Sunday, Mama mentioned that she had talked with our neighbor, Lida Utkin, who told her that Sashka came to their house two days earlier and asked if he could use their phone. (The Utkins were the only family on our block who owned a phone.) She overheard him telling somebody about a car accident and him being badly injured. She thought it was odd, but assumed it was probably some arrangement between Mila and Sashka. "Sometimes, teenagers behave so bizarrely."

"Why did Sashka do it?" Mama asked me.

"I don't know," I said. She didn't believe me. I saw it in her eyes. I cringed, fearing she'd ask me more questions, but she said nothing more.

If she had put her arms around my shoulders and tried to talk to me from her heart then, I'd probably have broken down and told her everything. The secret I was carrying in my chest was pressing on me like a gravestone. The heaviness of it was unbearable. But Mama didn't ask. She didn't know how. Or maybe she was scared of what she'd hear. Either way, I was left alone with my grief.

40. The Aftershock

For days, I lived in a haze, only half aware of what was going on around me. I flinched at the slightest noise, and my heart raced. The hardest thing was to be near Mama. It took all of my strength to smile and pretend to listen to her.

The only place where I could forget myself for a few minutes at a time was my work. But even there, listening to my students playing, I often felt a pang of panic and tears would start to pour from my eyes.

At night my brain came out of its stupor, and I would relive the attack over and over again—fighting, screaming, and always losing. Sometimes I woke, gasping for air, and saw Sashka's silhouette behind the bars of my closed window. I couldn't tell if it was my battered imagination or reality.

After weeks of this, I finally saw him. I had been avoiding going anywhere close to his house, but that morning I was late to a teachers' meeting and decided to take the shorter route to the bus stop. I turned the corner from Bagirskaya onto Gorky Street and there he was, standing at the gate of his house.

Startled I turned around, but he caught my hand. "Calm down," he kept saying as I struggled to free myself. "I won't hurt you. I just want to talk to you." He kicked his gate open and pulled me inside his yard.

For days I had been imagining our meeting. I wanted to face him, tell him how I felt, and demand to know why he had hurt me. But now, standing face to face with him, I couldn't utter a word. My tears choked me.

Sashka pulled me closer, wrapped his arms around me, and held me tight, waiting for me to calm down. "I love you," he said. "I'm sorry for hurting you. I didn't know what I was doing. I was drunk."

I wasn't afraid. I wasn't angry. All I felt was an endless emptiness.

"Let me go," I said. "Just let me go."

"I cannot live without you. I'll do whatever you want."

"I want you to leave me alone."

"I can't. If you tell me to die for you, I will."

"Die then. I don't care."

He pushed me away and reached into a pocket of his pants. My heart skipped a beat in panic. But instead of a knife, he brought out a cigarette lighter—a metal one with an impression of a spaceship and Yuri Gagarin's profile. Then he pulled up a sleeve of his sweater, exposing his smooth, muscular forearm. I couldn't guess what would come next.

"Tell me that you forgive me," he said.

"No. I never will."

With his thumb, he pressed the top of the lighter. It clicked and lit up. I expected him to start smoking, but he just watched the small blue tongue of the flame dance aimlessly in the cold air.

"Tell me you forgive me," he repeated. I shook my head.

Slowly, he lifted his bare forearm and placed his wrist above the burning lighter. Now I understood what he was trying to do.

"You can kill yourself. I don't care," I said.

He lowered his wrist until the flame was almost licking his skin. He didn't wince, but I saw he was in pain. His lips were parted, and his smile seemed frozen. His gray eyes turned black as his pupils dilated. The sickening smell of burning skin reminded me of the time when my father had singed a pig carcass with a blowtorch. I felt nauseous.

"Stop it!" I cried out, when I was unable to bear it anymore. I stepped closer and hit him on his smiling lips. He lowered his arms and stared at me. I continued slapping his face, beating on his chest, and calling him names. He did not defend himself and did not take his eyes off me.

"I cannot stand it anymore. I want to die," I sobbed. "Why didn't you kill me? Take your damn knife and do it now if you're not a coward. Do it. I'm not afraid of you."

At last, exhausted, I wept silently. He hugged me and said again that he loved me and wanted me to marry him. He swore he would never hurt me again and would not let anyone else hurt me, either. He told me how he stood outside my window every night, asking for my forgiveness. He showed me a red scab on the side of his middle finger where he had tattooed the date I wanted to block from my mind.

"It's a reminder to never hurt you again," he said.

I wanted so much to believe him. He was the only person in the whole world who knew what had happened to me, and he could understand.

He lifted me and carried me to the door of his house. Then he lowered me to my feet, took my hand, and led me inside. I didn't resist and followed him like a lamb, meek and obedient, to the slaughterhouse.

As time went by, I learned how to hide myself better from others. I started laughing again. I became more daring. People around me thought I was a cheerful and happy teenager, and no one suspected how I really felt.

Sashka and I continued on as a couple, and we got on well until it came to sex. I objected and resisted every time he attempted to undress me. He persisted, never taking my refusals as a sign to stop. Afterwards, I always cried.

Once, Sashka got mad at me, threw his shirts into his sports bag and said he was leaving me and this damn city. To my shame, I followed, begging him to stay. The willpower that I had once been so proud of was trampled. I was weak and scared. I said I loved him and couldn't live without him. He stayed, and everything continued.

When Sashka talked about our marriage, I no longer objected. We agreed to wed as soon as he turned eighteen. Until then, I begged him to be cautious and keep our relationship hidden from others.

"Spit on them all," he always responded. He never gave a damn what others said or thought about him.

In March, he came up with a new plan. "We don't need to wait another whole year. I know how to erase my birth date in the passport without a trace. I'll make myself a year or two older."

"Don't be a fool," I argued. "If anyone finds out, you'll go to jail."

"Nobody will notice," he assured me. "To delete a number and put a new one is as simple as to piss over two fingers."

"But even if you do it, what will we tell everyone? They all know that you're only seventeen."

"We're not going to tell anybody. We'll just go to the ZAGS (city registry office) and register our marriage."

"And then what?"

"We can move somewhere far from here where nobody knows us."

I didn't object. Perhaps making it legal would make things easier, I thought.

★ ★ ★

Sashka's technique of removing ink without a trace didn't work as well as he planned. The numbers on his passport disappeared, but the chemicals left a whitish spot on the page. On the lighter background, his new birth year stuck out like a pimple on the nose.

"No big deal," he assured me. "You see it because you know what to look for. Nobody else will notice."

In early April, we went to ZAGS and filled out an application for marriage. The clerk behind the desk scheduled our ceremony for the beginning of June, so that we'd have two months "to think it over and check your feelings." She told us to arrive half an hour early, bring our passports, the proof of the paid fee, and two people to witness our marriage.

The timing was perfect. Mama left with our apiary in the middle of April, and Papa took Andrusha there after his school year ended in May. Nobody would be home except me.

Sashka and I decided to trust our secret marriage to two of our friends—Boris, our childhood buddy, and Larissa, my coworker and college friend. We ask them to be our witnesses and wedding guests. We would hold our reception in Aina Café immediately after the ceremony at a table for four.

On a hot afternoon in June, we all gathered at the ZAGS. Larissa and I wore colorful minidresses and high-heel sandals, and she brought me a huge bouquet of gladioli. Sashka and Boris wore light shirts and summer pants. I laughed with them as we waited, trying not to appear more nervous than any bride would be before her wedding, but inside my guts were quivering.

The wedding procession in front of us entered the building, and Sashka flipped away his cigarette. "We're next." He took my hand and led me inside. Boris and Larissa followed.

We waited in a tiny, windowless passageway squeezed between two pairs of heavy double doors, one leading outside into the street and the other inside the ZAGS ceremonial room. As the clock ticked slowly, the armpits of Boris's shirt darkened with sweat.

Larissa pressed her back against the whitewashed wall, fanning her face and neck with a piece of paper. I felt heat coming from Sashka's body next to me.

At last, the door leading into the room flung open and the newlyweds, accompanied by a group of noisy friends and relatives, emerged. Laughing, they ran past us into the street.

The mixed feeling of fear and excitement made me almost jumpy.

We waited a few more minutes until the door opened again, and we heard our names. Sashka squeezed my hand and, to the sound of a recorded Mendelssohn's "Wedding March," we stepped into a large room and processioned along a red-carpet runner toward a wooden desk. The stern-looking woman sitting behind it looked up from her open logbook and invited "the bride and the groom" to occupy two chairs across from her. Boris and Larissa remained standing behind us.

She pressed the button on the tape-recorder, and we all grew quiet. On her request, Sashka handed the woman our passports and the proof of the paid fee. She checked the receipt first, then my passport. We waited while she entered my data in the Marriage Registration Log. When she finished, she took Sashka's passport and flipped through its pages. My guts sank.

First, she made sure that he had the Ashkhabad *propiska* (residency permit),[17] then she checked that there was no stamp of another marriage. Only after that did she open the first page. She looked up, comparing Sashka to his photo, and then examined the page. I held my breath.

---

17 A residency permit allowed a person to live in a given place. Without a *propiska* stamp, Soviet citizens couldn't get a job, be accepted to school, or marry. Residing anywhere in the USSR without a *propiska* was prohibited.

After a long, silent moment, she lifted a black phone receiver. Sashka and I exchanged glances as we listened to the whirring sound of the dial.

"Hello," she said to someone on the other end of the line. "I have a couple of young people here who want to get married. Could you please check the information on the groom?" Looking into Sashka's passport she dictated his name, date, and place of his birth.

She waited silently, the receiver pressed against her ear and her eyes half closed. Sashka shifted in his chair. I saw the moment the expression on her face changed.

"Yes . . . yes . . . yes. Thank you for the information. I'll talk to you later." The receiver made a metallic click when she put it down. Once again, she looked at Sashka's passport, then closed it, gathered all our papers in one small pile, and got up.

"By the rules, young man, I should report you to the militia for passport fraud. But I won't do it. I have a son of your age, and I don't want to spoil your future. Lose your passport and get a new one. And come back in a year if you or your bride don't change your minds."

Embarrassed and relieved, the four of us fled the room. Once outside, Larissa handed me my bouquet. I accepted it with an exaggerated solemnity, marched up to one of the plaster trash cans near the ZAGS entrance, and dropped it inside.

"That was a flop," Sashka said. "Let's go to Aina Café to celebrate."

41: The Discovery

Two months later, I realized I was pregnant. We couldn't keep our secret anymore. I was devastated. Sashka was elated.

"We'll have a son," he said. "*My* son."

I cried and begged him to do something, but he didn't have any clue where to go or who to ask for help. He offered to talk to his mother, but I forbade that. Instead, Sashka brought me his mother's old book about pregnancy and delivery. There was nothing there about how *not* to get pregnant or what a woman should do if she didn't want to be pregnant, but I found a sentence that said pregnant women shouldn't lift heavy objects or take hot baths, because both could result in miscarriage. So that was exactly what I decided to do.

My parents had a bedroom set that Papa had acquired *po blatu* (through connections). It was of good quality and very heavy, built of solid wood. That afternoon, I grabbed the foot of one of the beds and, straining, lifted it. I held it until my back began aching. The following morning, I could hardly get out of my bed. But that evening, I built a fire in our *banya* and sat in a bathtub full of water so hot I felt dizzy.

It didn't help.

Then I remembered somebody saying that if you added several drops of iodine into milk, making it look like cocoa, drinking it could result in a miscarriage. Just to be sure, I added extra drops and choked it all down. An hour later, I felt so sick that I feared I was going to die, but whoever was inside my belly clung stubbornly to it and refused to leave.

I tried to remember the conversations I had overheard and the books and magazines I had read. My experience equaled almost nothing.

I ran out of options.

Mama and Andrusha returned at the end of August to get him ready for the new school year. He was going to the sixth grade. Papa stayed in the fields with the apiary.

On the third day after their arrival, we were all sitting at the table having breakfast when suddenly I felt sick. I jumped up from the table and rushed outside. When I came back, still feeling crummy, my breakfast was on the table. Mama hadn't seen me all summer, and so now she tried to indulge me by making my favorite dishes, but I was afraid to touch it, thinking that I might throw up in front of Mama and my brother.

"Everything all right?" she asked.

"Yes," I said. "I just had to go to the bathroom."

The next morning, the same thing happened. "What's wrong with you, Mila?" Mama asked me after Andrusha left for school and we were alone. I was sipping my tea, afraid even to look at the plate on the table in front of me, stacked high with untouched pancakes.

"Nothing," I said,

"Are you pregnant?"

She was sitting across from me, her eyes concerned. Her question punctured the ripe boil of my grief, resentment, helplessness, and misery, and it all poured out in a stream of uncontrolled tears. I sobbed for a long time.

I expected her to be angry, to call me bad names, to shame me. I was ready for it. I deserved it. But Mama neither scolded nor comforted me. She just sat there, paralyzed with her own feelings of shock.

Looking back, I think she must have blamed herself for leaving me home alone so often, for giving me too much freedom when I needed her guidance, for allowing my friendship with Sashka, and probably for not explaining how relationships like ours could end.

She asked me if Sashka knew, and I said yes.

"And what have the two of you decided to do?" she asked.

"He said we can go away somewhere and live together."

Mama looked skeptical. "Where would you go? And how would you live?"

"I don't know. We can go to Norilsk where his father lives."

"Go to the Far North? Pregnant? Without *propiska*? Without a marriage stamp in your passports? And how are you going to survive with a baby on your hands?"

"I don't know," I said. I kept my eyes down, examining the pattern on the tablecloth. "Sashka said he'll take care of everything."

"Mila, stop being a child. You know your Sashka. He has all these fantasies in his head. But now it's time for both of you to look at things soberly." She sighed. "He is too young to get married until March of next year, and you will be too heavily pregnant by then. What will people say when they see you in a couple of months? How will I look into our neighbors' eyes?"

I wanted to tell her that there was not a minute during the past year when I didn't think about that, but I didn't say anything. The crease between her eyebrows deepened.

"I need to talk to your father," she said at last.

42: Gor'ko

I was afraid that my father would get angry and blame me—or Mama—for what happened. Instead, he looked unusually quiet and somber. He averted his eyes from me. I felt even guiltier.

To observe decency and save the family's reputation, my parents decided to arrange a wedding party before our relatives and neighbors noticed my growing belly.

"It will be a very small wedding," Mama told me, "with just the closest relatives, several neighbors, and a few of your friends. No more than thirty people. You can go to the ZAGS and make your marriage official after Sashka turns eighteen and the baby is born."

On September 17, 1966, Sashka and I sat at the head of a long table that stretched across the length of our living room and spilled through the open door into the kitchen. My aunts and uncles from both sides of my family—Papa's five and Mama's three siblings with their spouses—were all there. From Sashka's side, there was only Tamara and two of her close friends. Yulka, Boris and Larissa represented our friends and generation.

I wore a guipure dress with a white brocade lining that Mama made especially for the occasion. Sashka was in black slacks and a white shirt with his sleeves rolled up to show off his biceps. I could still see the self-inflicted burn on the inner part of his left forearm.

The table was crammed with food and an inexhaustible array of bottles. Mama ran like a hamster in a wheel, bringing out steaming dishes, taking away empty ones, adding bread to bread plates, pickles to pickle plates, and *oliviye* and *vinegret* (traditional Russian holiday salads) to salad bowls. At the request of a toasting guest, she'd sit down for a minute to raise her glass *za molodykh* (to the newlyweds), to their happy life, or to their parents, but then put it back on the table untouched and race to the kitchen again.

Papa was in his element, performing the duties of a hospitable host, toastmaster, and entertainer. My new mother-in-law sat at the table like Queen Tamara of Georgia, enjoying the offerings of food and drinks.

The Kondeykins didn't let anyone forget the Russian traditions. Their youngest brother's daughter was getting married, after all. Everybody had to drink to her well-being. Every glass had to be filled to the brim to signify that the newlyweds' home would always overflow with good fortune.

"*Pei do dna!* (Bottoms up!) Do not leave the evil at the bottom of the glass! Those who don't drink to the dregs don't wish well to the young couple."

From time to time, someone would stand and announce that their drink had turned "bitter." On cue, the guests chanted, "*Gor'ko! Gor'ko! Gor'ko!* (Bitter!)" To "sweeten" it again, Sashka and I had to kiss. We were timid at first, but the drunker our guests became, the more often they insisted we sweeten their vodka, and the more readily we complied with their demand.

I couldn't believe how fast everything had changed. Just weeks before, I was terrified that someone would find out about my involvement with Sashka; now we were encouraged to kiss in full view of my parents, relatives, and friends.

While the men went outside to smoke, and Mama and my aunts cleaned up and set the table for the dessert, we led our friends out to the yard to dance.

"Put on the *Beauty Queen* record," Sashka told Boris, and the familiar, rich baritone of Muslim Magomayev flooded the autumn air, sending an electrical charge through my body. Sashka pulled me to the middle of the group. "Let's show them how to twist."

Our guests closed in around us, laughing and cheering as we swiveled our hips and twisted our bodies in the popular dance that had recently reached Ashkhabad. Our friends joined in. The unbearable burden of the past year fell from my shoulders as I let my body move to the rhythm of the music. I felt as if I grew my wings back.

43. My Pinkerton

Contrary to the old Russian tradition, when newlyweds lived with the groom's parents, Sashka moved to our house. He, who had been a regular guest in our house for many years, struggled at first to feel at ease, especially with my father. Papa neither treated his new son-in-law badly, nor did he demonstrate much affection.

I continued teaching piano at the musical school, and Tamara arranged a job for Sashka at the Ashkhabad Television Studio. Every morning, he swore and moaned when I tried to wake him up.

"Damn this job! For the money they pay, I should just show up twice a month to receive my salary," he grumbled as he dressed.

"You thought someone would pay you for your beautiful eyes?" I rolled my eyes. "If you don't get an education, you have to be content with what you get."

"Who the hell needs your education? Your father finished only seven grades of school. Now he makes more money as a taxi driver than any engineer or doctor who sweated their best years over the books."

"No holidays, no vacation, only work, work, and work again. That's how Papa makes money. Is it what you want? No, Sashka, you're not made of the same dough as him."

Finally, I promised that if he went back to school, I would go with him. I didn't need another diploma, but it was the only way I could get him there. So four times a week, either in the morning or at night, depending on our work schedules, Sashka and I walked to The Shift School for Working Youth. Four years ago, when Yulka and I attended Evening School, we messed around with our friends, missed classes, and didn't care about learning. Now I was on time and paid attention, determined to help the father of my future child get at least a high school education.

At night, I would read aloud from our text books, because Sashka was too "exhausted after my stupid work" to bother studying. I tried to coax him to solve math problems or memorize a law of physics, which he said he needed "as a dog needs a fifth leg." On our way to school, he usually tried to convince me to skip classes and go to the movies. I remained as hard as a flint stone.

I was surprised to find out that I was good in math. I liked solving algebra equations, cracking and spitting them out one after another like sunflower seeds. The more challenging a problem was, the more stubborn and tenacious I became. My feelings of triumph annoyed Sashka.

"Why're you trying so hard? Nobody is going to give you a medal for it," he mocked me. I didn't know how to explain it to him.

Sashka tried to find every possible excuse to shirk his classes, especially on the dark winter evenings. Exhausted after a day's work and languid from the warmth of the heater and the monotonous voice of the teacher, he wasn't the only student who would droop, yawn, and struggle to stay awake.

Sometimes, one of Ashkhabad's familiar power outages would give us a reprieve. The whole district would plunge into darkness, and our principal would call the city power station. If they didn't promise to restore the electricity within half an hour, we were dismissed. Every time, the school howled with delight and rushed outside. In winter, even the teachers seemed happy to go home early.

One night, though, the power went off only in our school. Through the window, we could see the streetlights and the glimmers coming from windows of nearby houses. But it was too dark for us to continue the class. Several of the male students headed outside to smoke, and the rest of us sat quietly, talking and waiting for word from the school office. After about ten minutes, the school secretary announced that we could go home. The City Power Station had told her that this blackout wasn't their fault.

"Something is probably wrong with the school wiring," she said. "They will send an electrician tomorrow."

The next day, the problem was fixed and classes resumed. But the following week the school lights went off again. The second lesson had just started when it happened. Several minutes later, Sashka slipped into the classroom in the dark and sat next to me.

"What happened?" he asked, panting.

"Outage again. Where have you been?"

"I was smoking outside with the guys. Why?" he asked defiantly. And suddenly it dawned on me.

"You weren't here the last time the lights went off, either," I whispered.

"So what?"

"So, the teacher told us that last week somebody cut the wires."

"And you think it was me? You're simply Sherlock Holmes, my dear."

The following night, we had a school meeting. The principal told us that someone had caused serious damage to the school's electrical wiring. She said she suspected who the culprit was. If it happened again, she would report him to the militia.

"Did you hear what she said? What if she knows?" I asked Sashka after the meeting.

"Let her prove it first. *Ne poyman, ne vor* (Not caught, not a thief)."

When the third blackout happened, Sashka was in class. "Alibi is the proof of innocence," he whispered into my ear. I wasn't sure who had cut the wires that time, but I knew exactly who had instigated it.

The principal was beside herself. A uniformed militiaman came to our school. Sashka and several others were summoned to the principal's room, where they were questioned. But Sashka was right. Nobody was caught cutting wires, so nobody was to blame.

The blackouts would probably have continued if it were not for Borka's winter break. In February he came home from Moscow, where he studied forensic criminology at the Militia Academy. He and Sashka spent lots of time talking. I overheard snippets of conversation about "fingerprinting, forensic medicine, toxicology, ballistics," and more. When Borka went back to school, Sashka spoke of nothing but becoming a detective.

A year ago, those two had despised militiamen. Now one studied forensic science in Moscow, and the other was crazy about working in the Criminal Investigation Department of the MVD (Ministry of Internal Affairs).

At least the blackouts at school stopped.

A week after Sashka turned eighteen, he went to the Ministry of Internal Affairs personnel department to apply for a job. He stood in endless lines for doctors, officials, and clerks, gathering all the necessary references. He even managed to get a positive letter from the television studio, which he had quit after just three months.

After all the papers had been submitted, he waited, plucking the guitar strings in our room, curling up in bed with a book, or just sitting in silence and gnawing on his fingers.

After a week, the militia turned him down.

Papa came to the rescue, as always. He promised Sashka he would talk to a friend who held a high position in the militia. I didn't know what the price of Papa's big-shot-friend was—money, honey, or a tribute to their old friendship—but soon Sashka had a job in the city's militia.

I had never seen Sashka so elated. His job was to catch pickpockets in the Russian Bazaar area. His eyes burned with eagerness as he described the pursuits, shadowing, and nabbing of petty thieves. He seemed like he was still playing our childhood games. He invented tricks, pasted on a mustache, and changed his appearance so the bad guys wouldn't recognize him.

More than once, as Mama banged around in the kitchen and prepared dinner, she asked, "Do you know when your Pinkerton is coming home?"

44: The Maternity Ward

By the time Sashka started working for the militia, I was already home on mandated maternity leave. I had turned twenty in February and stopped work just a few days after.

According to the Labor Code of the USSR, maternity leave started fifty-six calendar days before a pregnant woman's due date and ended fifty-six calendar days after the baby was born. My leave would end in June, but by that time the school year would be over, and all teachers would be on our fifty-six-day summer break. I would have almost half a year of fully paid time with my baby. The timing was perfect.

All winter I wore a spacious cardigan and sweater to conceal my pregnancy. When I notified the musical school administration that I would need to leave soon, it came as a surprise.

Being pregnant wasn't something Soviet women showed off. Our attitude that sex was something shameful made us treat pregnancy as embarrassment, as well. Women hid our conditions as long as we possibly could, and if somebody did notice our situation, they would never say anything to us, but would whisper about it with others.

My time at home before my baby's birth was slow and relaxed, probably the best time I ever spent with my mother. For the first time we talked not as daughter and mother, but as women. She told me amazing stories about her family and her childhood, about the exile and escape to Turkmenistan. Several times a day, we sat and drank tea, sometimes with bread and jam, or pancakes and honey, or fragrant cookies fresh from the oven.

According to Russian superstition, it was bad luck to buy anything for a baby before its birth, so there was little we could do to prepare. Mama would have to take care of it all while I was in the hospital.

The only place where we cheated was when we asked my Aunt Pasha, who worked in a fabric store, to set aside a roll of blue flannel for diapers. No one doubted that my baby would be a boy. Sashka and I didn't even choose a girl's name, although Tamara suggested, "If it's a girl, call her after me—Tamara."

"She'll never die of modesty." Mama said, after my mother-in-law was gone.

My due date was April 11. As it approached, my body got big and clunky. In my sixth month of pregnancy, I could still do flips and handstands against the wall, much to Mama's dismay. But by my due date, I had gained forty pounds and looked like a fair-skinned, red-cheeked, stout *Kupchikha* (merchant's wife) from the painting by the Russian artist Boris Kustodiev.

I was ten days overdue when my contractions finally started, and I felt like an overblown balloon about to burst at any moment. Mama said we should go to the hospital.

After my registration at the maternity ward, the staff took me, alone, to a cold room, stripped me naked, and subjected me to the humiliation of shaving my pubic hair and cleansing my bowels with an enema. After that, a *nyanechka*[18] helped me into a hospital

[18] The lowest medical position in Soviet hospitals, something between a nurse's assistant and a cleaning lady.

gown and worn slippers and told me to follow her. On our way back down the hall, she squeezed the clothes I'd been wearing through a tiny window in the entrance door, where Mama was still standing. The maternity ward was a sterile environment, and no outside visitors or personal belongings were allowed. Russian women were isolated from everything comforting throughout their labors and deliveries.

Mama waved to me and whispered, "*S Bogom* (God be with you)." Her brown eyes were full of worry.

I followed the *nyanechka* up the stairs to a prenatal ward, where she pointed at an empty bed and walked away. Although it was late at night, the lights were on and several women were sitting, lying, or walking around the room—some silently, others moaning or whimpering. From time to time, I heard screams coming from the room behind the wall, which I assumed was where deliveries happened.

I waited until a doctor came in. She asked about the timing of my contractions. When she asked if my water had already broken, I said yes, because I had seen some spotting on my underwear when I changed into the hospital gown. She told me to lie down on my back and spread my knees. In a minute, she said, "You're not ready yet. Go to bed and try to sleep. You'll need lots of strength tomorrow."

The pain in my lower back and the clamor of women in labor kept me awake most of the night. By early morning, I noticed that most of the women around me were new.

I was sitting on my bed, bored and nervous at the same time, when I heard Sashka's familiar whistle coming from outside. I got up and waddled toward the window, but when I was in the middle of the room, something that felt like a big balloon of water broke inside of me. Warm fluid flooded my legs and spread across the floor.

"Nurse!" shouted one of the older women. "The girl's water broke."

Instead of the nurse, a *nyanechka* stormed into the room, holding a bucket and a mop. She looked furious.

"Who did this?" she yelled, pointing at the puddle on the floor. "You?" She glared at me as I stood in the middle of the room in my wet slippers, feeling terribly guilty, although I didn't know why.

She spat out insults in time to the swings of her mop on the floor. I started crying.

"Shame on you," one of the patients interrupted. "Aren't you a woman yourself? It's not the girl's fault. She didn't do it on purpose. Her water broke!"

"You're all the same. You fuck your stallions, and then come here and scream as if it's somebody else's fault. It serves you right, bitches!"

She stormed out of the room before anyone could respond. When the doctor arrived for the morning rounds, the older women complained.

"I'm unable to do anything with her," the doctor said. "Nobody wants to work here—it's a dirty and miserably paid job."

By the time they took me to the delivery room, I was physically and emotionally exhausted. I wasn't sure how much more I could take. But the midwife who helped me was a kind, middle-aged woman who told me she knew my mother. Not only that, she said she delivered me twenty years ago when my mother was almost as young as me. I wondered if Mama had asked her to assist me in my delivery. By then, I knew that most good things didn't just happen without help.

A woman on a table next to me screamed and cursed her husband. "I'll never let that asshole approach me closer than one meter."

"You all say it while you're here, but then a year or two later you come back again," her midwife replied.

At a quarter to seven in the evening I gave birth to my son. Dmitriy (Dimka or Dima) was born on April 21, right between the birthdays of the two most notoriously famous political leaders of our century, Hitler and Lenin.

I didn't get to touch my baby, or even see him, before they took him away. After what seemed like an eternity of waiting, the doctor came and stitched me up, and the nurses wheeled me to a new room.

The next morning, I woke up in the postnatal ward when a nurse called my name. "Kondeykina, take your medications."

I tried to sit up, but she stopped me. "You have to stay in bed until the sutures are removed."

There were eight or ten other women in the ward, all getting ready for the morning breastfeeding. When the nurses began to wheel in large carts full of newborns, I was as nervous as a young girl before her first date. *What does my son look like? What is his eye color? Does he have hair? Will I recognize him?*

The nurse read tags hanging on the babies' hands and handed them, one by one, to their mothers. Wrapped in white blankets and matching caps, they all looked identical to me. But new mothers reached their hands toward their child even before the name was called.

When the nurse handed out the last baby in the cart, my arms were still empty.

"Where is *my* baby?" I asked.

"Yours has a fever. We're not bringing him for breastfeeding today," the nurse said, and left without further explanation.

Every three hours, when the babies were brought in, I hoped to see my son among them. I worried myself sick as the day passed and nobody told me more than I already knew. While the other new mothers held and fed their children, I lay in bed with my face turned to the wall and cried.

Between the feedings, women trudged around in blood-stained hospital gowns and soiled hospital slippers, holding in place folded layers of cloth napkins between their legs with their hands. The only available warm water came from a silent, middle-aged Turkmen patient who somehow managed to sneak her water-heating coil into the ward. All day she sat cross-legged on her bed and drank green tea she heated in a glass jar sitting on her night stand. Every time she boiled water, she let one of the women pour a little into a bottle. They mixed it with cold water from a sink in our room and shuffled down a long corridor to the only bathroom, where they could wash themselves over the toilet bowl.

As the only bed-ridden woman, I had the "privilege" of being washed by the *nyanechka*. Once a day, she came with a large syringe full of a pink solution and ordered me to uncover myself and bend my knees. She doused me with the liquid and washed me with a piece of cloth connected to the end of a stick. It was beyond embarrassing, but I abided in silence.

The maternity ward reminded me of a prison: locked wards, no visitors, no flowers or outside food. Our only contact with our husbands or families was through scribbled notes delivered if we could "coax" a staff person to deliver it. A *treoshka* (a three-ruble bill) quietly stuffed into the pocket of a nurse or *nyanechka* could make difference, as could a gift to them of a chocolate bar or flowers.

I knew Mama and Sashka handed *treoshka*s around, because twice a day I got their short notes. I wrote back saying that I was fine, which wasn't true. I stayed sick in bed, worried to death about my baby and missing my home.

On the sixth day, they finally brought me my son.

"Choose which one is yours," the nurse said, as she showed me the cart full of babies.

"That one." I pointed. Even if she had showed me a hundred babies, I would have picked mine without a slightest doubt—big-nosed, big-eyed, with whimsically curved lips, he was his father's carbon copy. And he was lazy like his father, too. He lay next to my breast but didn't want to suck on it. I didn't have any idea how to make him eat. When the nurse came to take the babies back to the nursery, I told her about it.

"He'll figure it out when he gets hungry," she said and took him away from me.

The next morning, I woke up with a fever. The nurse said I probably had a cold. By the evening, I had bad chills. My swollen breasts were covered with purple knots and hard as rocks.

I wrote Mama a note: *If you don't take me home, I'll die here.*

Half an hour later, the head of the department walked into our ward. She told me to open my gown and examined my breasts. Then she called the charge nurse and started to yell.

"You've ruined the girl!" she shouted. "Look at her breasts! She has been here for five days, her baby is artificially fed, and no one told her that she had to express her milk! I'll fire you for dereliction of duty!"

They moved away from my bed, with the department head still berating the nurse. Not long after, the nurse came to my bed holding a basin of hot water and towels. She soaked the towels and applied them to my breasts, which I later understood was to make my milk ducts relax and dilate. But when she started massaging my breasts and squeezing my nipples to drain milk, I thought the torture would never end.

When Sashka came that evening, I wrote him a note: *I'm not staying here another day. Come tomorrow morning and take me and the baby home.*

Despite my doctor's objections, the next morning I got out of bed and announced that I was leaving the hospital with my son.

"I've never had such an irresponsible mother," she told me. "I cannot discharge you before your baby's umbilical cord stump falls off. You're subjecting your son to infection."

When neither persuasion nor threats helped, she made me sign a paper that stated I was leaving the hospital without the doctor's permission and under my own responsibility. I signed it with a flourish, picked up my child, and walked out of the hospital, vowing to never come back.

45: The Detective's Wife

Contrary to the doctor's opinion, both Dimka and I recovered well at home. At the end of May, Sashka and I went to the ZAGS to get our son's birth certificate and officially marry.

The office looked like time had frozen in the year since we were last here—it was the same desk, the same woman with a sullen face, and the same black telephone and registration book in front of her. It made me realize how much we'd changed in the last year. I was a mother now. Sashka had been working as a detective for several months, and he had settled into the routine and gained confidence.

The ZAGS woman recognized us. A semblance of a smile, like a shadow, drifted in and faded away from her face, but all she said was, "Where are your witnesses?"

Sashka and I looked at each other. It hadn't occurred to us to bring witnesses this time. We thought the legal marriage was just a formality to get our son's birth certificate.

"They were here last year. We thought one time was enough," I attempted a joke. She gave me a sour look.

"I cannot issue a marriage certificate without witnesses," she said, shutting the register as if putting a period to end our visit.

"Can you wait? I can get witnesses," Sashka said.

"No, I cannot. I have another wedding scheduled in half an hour."

“They’ll be here in five minutes,” Sashka promised. “Can I use your phone?” Without waiting for her permission, he picked up the receiver.

I wondered which of our friends could come on such a short notice.

“Anatoliy? Shebeko speaking,” Sashka said into the receiver. “I need a militia patrol now at the ZAGS on Svoboda Street . . . You come, too. I’ll tell you what it’s all about when you’re here.”

Five minutes later, I heard the howling of sirens and the screeching of brakes. The door of the ZAGS office swung open, and a whole group of uniformed men barged into the room. I recognized Anatoliy Lysenko, Sashka’s partner.

When they learned why they were there, two of Sashka’s coworkers laughed and agreed to witness our marriage.

“First you didn’t have any witnesses, and now you have too many of them,” the woman said, looking amused.

As she opened her register book, the phone on her desk rang. “Alo? No, everything is fine. No, no, no,” she said. “Nothing happened. A militiaman is getting married, that’s all.” She hung up and we continued with the procedure.

When she asked what last name I wanted to take, I answered, “My husband’s, Shebeko.” A few minutes later my son became Dmitriy Alexandrovich Shebeko.

Soon after our official marriage, Sashka came home with a gun. It was a Makarov semi-automatic pistol—a heavy, hawkish-looking thing. He loved it and showed it off every chance he got.

Officially, Sashka was supposed to turn in his weapon every night at the militia office, but in reality, the gun became a frequent guest in our house. I knew that if Sashka came home after midnight, wearing his shirt over his pants, it meant he hadn’t stopped at the office to drop off the gun. Sometimes, I smelled alcohol on his breath. The combination of the two terrified me.

The first night, he put the gun under his pillow.

"Are you going to sleep with it?" I asked.

"Yes. What's the use of having a gun if it's not near at hand? If something happens, I'll just have to release the safety and shoot."

"What could happen? Is someone after you?" It occurred to me that with his job, he could get into real trouble with criminals. I glanced at our son, sleeping in the corner of our room.

"Who knows what could happen," he said. "I have to be ready to protect you and my son."

I tossed and turned all night, worrying that in his sleep Sashka could accidentally put his hand on the gun and it would go off.

It didn't go off that night, but it wasn't long before Sashka's gun fired in our house.

Early one morning, I wheeled Dimka's sleep stroller to the warm kitchen, where Mama was already fussing with the dishes. We left Sashka sitting on the bed in his underwear, examining his gun.

"Hurry up. It's getting late," I said, closing the door behind me.

I was pouring water in the kettle and talking with Mama when I heard a loud bang. Dimka screamed in his stroller, and Mama scooped him up. I dropped the kettle and rushed to my room. My husband stood next to our bed, looking baffled but unhurt. There was a smell of gun powder in the air.

"*Chert poderi* (Dammit)! I removed the magazine and forgot that the bullet was in the chamber," he said.

He put his gun aside and examined the bookshelves on the wall across from our bed. There was a huge hole in the plaster, exposing the bricks behind it.

A shiver pierced my body. Just a few minutes before, I had stood in front of those very volumes of Alexander Pushkin's poems while I got dressed. Now the top of one book bristled like a scared cat.

After that, Mama refused to let me keep Dimka in our room overnight. "You're both out of your minds!" she said. "I won't let you have the baby while that gun is in the house."

Sashka and I were evicted to the tiny hut that Papa had built for Aunt Nastya. She'd moved into an apartment a few years before. We continued to eat and spend much of our time in my parents' house, and Dimka stayed with them all the time. Every night, Mama wheeled our son's sleep stroller into her and Papa's bedroom.

46: The Gold Rings

Before long, Sashka's youthful eagerness predictably gave way to overconfidence. His work in the militia opened many doors for him. He could walk into a store and ask for deficit merchandise, and the sales manager would get it for him even if they were not yet permitted to distribute it to the general public. Restaurant hostesses met us like old friends and ushered us to the best tables, and waitresses were all smiles and courtesy. We both knew the special treatment came mostly from people who had something to hide, and Sashka seemed to enjoy it.

Once, he showed up at my school in a cab and waited in the car while one of the students went to my classroom to tell me. I ran downstairs, thinking that there was an emergency with our son. Dimka was often sick at that time.

Instead, Sashka had come to show me a maroon patent leather pump with a fluffy adornment at the front that he had borrowed from the department store.

"Try it on. I've promised the saleswoman I'll bring it back in half an hour." He squatted next to me and helped me pull off my boot and slip the shoe on my foot. It fit as if I was born in it.

"What a beauty!" I said, admiring my foot.

"They haven't even started selling them, but the line has already stretched from the shoe department down the first floor and out into the street. I thought the crowd would kill me when I squeezed myself to the counter to talk to the saleswoman," he said, laughing.

"I cannot believe she let you carry it outside."

"We have a score to settle with her. She'll do whatever I ask if she wants to work there. So, do you want them?"

"How much are they?" I asked.

"Don't worry. I'll find money."

Later, a coworker who had watched the whole scene from a window told me, "You're such a lucky woman. He treats you like a queen."

And she was right. In public, Sashka was courteous. He brought me flowers, opened the door for me, and offered his hand when I exited a bus. Most of all, he liked to give presents, and he always did it with pomp. In fact, I wasn't sure what he loved more—to see me happy or to impress everyone with his generosity.

For my birthday, he gave me a gold ring with an alexandrite gemstone. "Alexandrite from Alexander," he said with a grin, putting it on my finger. "The salesman said that alexandrite is a special stone. It changes its color, depending on the daylight. Watch it and you'll see."

I was thrilled. The only gold ring I owned was a modest wedding band on my right hand. And he was right; the bluish-green stone he put on my finger in the morning turned to violet by afternoon, and dark purple with a red tint when the daylight faded.

"Look at it now!" I ran from Sashka to Mama, showing them my finger. He beamed with pride.

That evening, when our family sat down at the dinner table, Papa reached into his pocket and produced a small box. "Here's to you from Mama and me," he said. "Happy birthday!"

I opened the box and found another gold ring, this one in the shape of a flower, with a sparkling ruby in the middle.

"Oh, thank you! It's so gorgeous! I love it!" I kissed him and Mama and put my ring on my middle finger, next to Sashka's.

During dinner, I purposely held my hand on the table for everyone to see.

Sashka ate silently. When we went back to our room after dinner, he asked me to take off my alexandrite ring and give it to him.

"Why?" I asked laughing. "It's my ring now."

"I want to look at it closer," he said.

I took off my ring and handed it to him. He lifted it to his eyes and his lips curled into a sneer as he pressed it between his thumb and index finger so hard that the stone popped out and the ring lost its shape.

"No!" I shouted. "What have you done?"

"Not a big loss for you. You liked your father's present more than mine," he said.

I couldn't stop crying, and eventually Sashka promised to take the ring to the jeweler to fix. When he brought it back, the small gold prongs holding the gemstone were no longer even.

Occasionally, Sashka came home for lunch with one or another of his coworkers in tow. They all were young, friendly men in their twenties, and when they were around, Sashka was a generous host and a loving husband and father. He would show off our son's latest achievement to his guests, and they all laughed as our fat toddler stomped around the veranda.

When everyone else went home, though, his cordial mood was replaced by suspicion and jealousy.

"Why did you smile at him?" he questioned me.

"I tried to be nice to your friend."

"You were flirting with him."

"Oh, don't be a fool, Sasha. I wasn't flirting with anybody. He was our guest. Would it be better if I were surly with him? If you don't like the way I behave, then don't bring him or anybody else to our house."

"Now you're reproaching me for bringing my friends here," he screamed.

"I'm not reproaching you. I just don't like that you distrust me. And I don't like you yelling at me, either."

"Of course, I always have to do what *you* like. What if *I* don't like something?"

"You just told me what you don't like, remember? That's how this argument started."

He went on and on, clinging to my every word and going in circles until I lost the thread of our conversation and my temper. No matter what we argued about, he made it my fault. When I'd try to rehash our argument and figure out how it all started, I couldn't reconstruct our conversation.

One of Sashka's co-workers—a copper-faced Armenian named Akop—started to come to our house more often than the others. Akop was my husband's detail supervisor, and so I always tried to be courteous and respectful without revealing my dislike for him. More than once, I caught his eyes roaming over my breasts and figure while I carried dishes or chased our toddler around. His slimy smile made me blush.

Oddly, Sashka didn't seem to notice anything and kept bringing his boss with him.

One day, he told me that Tamara had invited us and Akop to her house for supper. I went reluctantly, but to my surprise, the evening went well. I relaxed and enjoyed myself. Tamara flirted with Akop, who told us lots of Armenian Radio jokes. These had recently become very popular.

"This is Armenian Radio. Our listener asked us, 'What is an exchange of opinions?' Our answer is: When you walk into your boss's office with your opinion and walk out with his."

"Exactly!" Sashka laughed. "That's what happens to me all the time when I walk out of your room."

The more we drank, the bolder his jokes became. "This is Armenian Radio. Our listener asked us, 'What is the most permanent feature of our Socialist economy?' Our answer is: Temporary shortages."

"This is Armenian Radio. Our listener asked us, 'What if socialism was built in Greenland?' Our answer is: First snow would become available only through ration cards, and later it would be distributed only to the KGB officers and their families."

After we finished the meal and our drinks, Tamara went to the kitchen to bring out a dessert. Sashka, Akop, and I sat at the table, talking.

Suddenly the lights in the house went off.

"Sashka, it's probably the plug again. Come down and check it," Tamara yelled from the kitchen.

"Dammit," Sashka swore. "I'll go and see what happened."

I heard him push his chair away from the table and walk toward the hallway. Akop and I stayed in the dark room. For a few minutes, there was an awkward silence. I was not surprised when I felt his heavy, hot paw on top of my knee. Disgusted, I jumped up and bumped into a corner of the table just as the lights came back on. Squinting in the sudden brightness, I saw Sashka standing in the doorway.

"*Oi-oi-oi*," I moaned, rubbing my thigh. "I wanted to go and see if I can help you and ran into the corner of the table." I wanted to yell and slap that stupid, smiling bastard who sat as if nothing had happened, but he was my husband's boss. I knew Sashka would beat the hell out of him if he knew what happened, and then he'd lose his job.

Sashka approached the table, opened another bottle of vodka, and poured it to Akop and then to himself. "To our faithful wives," he said with a smirk.

After the party ended, my husband didn't say anything to me, but Akop's visits to our house stopped.

Later, Tamara told me that the blackout had been staged. At Sashka's signal, she left the room to bring the dessert. After rattling the cookware in the kitchen, she went to the hall and unscrewed an electrical-meter plug, plunging the house into darkness. Then she waited for a few minutes and screwed the plug back into place. The whole time, Sashka stood in the doorway, ready to take his guest and me by surprise.

"He loves you and rages because he is jealous," Tamara said. "Show him that you're jealous, too. Men love it."

"I'm not jealous," I told her.

"Can't you fake it?" She rolled her eyes. "You have to be cunning with men. Never tell your husband all the truth about yourself. The less he knows, the better for him."

The truth was I didn't need to fake it. I saw how women clung to him at parties, how they looked at him with their beckoning and promising eyes, how they followed him outside to have a smoke. Yes, I was jealous, but I'd rather die than show it to him or anyone else.

More and more, I could see the truth about my husband—Sashka was obsessive, selfish, and brooked no argument. He never accepted critique, never admitted a single mistake, and never considered anybody's opinion that contradicted his own.

I wasn't an angel, either. Stubborn and uncompromising, I was always ready to prove my own case. I was too proud or too strong-willed to show him that my guts sank with fear when he entered our hut filled with alcohol, anger, and jealousy.

We both were competitive and, for me, revealing my weakness meant losing.

It didn't help that our intimate life never improved. During the day I was my own strong and boisterous self, but when night fell I became jittery. I tried to delay going to bed, finding things to do and hoping my husband would fall asleep without me. Then I'd sneak into bed and lie silently, trying not to wake him up. Sometimes he touched or embraced me in his sleep, and my heart skipped a beat. I longed for his body, and I was repulsed by it. I wanted it, but whenever he tried to initiate sex, I suddenly felt a bolt of panic. Losing the perception of time and reality, I cried and fought him off again and again.

Sashka and I never spoke about the afternoon he raped me, nor did I share my darkest secret with Mama or anybody else.

47: A Step Forward

I continued to debate politics with Papa, although my earlier idealistic ideas about how the system worked had changed. I acknowledged the existence of corruption in our country, but unlike Papa, who blamed communists for getting bogged down in deceit, I insisted that the Party and the socialist system were not at fault. In my opinion, the Soviet machine skidded and threw dirt from under its wheels because a few immoral and greedy individuals had penetrated the profitable, cushy jobs, and then used their position to rob our country.

"The crooks occupied every place where they could find a tasty morsel and became parasites who fatten themselves at the expense of our society. We need honest and high-principled citizens to clean our country of that trash," I fumed.

"Nonsense," Papa objected. "A fish rots from the head. Nothing will ever change while the Communists are in power."

"If you and I sit here and argue, nothing will change. But if we fight the crooks, we'll eventually win."

"So, why are you sitting here then? Go and fight them!" Papa retorted with a sneer. He reached into his jacket pocket, pulled out a pack of *papirosas*, tapped one out, and put it into his mouth. I understood that our dialogue was over and retreated.

He is right, I thought. What's the use of arguing, if I myself haven't moved a finger to change anything? But what could I do without having any authority?

After much thought, I decided to study law at the Turkmen State University.

There were different ways of achieving something in the USSR, I reasoned. One was doing it on your own—relying on your own brain and abilities. The other two were *blat* and *vzyatka*.

Blat meant using the help of acquaintances, relatives, or friends who had connections. You could get a good job, acquire a voucher to a health resort, obtain a pass to a famous musician's concert, or just buy a good book *po blatu* (through connections).

Vzyatka (a bribe) could be given in the form of money or a gift. The price was set by the bribe-taker and depended on what you were hoping to get in exchange—a new apartment, a good job, a driving license, or maybe an out-of-turn telephone in your home.

I decided that I would enter the University on my own.

At the time, one of my private students lived with his grandmother, who was a teacher at the Turkmen State University. After one of our lessons, I told her about my desire to go to the university and asked her advice on how I should proceed. It was already May, and the university would soon start accepting applications.

"What program are you going to apply to?" she asked.

"Law school," I answered.

"Oh, it's almost impossible to get in there. Last year it was so overcrowded with applicants, that even a Gold Medal[19] graduate

[19] A secondary school student with excellent grades in both their school subjects and their final examinations was awarded the Certificate of Secondary Education (also called a Maturity Certificate) with a gold

was turned down. Have you considered the Russian philology or the foreign languages programs? They are easier to enter, especially the first one."

"No, I want to study law," I said firmly.

She shrugged. "I'll try to find out this year's admission requirements and let you know the next time you come."

A week later, she told me that the law school accepted applications only from those with Turkmen ethnicity. "Even if you were a Turkmen, you won't be able to get in," she told me. "I have a friend there, and he told me in confidence that bribes and solicitations from high-ranking people have been collected, and the dean already has the final list of new students."

"Without entrance exams? How could that be?" I asked.

"They'll still have to take the entrance exams, but it's a joke." She studied me. "Why do you want the Law School, anyway?"

"I hoped to find a job in law enforcement."

"Take my advice," she said. "Apply to the foreign language program. It's becoming more popular, and one of last year's graduates found a job at the KGB. He is very happy."

I had never considered studying foreign language. Where would I use it, I thought, except teaching at school? The only foreigners I ever saw were the rare groups of East German tourists. I'd rather teach one student at a time to play piano than a class of blockheads to speak a language they would never have the opportunity to use.

But the university professor's suggestion made me reconsider.

"I don't know any languages," I said. "In middle school, I studied English, then I took a year of German in the musical college, and in evening school we didn't have foreign language."

"Don't worry. If you get in, you'll start with the alphabet, anyway."

---

medal. The medal significantly improved the student's chance to be admitted to a higher educational institution.

"But how will I pass my entrance exam?" I asked.

The woman smiled. "I can help you. Choose which language you'd like to study, either English or German, and start your application process. Memorize one or two of the required conversational topics that they give you to study for the exam. You'll have to say at least something."

Was she offering to use her influence? "If you help me get into the university, I'll teach your grandson for free," I offered cautiously.

"Good," she agreed without even blinking.

I left that conversation feeling bizarre. The purpose of going to the university was to get a job where I could fight corruption, and now I was using *blat* and *vzyatka* to get into the university. *It's the only way I can achieve my goal,* I tried to convince myself.

I decided to apply to the English program. A week before the entrance exams, I went to a review of English grammar. The meeting room was full of young people, seventeen- and eighteen-year-old quick-eyed kids who had recently changed their school uniforms for minidresses and short-sleeved shirts. What was I doing among all these teenagers, I wondered. When the instructor began the "review," he may as well have been discussing Chinese grammar, instead of English. Past perfect, future in the past, and passive voice verbs all sounded absolutely alien to me.

But still, on the first of August I went to the third floor of the university and waited in the corridor for my turn to take my exam in English. I arrived at eight o'clock in the morning and waited until almost noon while all of the other applicants filed in and out—some left happy and smiling, while others averted their eyes, dejected. I clasped my examination slip in my sweaty hands and contemplated ways to retreat.

"Ludmila Shebeko," a woman at the door called.

I exhaled and entered a wide, sunlit room. At the front, the examiner listened to an applicant babbling something in English. Two or three students sat at desks, preparing for their exams. They each had been randomly assigned a topic after they entered the room, and they had thirty minutes to prepare themselves for their conversation with the examiner. Of the twenty possible conversation topics, I knew only enough basic English to tackle two—"My Family" and "My Biography."

The assistant showed me to a desk that was covered with small white pieces of paper.

"Take a ticket and tell me its number," she said.

I scanned the desk and wished myself good luck. I pulled a ticket and read, "Number Seven."

She recorded the number in her register, then rummaged through her papers and handed me my assignment sheet and a thin book. It was a condensed version of *The Adventures of Huckleberry Finn* by Mark Twain. She showed me an extract of the text that was marked with a pencil.

"You have to read it, understand it, and be ready to answer the examiner's questions. Your second task is written on your ticket. Take a seat and start preparing for the exam," she said.

I chose a desk at the end of the room and sat down. I had read *The Adventures of Huckleberry Finn* in Russian when I was in the sixth grade. Scanning the English text, I recognized some of the English words, but I couldn't understand a single sentence. Nor would I be able to "speak on the topic of Great Britain," which was the second task outlined on my ticket.

I was about to get up and leave when the examiner called my name. I got up, gathered my papers, and made my way slowly to the examiner's desk. I was the only student left in the room.

"What's your name?" the examiner asked me in English, when I came up to her table.

"Ludmila Shebeko," I answered feeling a tiny bit of satisfaction. *I got this one!*

"Take your seat," she said. I didn't understand and continued standing in front of her.

"Sit down," she repeated slowly. I lowered myself onto the chair in front of her.

She was a young woman, probably in her early thirties, with a round face and soft eyes that looked at me with encouragement.

"What do you want to start with?" she asked. I shrugged. My hands were trembling, and I wasn't sure I could say a single word in Russian, let alone English.

"Let's start with the last task. Which topic do you have?" she asked in Russian.

"Great Britain," I said hopelessly.

"If you don't know it, start with whatever you've learned. Just don't sit silently." I saw she was trying to help me, but instead of relief, I felt ashamed. *She thinks I'm dumb.*

"My name is Ludmila," I started in my best English dialect. "I em tventy-von years old. I have a family: a mozer, a fazer, a brozer, and a little son. My son's name is Dima. He is a toddler. My brozer's name is Andrey. He is fifteen years old. He is a schoolboy." She listened to me, nodding. "My mozer's name is Valentina. She is forty-two years old. She is a housevife. My fazer's name is Ivan. He is forty-seven years old. He is . . . " I continued to describe my uncles, aunts, and cousins. Perhaps I could continue like this until she let me go. But eventually, I ran out of people. "I love my family," I finished.

"Good," she said, and then switched to Russian again. "Let's go to your reading task. Did you understand the text?"

"Not really. But I know it's about Huck Finn when he travels down the river with Jim," I said, thinking about the picture I had seen on the previous page.

She asked me to read several sentences from the English text. Stumbling on every word, I did. Then she asked me which school I graduated from. I waited while she wrote something in her papers. Then she took my exam slip, filled out the first line, signed it, and handed it back to me.

I waited until I closed the door of the exam room to look at the slip. In the English Language column was the grade 4 with *Khorosho* (Good) next to it.

So that's how it works, I thought, feeling baffled and relieved that it was over.

I passed two other, much easier entrance exams—History of the USSR and Russian Literature—and became a student of the Turkmen State University.

48: Repeating Mama's Fate

Many nights, Sashka and I sat head to head in the darkness of our bedroom, listening to his new shortwave transistor radio. He would turn the knob, trying to catch the Western radio stations that broadcast into the Soviet Union in Russian: *Radio Svoboda* (Radio Liberty), *Golos Ameriki* (Voice of America), or the BBC. We called them "enemy voices." Through the hiss and squeal of government jammers, they talked about events in our country and abroad, criticized our Soviet system and government, and praised the Western way of life. We knew it was a slander and didn't bother to listen. We were there for the music.

When the news eventually stopped, we could hear Beatles songs, jazz, or rock. Sashka and I both reveled in the sounds of the hostile but compelling world, where people could freely create and listen to whatever they wanted. "The decaying capitalism rots,'" Sashka would say, "but it smells so good."

At the end of August 1968, we heard a snippet of news that attracted our attention. Sashka stopped twisting the knob and we leaned closer towards the ribbed-plastic surface of our *Spidola* transistor radio. The announcer said that the Soviet Union and its Warsaw Pact allies—East Germany, Bulgaria, Hungary, and Poland—had invaded Czechoslovakia. Soviet tanks were rolling through the streets of Prague.

The "enemy voices," of course, had the story completely inverted. What they called a Soviet invasion was in reality our fraternal assistance to the working people of a friendly country. Ordinary Czechs and Slovaks were grateful to the Soviet government for our help. They greeted our soldiers with flowers and smiles. This was simply anti-Soviet propaganda, another attempt of our enemies to tarnish our country.

What would you do, we asked each other, if a house was on fire and people were trapped inside? Would you ask their permission to break into the house? No, you'd rush inside and save them. The same situation was in Czechoslovakia; our friends were in danger, and our duty was to interfere and help them. The logic seemed faultless.

Out of all our friends, Sashka and I were the only couple who lived "separately" from our parents. When we held a party, our tiny hut could hardly hold all our guests. They danced in one room, drank in the other, and smoked and talked on the porch.

Sashka was the heart of the gathering. He drank, played his guitar, and sang. The more alcohol he consumed, the rowdier he became, and the more nervous I grew. Over and over again, I caught myself thinking that I was repeating Mama's fate. Exactly like her, I tried to stop him, stepping on his foot under the table, whispering in his ear, and hiding alcohol or pouring the remains out after the party. My guts tightened when our guests left. Without my parents being under the same roof, I had to deter Sashka's drunken rages on my own.

If I had once been proud that I was the only one who could subdue him, now I understood that I had been playing with fire, and one day it would destroy me.

Years earlier, when I accused Papa of alcoholism, he told me, "I'll see who *you* marry. You might find one who doesn't only drink but beats on you."

"I'd rather be alone all my life than live with a drunkard like you," I had retorted.

Now, I acknowledged, Papa could have been right. Sashka didn't dare lift his hand to me, but once, during one of his drunken outbursts, he pulled his gun on me. I had told him that if he didn't stop drinking, I would divorce him. His "answer" stared at me with its dark round eye.

The next morning, I told Sashka that his behavior had been so unruly that I had thought about calling the militia. It was not true, but I wanted to scare him into thinking that he could lose his job.

Reporting a husband to the militia was the last thing I wanted to do. Most of the time, the militia refused to deal with domestic violence calls. But even if they came, they would scold the abusive husband like a kindergarten teacher would scold a mischievous student and then leave the embattled wife on her own with her abuser. Complaining to friends or neighbors had a similar outcome. We had a saying about this: *Ne vynosi sor iz izby* (Don't take out the trash from your house in public).

Once, he showed up late at night covered in blood. His shirt, pants, and even his socks were soaked with it. His clotted hair covered an ugly gash. He smelled of alcohol. I helped him undress and cleaned his wound. Wincing with pain, he told me that he had attempted to detain a man on the militia's wanted list, but the man's friends stood up for him. One of them hit Sashka on the head with a guitar and knocked him down.

"Where was your gun when you needed it?" I asked. "They could have killed you."

"It would have been better for them if they did. Now I'll get all of them, and they'll cry bloody tears," he promised.

A month later, he recognized one of the guys on the street. Either the poor bastard resisted arrest, as my husband claimed, or Sashka took revenge. He shot the man. A bullet went through his victim's lung and almost killed him. The militia launched an investigation.

For weeks, my husband looked darker than a thunder cloud. The official ruling was that he had not only exceeded his authority but also had mistaken the guy and shot the wrong man. The incident was hushed up, and Sashka regained his usual aplomb. The incident only served to reinforce his belief in his own impunity.

Power made him believe that he was immune to the law he had been charged to protect. He used his position to settle his own scores with people. He subpoenaed a guy who he thought was hitting on me. The innocent man complained to me later that my husband had threatened to lock him up if he ever saw us together. Another time, Sashka beat on Tolik, who had been my friend since we were toddlers.

His endless jealousy and drunken antics went on and on. I grew weary.

49: Escape

Sashka was angry that I entered the university without his consent. He brushed aside my arguments in favor of education and a better future as a pretense. He accused me of shopping for another man. Trying not to escalate our disagreements further with money problems, I kept my teaching job at the musical school.

After six hours of sitting in university auditoriums and classrooms, I hurried to the musical school to teach my students. When I finally got home, Dimka was too sleepy to play with me, and I had to put him to bed. He was growing, and I was missing too many of the cute things he did and new words he learned.

At night, when everyone else was asleep, I pulled out my *Bonk's English Language* textbook and turned on a table lamp, hoping not to wake Sashka. I finally sneaked into bed at two in the morning, with English words and phrases swarming and buzzing in my head like a disturbed beehive. It seemed as if I had just closed my eyes when the alarm clock on my desk unceremoniously declared that it was time to start a new day. I felt like a machine programmed for incessant operation.

But no matter how hard it was, I never considered quitting the university. I would finish what I started at any price, so that no one—especially myself—could call me a weakling or a coward. My husband's objections only made me more determined to go on.

At twenty-one, I was the oldest student and the only parent among more than 60 freshmen. Knowing why the university admitted me and how far behind I was when I started, I was always afraid of embarrassing myself in front of my teachers and classmates. But at the end of the first term, I passed my midterm exams with excellent grades and was given an enhanced stipend of thirty-five rubles a month. It was seven rubles higher than any other first-year students got. For the first time in my life, I felt satisfied.

Even with my teacher's salary and enhanced stipend, we depended on my parents' financial help. And of course, I couldn't have done any of it without Mama's parental support. She was a real mother for my son, who she adored and spoiled like she had never spoiled me or my brother. Not a word of reproach or complaint ever came from her mouth towards me.

Still, in the evenings after everybody was fed and Papa's and Andrusha's clothes hung washed, ironed, and ready for the morrow, and when the dough for the next day's *pirozhki* had been put under a blanket and Dimka had stopped tossing in his bed, Mama sat silently on her veranda, listening to the radio or just thinking about something of her own. Looking at her sunken eyes and overworked calloused hands resting on her lap, I saw how exhausted she was.

How much I regret that we were so restrained in expressing our feelings for each other back then. How I wish to turn the time back and tell her how much I love her, how infinitely I appreciate her devotion and sacrifice, and how sorry I am for being so selfish.

In spring, Mama took Dimka with her to the Kopet Dag Mountains with the apiary. Like my brother and I before him, now my son would spend his summers in the mountains, plains, and deserts of Turkmenistan.

I didn't have any reservations about letting him go, but once they were gone, I realized I didn't have anybody to go home to. I was tired of Sashka's constant showdowns and nitpicking. After work, my legs didn't want to carry me to a bus stop. I loitered around town and lingered in front of store windows. I killed time until the stores closed their doors and the lights in their windows went off.

At the end of June, I finished the first year of my studies at the university with honors. The musical school also let its teachers go for the vacation. Instead of being happy to have all the time to myself, I paced inside our four walls, like a hunted animal that had gotten herself into a trap. I was pregnant. The idea of having another child was out of the question.

While I was a student at the musical college, I had been terrified to pass the state-run abortion clinic on my way to school. It was a long, one-story structure, and when the windows were open, I could hear the clanking of metal instruments, moans of women, and an occasional scream. Now I had been there three times in two years.

The first time was when Dimka was seven months old; as soon as I stopped nursing him, I got pregnant. After that, no matter what I tried and how carefully I calculated "safe" days, every six months, as if on schedule, I ended up in the clinic. I never told Mama. Sashka knew about my pregnancies, but he dumped all the decisions on me.

My husband didn't display much attachment to our son. He showed interest in him only when there were people around. Dimka was a beautiful toddler with large gray eyes, blond hair, and a sweet face. He began walking at nine months and always attracted lots of smiles. Sashka looked proud when others were amused by our son, and when they told him that the boy was his own carbon copy. But he rarely held our toddler or played with him when we were alone. He was especially annoyed when Dimka was sick.

"What kind of a man will he be if he whimpers at the slightest pain?"

"He is a nice child. He never cries when he feels well." My maternal protectiveness rose. "Instead of complaining, take him in your arms and try to calm him down. He is your son."

"When he grows up, I'll teach him lots of things. Now he needs his mother," was his answer.

This time, I didn't tell Sashka about my pregnancy. I didn't want to be a wife anymore. I wanted an escape.

After my strength came back following the abortion, I took a trolleybus to the Aeroflot Ticket Agency. After five hours in line, I emerged with a ticket to Frunze, the capital of the Kyrgyz Soviet Socialist Republic. I hadn't planned to go there, but all of the tickets to the favorite destinations of the Soviet people—Moscow, Leningrad, the Black Sea, or the Caucasus resorts—were sold out. Amid the summer holidays, when everyone tried to escape the scorching heat of Ashkhabad, it was almost impossible to buy a ticket to any of those places on short notice.

I didn't know a single person in Kyrgyzstan, but it didn't matter. I couldn't be picky about my destination when I was running away from my husband. Only when I had the plane ticket in hand, did I realize that I was really going to leave my husband, not for a short time as before, but for always.

As if he suspected, Sashka came home early that night and brought me a present, a small, gold-plated bracelet watch. He took it out of his pocket and put it on my wrist.

"What's the occasion?" I asked.

"I just wanted to give a gift to my wife," he said. "Can't I do it just because I love you?"

I felt a pang of guilt. "Thank you," I mumbled, staring at the watch. It looked elegant, but I didn't want it. I had already distanced myself emotionally, and it seemed wrong to accept anything from him. I pretended to examine the watch and noticed fine scratches on its tiny oval face.

"Where did you get it?" I asked.

"I bought it. Do you like it?"

"Where did you buy it?" I insisted.

"Look, I'm giving you a present, and you're questioning me. What difference does it make where I've gotten this damn watch? I've stolen it! Does it sound better to you?"

"Not really."

"Then what do you want from me?" His eyes narrowed.

"I don't want anything from you, including this watch. This watch is not new. Somebody has been wearing it."

"Damn it! Why do you always have to spoil everything? I've confiscated it from a petty thief. It's nobody's watch. No one is looking for it. Are you pleased now?"

"At least I know the truth," I said, taking off the watch from my wrist and handing it to him. "It's stolen. I don't want it."

He snatched it, took a swing, and dashed it against the wall. Tiny shards of glass and springs sprinkled in all directions.

He pulled a cigarette from his pack and clicked the lighter, again and again. It didn't produce any flame. He cursed and stormed out the door.

I collapsed on our bed and burst into tears, feeling like a fly that had hit a spider web. I wanted to break out of that web and run without looking back.

The next morning, after Sashka left for work, I went to Mama's house and found our brown suitcase with metal clasps and corners. I kept my hands busy with ironing, folding, and packing my clothes while my head tried to compose the letter I would leave for my husband.

I wanted to vent all the resentment and frustration that had accumulated in my heart over the years. I wanted to tell him how much he had hurt me and how hard I had tried to forget everything; how I had believed when we married that he truly loved me and would be a good husband and a loving father; and how frustrated and disillusioned I had eventually become when I realized that wasn't true. I wanted to say so much, but when I sat down at the desk, I realized that whatever I said wouldn't be enough. I pictured Sashka's sarcastic smirk and his icy eyes reading my letter.

I took a pen and wrote, "I cannot live like this anymore. Don't try to find me. Mila."

When the plane took off and started gaining altitude, I took a deep breath. The anxiety of the last months disappeared as if someone had turned a switch inside me. Instead, I felt only weariness and emptiness. *I've done it. I've done it. I've done it.*

I pressed my back into the chair and closed my eyes. Sashka would never forgive me for my audacity. I didn't want to think about what would happen when I came back.

Unexpectedly, my trip turned out to be lovely. I stayed for a couple of days in a hotel in Frunze, and then went to Cholpon Ata, a small town at Lake Issyk-Kul. I was stunned by the untouched beauty of the alpine lake with its white sand beaches and crystal-clear water. Surrounded by the Ala-Too Mountains, it reminded me of a gem embedded into a beautiful setting.

But all the beauty could not stop me from worrying about what would happen when I came back home.

I flew back to Ashkhabad three weeks later, in time to prepare for my fall terms. Sashka was no longer in the hut in my parent's yard, and his things were gone. A friend told me that he had been kicked out of the militia for a drunken shooting rampage at the zoo area.

"After you left, he looked for you everywhere. He was always drunk and madder than hell," my friend told me. "Be careful."

A couple of weeks went by, and when Sashka didn't show up, I went to the courthouse and filed for divorce. The court required three months waiting time to allow for the "reconciliation of the spouses," but I knew that would not happen. As it turned out, though, my marriage was not over yet.

50: A Soldier's Wife

At the beginning of November, I bumped into our friend Boris. "Sashka received a subpoena from the military enlistment office," he told me. "He's being drafted into the army."

All able-bodied Soviet men over the age of eighteen were subject to a mandatory military draft and at least two years of service for their country. Sashka had avoided it until that point because of his militia job, but now that he was unemployed, the government caught up with him.

The timing was awful. Divorcing a husband who was in the army was a shameful act and in the eyes of my compatriots it was considered a betrayal. Everyone knew that it was the duty of a Soviet wife to support her husband during his service to the Motherland.

"The army alters people," people told me. "He will be a completely different person in two years." I didn't believe them.

Sashka was drafted to the Internal Troops of the MVD, ironically the same organization that had fired him several months earlier.

Trapped by the change of circumstances, I resigned myself to being a soldier's wife. At least, I reasoned, he would be sent somewhere far away, and I wouldn't have to see him.

The day before his departure, Sashka came to our house to say goodbye. It was the first and only time I saw him after I fled our marriage the summer before. We sat at the table and drank tea.

His head was already shaved, and he looked unusually subdued. He held Dimka on his lap and said he loved me. If I waited for his discharge, he promised, everything would be different. He swore that he would never hurt me again.

I was silent. The web that bound me to this man still held me fast, no matter what I did to escape.

On the conscription day, I played the role of the supportive wife and went to the train station with Sashka and his mother. The platform was full of bald draftees surrounded by parents, buddies, and girlfriends, and the three of us stood in a small circle while Tamara gave her last instructions to her son. He smoked absentmindedly, pretending to listen. The time passed slowly.

At last, the locomotive shrieked a long whistle, letting passengers know it was time to get into their cars. The crowd stirred. The new soldiers shouted their last farewells, kissed their families, and ran to their carriages. Sashka didn't move.

"Are you going to wait for me?" he asked me.

I felt a lump in my throat. He grabbed my shoulders.

"I'm not going anywhere if you don't answer my question." The train shrieked two more times and began slowly moving. Everyone was yelling—the departing men from the open windows of their carriages and the remaining families from the platform.

"Go," I said. "Your train is leaving."

"Are you going to wait for me?" He was shaking me. "Tell me." The train started gaining speed.

"Yes," I squeezed out. "Go."

"I'll write to you when we get to the destination." He kissed me, ran, and jumped on the footboard of a passing car.

"Don't cry, sweetie." An elderly woman touched my arm. "He'll be back in two years. The time flies so fast."

The next day, I went to the court and withdrew my divorce application.

A month after Sashka left, I received his first letter. He was in a boot camp in Siauliai, in the Lithuanian republic. After three months there, he and the other cadets would take the oath of enlistment and would be sent to different parts of the Soviet Union for their permanent service.

He wrote that his superiors were stupid, and he had almost beaten a sergeant who was bullying young recruits. He was already sick of the army and missed Dimka and me.

I sent him a picture of the three of us that was taken during his last visit.

In January, a telegram arrived. All it said was, "Come urgently. Sasha."

I didn't know what to make of it, but when I showed Tamara, she panicked. "Something is wrong. You must go to him."

My university semester was over, so after I took my last exam, I went to the Aeroflot Agency and bought a ticket to Riga, the capital of the Latvian republic and the closest airport to Siauliai. From there, I would take a train.

I arrived in Siauliai in the afternoon, left my suitcase in the luggage storage at the station, and set off immediately through the snow in search of the military training unit.

All I had was an address written on a piece of paper. The few people I met on the almost-deserted streets shrugged when I asked them for directions. Nobody understood Russian. Nobody even slowed down to look at the address I showed them.

The temperature dropped. My toes grew numb from cold. Early winter twilight fell on the city, and I started to worry that I wouldn't be able to find my husband's unit before dark. I had almost lost hope when I saw a man dressed in a shabby sheepskin coming out of an alley.

"Excuse me," I pleaded, expecting him to pass by as everyone else had. "Could you please help me?" The man stopped and looked at me in surprise.

"*Mogu, yesli khorosho poprosish*," he said in Russian. It was what Papa used to say when I asked him if he could help me, too. "I can, if you ask me well."

"I'm so glad to see you. I'm looking for the Interior Troops Training Unit, but local people here don't understand Russian."

"They all do. They just pretend not to."

"But why?"

"Because they hate you."

That was the last thing I expected him to say. "Hate me? What have I done to them?"

"You're Russian, and that's enough. They consider all Russians to be occupants."

"The occupants? But the Russians freed them from Germany during the war," I said.

"They say they'd rather be under the Germans. There was more order then."

"What about you?" I asked.

"I'm Gypsy. They don't like me, either. What are *you* doing here?"

"I came to see my husband. He's in the MVD training camp here. Do you know where it is?"

"Sure. It's just two blocks from here, behind that corner." I thanked the man and went in the direction he pointed. I soon came to a long fence with barbed wire on top. I followed it until I found a military checkpoint. After a lengthy explanation of who I was and why I was there, I sat on a wooden bench while the guard called his superiors.

While waiting, I examined the posters on the walls of the room. "People and the Army are united," one of them said. Another poster depicted a soldier talking on the phone. "A chatterbox is a find for a spy," it said.

Finally, the door of the checkpoint swung open, letting the frosty air rush inside, and a soldier in a gray greatcoat and tarpaulin military boots stomped in. Although I expected to see Sashka, I didn't recognize him at first. He looked just like every other soldier.

"What happened?" I asked after he hugged me.

"I'll tell you later," he said, handing a piece of paper to the guard. It took another half an hour before we stepped into the snowy, dark street.

"What happened? Why did you send that telegram?" I asked again when we were outside.

"Nothing happened," he said. "I missed you." He stopped in the middle of the street, pulled me to his chest, and began kissing me. His winter overcoat reeked of tobacco and wet wool.

"Stop it, Sashka. People will see," I said, slipping from his grasp. "What do you mean nothing? Your mother is scared to death. I left my job and our son and rushed here because of your telegram, and now you're saying nothing happened?"

"So now you're not happy because I didn't break my neck?" he asked. "Sorry I couldn't give you such a pleasure. Here I am, safe and sound."

For once, I didn't rise to his taunts. I didn't travel almost four thousand kilometers to get into an argument with him.

"Your mother gave me a food parcel for you," I said. "It's in the luggage storage at the train station. Let's check into a hotel first, and then we can go to the station to get it. We can buy some milk and bread for tomorrow morning."

Not far from the train station, we found a small hotel. The middle-aged woman at the desk had a face as impenetrable as tank armor. She shrugged and shook her head to our questions at first, but eventually, after a lot of gestures and her careful inspection of the marriage stamp in my passport and Sashka's furlough certificate, she checked me in.

On our way back from the train station, we stopped at a small grocery store. I gave Sashka a five-ruble bill and stayed outside with my suitcase and Tamara's box. When Sashka came out, he was holding a brown paper package. From the pocket of his soldier's coat peeked the neck of a vodka bottle.

"Well," he said with his old grin, "we're armed now." My mood dropped to match the frosty air.

I spent three days in Siauliai, but Sashka had only been able to get a twenty-four-hour furlough. He got himself drunk on the first night and spoke with contempt about his superiors. He boasted that the cadets, even the older ones, respected him.

If the army changed people, it had so far missed my husband. I was relieved when he had to go back to the camp the next afternoon. Seeing him had only reinforced my decision to divorce him as soon as I morally could.

I spent the rest of my stay in the hotel room. I didn't want to go out into the cold, gray city with its surly people who hated me because I spoke Russian. When Sashka left, the hotel clerk's curiosity prevailed. The woman at the desk who couldn't understand me the night before suddenly remembered her Russian. She wanted to know where I came from, what I was doing in Siauliai, and if my husband and I had kids. By the time I left for the train station two days later, she was smiling and inviting me to come back again.

On my last night, Sashka showed up. He said he had gone AWOL and had to be back before the wakeup call. I didn't welcome him, but I didn't object, either. It didn't matter now. My decision was already made. Our marriage was over, and I would never be back.

51: Job Training

At the beginning of my third year at the university, our schedule changed, and our classes all happened in the afternoon and evening. This conflicted with my musical school job, and after six years of teaching piano, I had to resign. With a heavy heart I went to the musical school to say goodbye and to get my *trudovaya knizhka* (work-record book).

I was sad to leave for many reasons—in part, because I loved my students and enjoyed working with them. But also, I was determined not to depend entirely on my parents. I was an adult, and a mother. I had a responsibility to earn my own living and support my family.

In the end, I didn't have to worry. After just a couple of weeks I found a job as an accompanist for a team of gymnasts in the Dynamo Sports Society.

While I still worked long hours and studied late into the night, my student life gradually developed into something more than endless worries and anxiety. I made new girlfriends who loved to joke and laugh in the corridors and pass notes during lectures. In particular, I befriended Olga Fandeyeva—a tall, thick-boned, smiley woman three years younger than me. Our close relationship replaced what I'd lost when Yulka moved to Moscow a year before I entered the university.

Olga and I played hooky and went to movies and we always celebrated holidays and birthdays together, most often at my house. The only male we allowed into our circle of friends was Dimka, who everyone called *Syn Polka* (a son of the Regiment).

At about the same time, I started training for another kind of work. Although university students were exempt from the military draft, we were all required to take military training courses. The male students were trained to be soldiers, and the women were schooled as nurses. After graduation, men were drafted to one year of active duty at the rank of junior lieutenant, while the females were registered as military nurses-in-reserve, liable for service in wartime. During peace, we had to take periodic refresher courses.

"Don't mess with the military faculty," upper-class students told us on the first day. "No skipping lessons, no coming unprepared. For the slightest offense, you can be kicked out of the university."

For two years, we were drilled one day a week in general therapy, surgery, traumatology, and infectious diseases. We learned how to write prescriptions, administer medications, apply bandages and splints, and give shots. We practiced on each other, playing a nurse and a "wounded soldier." The teachers were so strict, and taught us so meticulously, that we wondered if they thought that after graduation we were going to become medical specialists, not English teachers.

Fortunately, the Cold War that raged between the Soviet Union and the United States didn't turn into a "hot" war, and the bloodshed missed my generation. But from then on, it was my job to administer injections of antibiotics to my son and vitamin shots to Mama, to place *banki* (suction cups) to Papa's back when his muscles were sore, and to measure the blood pressure of whoever needed it.

52: The Capitalist Sharks

At the end of September of my fifth university year, I was getting ready to start my senior thesis and looking forward to graduation the next spring.

The bell had just announced the beginning of classes when Olga and I were summoned to the office of the dean of the foreign language department—"with your belongings, please." Sensing trouble, we stuffed our books and notebooks into our bags. *What have we done wrong?* I wondered.

We found several other high-achieving students from our class in the reception area of the office. Nobody had a clue why we were there. Finally, we were ushered into the dean's inner office.

"You've probably heard that a very important cultural event is going to take place in Ashkhabad," the dean began. "The UNESCO International Conference on the Social and Cultural Development of the Countries of Central Asia in the 19th and 20th Centuries will start tomorrow. Participants are arriving from all over the world, and most don't speak Russian. They'll have qualified interpreters translating for them during the sessions. But the organizers need more English-speaking people to help at the accommodations. The Central Party Committee has requested that the university dispatch our best graduate students to assist hotel staff, so starting immediately, you are dismissed from classes until the end of the conference."

He said something about the trust placed in us, our responsibility, and something else, but I could hardly hear him. What an opportunity!

Although I'd been studying English for four years, I had only ever heard English spoken by native speakers once. The previous summer, I had gone to Leningrad with a group of Ashkhabad tourists. During our visit to the Hermitage Museum, I noticed a small group of foreign tourists standing in front of one of the French Impressionist paintings and speaking English. I drew closer and listened, but to my disappointment and shame, I could understand only half of what they said.

That memory troubled me as I walked into the Hotel Ashkhabad. My fellow students and I were greeted by a man in a gray suit and tie.

"Good afternoon," he said. "My name is Georgiy Ivanovich. I'm a KGB officer."

He was probably in his mid-forties, with a clean-shaven face, calm voice, and attentive eyes. I had never met a KGB agent before, but this was exactly how I imagined them to look.

Georgiy Ivanovich told us that three hundred scholars from twenty-three countries would take part in the UNESCO conference. "There will be many more people than that, because of the interpreters, journalists, and spouses of the participants who are coming as their guests," he said, "and they will come from all over the world, including our rivals from capitalist countries such as West Germany, Finland, Great Britain, France, Italy, Denmark, and the USA. All of the foreigners will stay here in Hotel Ashkhabad. Your responsibility will be helping them and the hotel staff communicate with each other."

I was going to swim in the same waters as capitalist sharks. My head was spinning with excitement, and I was very glad that I'd chosen to study English.

Georgiy Ivanovich paused and looked us over. "Be polite, but vigilant. Talk to them. Pay attention. Listen to what they say and what they're interested in. If you notice or hear anything strange in their behavior, report it to me or my partner. One of us will always be around."

"What do you mean by strange behavior?" I asked.

"If a foreigner asks you to help him find somebody in Ashkhabad or to pass a letter or a package to someone, or if he asks too many questions about our life or just seems overly curious, tell me about it. It could mean nothing, but I'd like to know."

Nothing about Georgiy Ivanovich's request struck me as unusual. He was a KGB agent, and it was his job to protect us from enemies inside and out. The more I listened to him, the more I wanted to get a job in the KGB after graduation.

The students were assigned to different parts of the hotel. My friend Olga was sent to the restaurant to help the staff during meals, someone else went to the reception area, and I was told to assist a saleswoman at a *valyutnyi magazin* (foreign currency shop).

This was an exciting opportunity, because normally, Soviet citizens were forbidden to even enter a *valyutnyi magazin,* let alone shop there. These were state-run stores that sold luxury goods to foreigners and high-ranking officials who had access to foreign money or special checks. Normal Soviet citizens were legally forbidden from having foreign currency, and I had never seen a *Beriozka*, as the chain was called, in Ashkhabad before.

Now, as I chatted with the saleswoman, I tried not to gawk at the shelves of unfamiliar delicacies, funny-shaped bottles with colorful labels, packs of filter cigarettes, and colorful garments. The woman's sleek face, with her thick covering of imported cosmetics, was distracting enough.

That night I stayed up late, learning the names of foreign currencies and English phrases about shopping I thought might be useful in my job. But as it turned out, I wasn't destined to talk about American dollars, German marks, French francs, or Italian lire.

When I got to the hotel the next morning, Georgiy Ivanovich sent me to interpret for an emergency doctor who was visiting a few sick guests. Soon, what started as a few bouts of stomach issues turned into full blown disaster.

It turned out that while the conference participants discussed the civilizations of Central Asia at plenary meetings, the event organizers had arranged for the guest spouses to get acquainted with it in person. They arranged organized tours to museums, Turkmen rug factories, and other attractions.

On their first afternoon, the guests had visited a collective farm. Everything they saw looked nice—animals were well fed, buildings were sturdy, there were no hungry dogs on the streets, and all of the children wore shoes and went to school. The idealized farm they saw bore little resemblance to what I witnessed in the fields of rural Turkmenistan during those long-ago summers with my parents.

After touring the farm's cotton fields, the foreign guests were invited to sample authentic Turkmen cuisine, and that is where things went badly.

Exhausted and flushed from hours spent under the scorching afternoon sun, the guests were seated on a *topchan* (raised platform for eating) strewn with beautiful Turkmen carpets and laden with local treats—fragrant, honey-sweet melons; translucent grapes; bursting-at-the-touch-of-a-knife watermelons. There were trays of tomatoes, cucumbers, and herbs surrounding a huge platter of steaming pilaf and still-warm *churek* (flat Turkmen bread). How could anybody refuse trying it all?

The foreign guests gulped down glasses of cool water and ate liberally from the fruit platters, and their foreign digestive systems, not used to Turkmen food, revolted. Within hours, the better half of our international group was down with devastating diarrhea.

It was a hectic night. I was called from one room to another to translate for doctors and their unusual patients. At first, I was embarrassed to translate questions about stool consistency, toilet visits, or other symptoms of the patients' misery. Such words as *diarrhea, nausea, bloating,* or *vomiting* were not part of my English vocabulary. I had to substitute them with wordy descriptions or even gestures. But since every patient had the same problem, and every visiting doctor kept asking the same questions, I soon became a pro in gastro-intestinal English.

Everything was different about these people. And funny too. One woman, for example, called for the doctor and I to enter her room, where we found her completely naked and lying prostrate across the bed. The weather in Ashkhabad that week was hot and the hotel lacked air-conditioning. She remained that way for the length of our conversation, and was not at all shy about it. The doctor, while talking to her, studied the wall in front of him.

Another conference wife, gaunt from several days of diarrhea and dehydration, asked the doctor, "What would you recommend I drink—vodka or cognac—at the reception party tomorrow?"

The doctors came, gave their recommendations, and left. But since I stayed in the hotel around the clock, patients started to turn to me for advice. I wondered if they understood that I was neither a doctor, a nurse, nor a dietician.

"Hi Mila," a woman greeted me on her way to the restaurant. "I feel better today. Can I order a steak for dinner?"

"I don't think it's a good idea. I'd stay another day or two on a lighter diet," I told her.

When we weren't working, Olga and I spent time with the Soviet scientists, three middle-aged Moscow men who buzzed around us. We took them for a walk around the city and showed them the places of interest. They took us out to dinners and treated us to delicacies. When one of them learned that I loved black caviar, he ordered a bowl of it.

"You should eat as much as you want," he said. "I want you to remember the time when you ate black caviar with a soup spoon."

Olga and I drank champagne, laughed at jokes, and enjoyed our conversations with the world-renowned scholars. We felt flattered. But we were not naïve. "They are professors of science," I told Olga, "but the thoughts in their heads are the same as in a truck driver's." We stayed together and didn't let the professors get too close.

Georgiy Ivanovich sought me out every day, and we chatted when I had spare time.

"Something interesting for me to know?" he asked when I bumped into him on the stairs.

"Not unless you're interested in how many stools a day our guests are having," I told him.

"No thanks," he laughed. "Let it be their top secret."

I liked talking with him, but I also worried. I felt he expected more than my funny stories, yet I didn't have anything suspicious to report.

"I like these Westerners," I told him once. "They remind me of children—happy, open, and friendly. They don't know simple things; their questions are often naïve, but they are good-natured."

His face became serious. "Don't be fooled by their behavior. They are not as simple as you think."

"But they're not as suspicious as we are," I said, and immediately regretted my words.

"We're not suspicious. We're vigilant. We live in the hostile world that hates us. Your *friendly* Westerners would be happy to choke you at the first opportunity."

"It's hard to believe." I knew better, but I couldn't stop myself. "I think there are good and bad people in all countries." He smiled at me, but his eyes stayed flat. My words had annoyed him.

I should have kept my tongue behind my teeth, I thought. Mama is right scolding me for my inability to hold my opinions back. But I don't understand why we are trying so hard to please foreigners if we think they're our enemies. Why do they stay in the best hotels, where ordinary Soviet people are not allowed? Why do we have *Beriozka* stores where they can buy anything they need and we, the citizens of this country, have to stand in lines to buy a pair of decent shoes or even food? Why do we hate them and envy their way of life? It's not the foreigners' fault. They probably don't even know about it.

53: The Roasted Rooster

I graduated from the university and defended my thesis on *Aphorisms and Phraseological Units in Oscar Wilde's Plays.* I was the proud holder of a "free" diploma, which allowed me to find any job I wanted.

The "free" diplomas were rare and coveted, given only to honor students with "red" diplomas (cum laude) and those who had health or family reasons to stay in the city. The rest of the university graduates would receive their diplomas only after working for three years at assigned teaching jobs, usually in remote, dusty small towns on the periphery of civilization. Students whispered together about teachers stuck in rooms with tiny windows that faced unpaved streets, with no entertainment and primitive outhouse buzzing with green flies.

As a single mother with a small child, I got off the hook. But my fellow students also made every possible effort to evade the placements—feigned illnesses, bribes, even hasty marriages. As a result, many remote Turkmen schools were left without English, German, or Russian teachers. Only a few, including my friend Olga, went and worked the allotted time in the most difficult conditions.

Teaching was not my plan for my degree, anyway. *Komitet Gosudarstvennoi Bezopasnosti* (the Committee for State Security) was my first choice, but I didn't know what the procedure was for applying for a job with the KGB, so I just went to the Ashkhabad headquarters to find out.

My legs felt weak as I climbed the granite steps of the big, gray building on the corner of Karl Liebknecht Boulevard and Svoboda Prospect. I paused at the top of the stairs, collected my courage, and pulled the wooden bar-handle of the massive door.

After the bright summer light, the inside was dim and cool. On my left, I saw a uniformed officer sitting behind a desk.

"Who did you come to see? On what issue? Your passport!" he demanded.

After he entered my passport data in the register, he called someone and reported my job inquiry. Then he pointed to chairs on the opposite side of the hall and told me to wait.

Fifteen minutes later, a man in civilian clothes came and asked me several questions about my education, work experience, and criminal record. Satisfied with my answers, he handed me an application and led me to the door.

The application I brought home was exhaustively long. It felt like somebody was stripping me naked and then pulling off my skin, too, to check what I was hiding underneath it. They wanted not only information about me, but also names, birthdates, places of birth and death, employment history, political views and affiliations, social origin, *natsional'nost'* (ethnicity) of all my relatives. They asked if any relatives resided abroad or had resided in German-occupied territories during the Great Patriotic War. To answer questions about my grandparents, I had to let Mama into my enterprise.

The thought of my grandparents clouded my optimism. Was I fit to work in the KGB if I was the grandchild of *kulaks*? Even though in the column about their social origin I wrote "*iz krestyan*" (from peasants), it would be clear that they had not come to Turkmenistan from Russia in the 1930s to bask in the sun.

Those weren't the only "dark spots" I had in my biography, though. I also had to explain my housewife mother with a criminal record, my "capitalist" father whose apiary was a splinter in the socialist system, and my husband and his spotty work record.

"Don't build up too much hope," Mama told me after I returned my completed application to the KGB. "They don't take people from the street. To get a job in this kind of place, you have to be the daughter of a big shot."

Still, a neighbor told me that a man had been snooping around our neighborhood, asking people about me.

After a month of worrying, I called the KGB staff department to inquire.

"You didn't pass," a man told me, and then hung up. He offered no explanations and no comforting words. I felt like somebody had slapped me on the face without even saying what for.

I was still stewing over my failure when I bumped into a former university classmate, Lilya.

"It's a pity you couldn't make it. Where will you apply now?" she said.

"Didn't make what?" I asked, astonished. I hadn't told anyone but Mama about my application.

"It's all right, don't pretend. I know you applied for a job in the KGB and they turned you down," she said easily.

"How did you learn about it?"

"A friend in the KGB told me."

"Why you?"

"He knew I graduated with you. About two weeks ago, he asked me if I knew you."

So they had questioned my school contacts as well as my neighbors. "Do you know why I didn't get the job?" I asked.

"As a matter of fact, I do. I asked him about it the other day. He didn't want to tell me— 'confidential information . . . I cannot discuss it . . .' you know—but then he gave in. He said it was because of your contacts with foreigners."

"What foreigners?" I asked. And then it dawned on me. It was my work as an interpreter at the UNESCO conference the previous fall. I remembered Georgiy Ivanovich asking what our foreign guests talked about and what they were interested in, and my flippant, ambiguous answers. I hadn't cooperated and even more, I had shown sympathy for them and said they weren't all evil.

If that's what it took to be part of their ranks, I thought—spying on people and reporting every passing comment to the KGB—then no thanks. I was glad they decided I wasn't one of their own.

"What's done is done for the best," Mama said when I told her the news. My bitterness gave way to a feeling of relief.

After my failure with the KGB, I wasn't sure whether it was worthwhile to apply for work at the Ministry of Inner Affairs since Sashka had been sacked from their Criminal Investigation Department. Even though we hadn't lived together for more than four years, we were still legally married, and I understood that my chances of getting a job in the same organization were flimsy. Nevertheless, I decided to try.

Compared to the KGB, the people at the Ministry of Inner Affairs were friendly and open. I talked to real people who interviewed me in their offices, and I could see their eyes and read their faces. When I mentioned my concern about Sashka's record, the man who interviewed me said, "Don't worry. You're not responsible for your former husband's mistakes."

When he asked what department of the militia I would like to work in, I did not hesitate. "OBKhSS." This was the group that controlled economic crime and corruption. My interviewer nodded but told me that the only open position they currently had was for an inspector of *Detskaya Komnata Militsii* (the Youth-at-Risk Department).

"Don't worry," he added. "When you get into our system, it's easier to move you from one department to another. You'll just have to prove you're a worthy candidate for an OBKhSS job."

Three weeks later, I came for an interview with the chief of the personnel department of the Ministry of Internal Affairs. The inspector of human resources had told me I had passed all the other checks, and meeting the chief of staff was the last step.

The appointment was scheduled for late afternoon. When I walked in, the chief of staff was sitting at a table, talking to someone on the phone in Turkmen. Without interrupting his conversation, he nodded to me and gestured for me to take a seat. He was an imposing man of forty-five or so with cropped dark hair just touched with gray at the temples. His hands, which had apparently never seen hard labor, were sleek, and I noticed a heavy gold wedding band on his right ring finger.

He hung up and pulled a thin folder from a stack on the side of his desk. While he was leafing through it, the door opened, and a man in civilian clothes entered the room. He looked older, shorter, and heavier. The Chief of Staff got up and reached with both hands to greet the newcomer, whose appearance and behavior exuded superiority. I wondered who he was and why he'd come to my interview.

The man eased his fleshy body into a chair. Something about him reminded me of a bulldog impatiently watching his meal being prepared.

There wasn't much of an interview. Neither man asked any questions about my background or my education. They were more interested in finding out whether I had friends or acquaintances working in the MVD system. The conversation was informal. They talked as if they already considered me one of their staff. At one point, the older man asked me about my age, and when I told him he said I was too old to make a good career. Then the two of them made some calculations and decided I would be able to rise at most only to the rank of major or lieutenant colonel before retirement. That was something I had never considered before—ranks, retirement, pension. All that seemed to be far in the future.

"Call me on Monday. I'll tell you when to meet with the head of the *Detskaya Komnata Militsii*," the major concluded, closing the folder and putting it aside. "Are you willing to wear a militia uniform?"

"Yes, if I have to," I said. The interview was over. I got up.

"You'll look good in a militia uniform," the bulldog said, sizing me up. "You have a nice figure. Stop by my office when you wear it. I want to see it." His wet red mouth stretched in a smile. *Who is he? He sounds as if I should know him.*

He turned to the major and said something in Turkmen. I could understand only a few words.

"One more thing," the chief of staff stopped me. "We have to *obmyt'* (drink for) your new position. Invite us to your house on Saturday and bring a friend. Let's relax together."

His proposal sounded so inappropriate that at first I thought it was a joke or a test. "To relax together" was definitely suspicious.

"I live with my parents," I said brightly. "They'll be glad to have guests. My mother is an excellent cook." They both shook their heads.

"Can we go to your friend's place?" the major suggested.

"No, she lives with her husband and son," I lied just in case. I didn't have anybody in mind, but the whole notion of "relaxing" with these two men was disgusting. "I can invite you to a restaurant and bring my friend with me," I offered. Having noticed the sour expression on their faces, I added, "I'll pay for everything."

"It's not a problem," the bulldog said. "I have a nice place in Firyuza. Just bring your friend with you and we'll go there."

The fog of suspicion froze into a heavy chunk of ice inside my chest. "No, I can't. Sorry," I said.

The bulldog cursed in Turkmen, and the chief of staff frowned.

"Give me a call on Monday," he said, his voice suddenly dry and scratchy like emery paper.

When I returned my visitor's pass on the way out, the guard asked me, "Is the minister still at the chief of staff's?"

"Who?"

"His secretary said he was there." I didn't answer.

When I called the personnel department on Monday, the inspector of human resources answered.

"Sorry," he said. "Your nomination has not been approved."

"But I was told—"

He interrupted me. "We found a more suitable candidate for this position." Then I heard the click of him hanging up. As I stood there holding the dead handset, I felt that my whole world had just turned upside down.

Papa was right. Once, in the heat of one of our political debates, he said, "You'll understand it all when a roasted rooster pecks you in your ass." Now, blankly staring at the handset, I at last understood.

It was the fall of 1973. I was a twenty-six-year-old idealistic fool whose world had crumbled like the toy kaleidoscope that I took apart when I was a child. I wanted to see the magic inside it. Instead, I found a bunch of broken glass—pathetic rubbish instead of a fairytale world of unprecedented beauty. Feeling deceived, I wept.

54: The Bitter Awakening

In the spring of 1974, my parents sold their apiary. Tiny mites had been sucking the life from local honeybees, reducing numbers in colonies across our region. The invading pests had not been studied, and no one knew how to fight them. Mama sprinkled tobacco inside every bee colony. It irritated the bees and made them move and scratch, which caused the parasites clinging to their bodies to fall off. Once, she showed me a white piece of paper, which she had put at the bottom of a beehive to see the results of her treatment. It was covered with microscopic reddish bugs, the killers of her dear *pcholki* (honeybees). But, in spite of her attempts, the number of our bees kept declining. All they could do was sell the remaining beehives. It was a major financial blow after providing most of our income for more than twenty years.

That summer, I applied for a position as an English-language teacher with an Ashkhabad school that happened to have a music center called Echo. When the principal learned that in addition to my university diploma, I was also a piano teacher, she was thrilled. "Our school is a perfect place for you," she told me.

And at first, it seemed to be. I taught English in the morning and piano in the afternoon. My principal was a member of the Communist Party, and she was what a *real* communist was supposed to be—honest, principled, and clean-fingered. She ignited her teachers with her passion and enthusiasm and never failed to praise us for our achievements.

"*Umnichka!* (Whiz kid)," she would marvel at a teacher's excellent performance. "I'll record an acknowledgement for your achievements into your *trudovaya knizhka* (employment record book)." And she followed up. During my four years of teaching, I had three acknowledgements from the school administration.

In my second year as a teacher, the principal increased my school hours and appointed me to be a *klassnyi rukovoditel'* (class master) for a fourth grade—forty-two ten-year-old children. After that, my working day did not stop with the school bell. I was busy with extracurricular activities: class hours, individual work with students and parents, educational work in cooperation with other teachers, Pioneer and Komsomol organizations, preparations for class and school events, field trips, and much more. All that work added up to just a ten-ruble raise, less than one percent of a teacher's salary but I did not complain.

What got me, though, was the "ideological and patriotic education" of the schoolchildren, which was a part of a class master's responsibilities. Nothing had changed since my own childhood: the same Pioneer meetings, Pioneer heroes, Pioneer symbols, and the same empty talk about supremacy of our Soviet system and promises of a bright future. My fourth graders' eyes sparkled with the same light of excitement that mine had almost two decades earlier. I had to look into their eager, trusting eyes and tell them things that burnt my tongue to say. Was it moral to teach kids something I don't believe in myself, I wondered. Eventually, they, too, would come to understand all the lies and duplicity of our system.

The last straw came at the beginning of my fourth year at the school.

I was called to the room of the deputy director for educational work. "Are you aware of what Oleg K. has done?" she asked when I entered. Her question did not surprise me. Oleg was a lazy and cocky boy, notorious for his bad behavior. I spent more time disciplining him than any other student in my class.

"What did he do this time?" I said.

"I was informed that he wiped the blackboard with his Pioneer tie." Her voice rang with indignation. "It tells me that the patriotic education in your class is poorly conducted. We must condemn his behavior at a school meeting. Be sure his parents come, too."

"Let's not rush it. I'll talk to Oleg first," I offered. "He's not a bad boy. Calling his parents to school could only make it worse. His father is abusive, and I'm afraid he will beat his son."

She didn't say anything, and I took it as an approval.

The next day I was summoned to the deputy director's room again. There I found the school's Pioneer Leader and Oleg's father, a sullen man with a baggy eyes and puffy face. He looked hung over. It was the first time I met him. Usually Oleg's mother came alone to teacher-parent meetings. She sat near the back wall, behind the other parents.

The man stared at us with a challenge. When the deputy director told him about his son's offence, he chuckled. "So what?"

"How could you say that? By his act, your son disgraced not only the honor of a Soviet Pioneer, but the honor of our school Pioneer Organization," the Pioneer Leader interjected. "We have to raise the issue of his temporary expelling from the Pioneers."

"Who needs your organization?" Oleg's father scoffed. "Stop filling my son's head with your nonsense."

The Pioneer Leader swallowed the air like a fish thrown ashore. "Now I understand where the wind comes from," she mumbled.

"Ludmila Ivanovna," the deputy turned to me. "What do you think about all this?"

It was the question I had been trying to answer for myself. I loved working with children, but a school, even a good one like this one, was part of the system. No matter how much I tried to be honest, I could not deviate from the main task of the Soviet school—to educate the younger generation in the spirit of Communism. I no longer believed in that bright future, nor was I willing to tell half-truths. There was no other way for me.

I got up and left the room. I would rather be hungry than fooled and brainwashed. The next morning, I submitted my resignation, and I went back to teaching the piano at the musical school. From then on, my life went without any big surprises or shocks.

55: June, 1983

My father was dying. He was not supposed to. Doctors said that he'd suffered a mild stroke which had affected his speech and that he'd recover quickly. They did not know a damn thing, those doctors. Papa was slipping away from us, and every new day brought new changes.

He had walked into the Neurological Clinic with my mother at his side at the end of April. Now it was the beginning of June and he lay in bed in a coma, eight patients in the ward, too hot, too crowded, no air conditioner. The smell of urine and chlorine was overwhelming.

I noticed the first signs of his disease in February. We'd gathered at our dinner table to celebrate my birthday, the usual hodgepodge of people: relatives, friends, acquaintances, all who remembered to come. Papa got up to make the first toast. I could see him standing across from me with a shot of vodka in his outstretched hand. He had put on some weight; his slim waist and lean thighs had become slightly heavier, but his shoulders were still wide and his back straight. He was always the first to open any feast, be it a birthday, wedding, or wake. Those were not brainy toasts; he erred in confusing words or mispronouncing non-Slavic names, but his good nature and openness made up for his slips. He liked to toast people and they loved him.

"Hey, Papa, why are you stuttering?" I asked after our guests downed their drinks and bent over their dinner plates.

"I don't know. I've noticed it myself. It could be my dentures," he said

By the beginning of April, his stuttering became worse. His smoker's cough, which had been tormenting him for years, worsened also; he gasped at night, and spat out some thick yellowish-green mucus on newspaper pages he kept under his bed. I'd throw them away when I washed the floor in my parents' bedroom.

In no time, he had turned into an old deteriorating man. It was painful to see him coming home from work in the evening, haggard, barely dragging his feet, depressed.

"You have to stop working, Vanya. Go to see the doctor," Mama kept telling him.

"What do they know, your doctors? They're all *konovaly* (horseleeches). Your Gorbacheva already buried me ten years ago." Dr. Gorbacheva was our family physician who had been working in our Lenin district Polyclinic. Years ago, when Papa had problems with his stomach, she told him if he didn't stop drinking, he'd die from stomach cancer as his brother Mikhail did. Papa had been avoiding her ever since.

"You cannot work in your condition," I supported Mama. "You're almost sixty-two. You should have been retired for two years by now."

"And what will I do if I retire? Sit home and see you starve?"

"It's the eighties, not the thirties now. Nobody starves to death anymore. And you're not the only one who makes money in our family. Andrey and I work, too," I said.

"Can you live on what you make?"

"The other people do. You keep forgetting that we're not kids anymore. We already have children of our own."

"You'll go begging without me." He waved me off like a fly.

Since selling the apiary in 1974, Papa had been working as a truck driver, delivering crates of wine and vodka from Ashkhabad *VinZavod* (winery) to liquor stores around the city. Apart from his regular wages, he made some extra cash by helping to load and unload the truck. He also took advantage of a breakage allowance of two bottles per full truckload, which, if he was really careful, he could either take home or trade for cash. How many truckloads he delivered and unloaded during his shift I didn't know. Looking at his gaunt face and sunken eyes at the end of the day, I'd say more than one or two. Sometimes he complained that he had broken a crate of bottles and had to pay back all the money he had earned.

I remember Mama put his dinner on the table, got a sweating bottle out of the fridge and silently poured him a shot of vodka. He washed it down, drew a sigh, and sat for a long time, staring at the empty wall in front of him.

"Eat Vanya, everything is getting cold," Mama cajoled him.

"I can't. Give me another one."

She filled his shot again, without objections, and sighed too. He drank it and began eating, slowly, reluctantly, his head hanging low over his bowl of borscht. Then he pushed the unfinished soup bowl away, declined Mama's persuasions to eat a little meat, and shuffled outside to smoke.

He stopped socializing. All his *sobutyl'niki* (drinking buddies) had disappeared. He became thin, gloomy, and withdrawn.

In the middle of April, the day came when Papa wasn't able to go to work. Mama called the Polyclinic. Dr. Gorbacheva came for a visit, examined him, and said that he had probably had a mild stroke. She wrote out a *bol'nichnyi list* (sick leave) and a hospital referral and left.

Soon, he was admitted to the Neurological Clinic. The physician's prognosis was encouraging. The doctor assured us that Papa's stroke had only affected his speech, nothing serious, and that he was going to be all right. To speed up his recovery, she advised us to bring him the ABC Book to practice reading letters and simple words and do easy math problems to stimulate his brain.

We rushed into action. Every morning, Mama or I took him to a small hospital yard, found an empty bench, and did our homework. I remember him grinning, like a kindergartener, who managed to sound a letter or give the right answer to a simple problem.

On the 9th of May, we brought him home to celebrate Victory Day. It was the last time we sat at the same table with Papa, our decorated war veteran. He was happy to be home but looked subdued.

Soon our hospital yard lessons had to be stopped. Even a trip to the bathroom, which was located at the end of the corridor, became a challenge. The doctor didn't know why, in spite of her expectations, Papa's health was deteriorating so fast. They dragged him to x-rays, ultrasounds, and ordered all kind of tests but only shrugged their shoulders.

Looking at his listless body, prostrate on the narrow hospital bed, I recalled how several years ago, when his sister, Aunt Nastya, was dying a long and painful death from esophagus cancer, he told me if something like this ever happened to him, he knew how to stop it. Poor Papa, he believed he was the master of his own fate.

The first part of June was unbearably hot. Mama, Aunt Pasha, Papa's younger sister, and I were staying in turns at his side. There were eight beds in the room, standing like soldiers side by side in two formations of four with a narrow aisle between them. The beds were placed so close to each other that it was almost impossible to fit a chair between them. Anyway, to find a chair was a problem and I sat on the edge Papa's or his absent neighbor's bed, while the latter wandered outside in hope of catching a little breeze. The temperature had risen to forty-two degrees Celsius (107.6 Fahrenheit). Inside, prostrate from the heat, I was fanning, in turns, my unconscious Papa and myself with a folded newspaper.

When I was unable to tolerate it any more, I went one block to the *Zelyonaya Zona* (Green Zone), a wide esplanade stretched between Karl Marx Square and *The Tulip*, a monument to the Turkmenistan soldiers who had died for the liberation of our Soviet soil from the German invaders. There, I sat on a bench in the shade of an acacia tree, surrounded by a sea of blooming yucca plants. Their towering clusters, heavy with white bell-shaped flowers, tormented me with their incongruous beauty, intensifying my pain and devastation. The contrast between the beauty of nature and my grief and feeling of guilt was jarring.

Tears of remorse ran down my cheeks as I thought how unfair, cruel, and egoistic I had been all my life towards Papa. Everything he had bestowed on me I had taken for granted—his love, his generosity, his devotion. He had never asked anything in return, he only needed my understanding, and I hadn't given him even that much.

I recalled how mad at him I had been and how I had fought his every attempt to bash our Socialist system and its Communist leaders. Even later, when I was older and when the rose-colored glasses had fallen from my eyes, I still argued with him, trying to protect the shards of a bright future and fraternal friendship myth that had been trampled by Soviet tanks, first in Czechoslovakia and then in Afghanistan. I had never admitted to him that I had been wrong.

But most of all, I punished myself for refusing to listen to his stories about the war, *his* war, that human grinder and destroyer of souls he was thrown into at age twenty. When sober, he had rarely mentioned it, but warmed up by alcohol, he became sentimental and loosened his tongue. "I don't want to hear your drunken war stories," I would cut him off. It had never even occurred to me that being drunk was the only way he could bring himself to talk about it.

How could I have been so callous? That war was the most memorable time in his life. He had survived it and came back a winner. What right do I have to judge him? I have denied him simple benevolence and understanding; in exchange I took for granted his generosity, I cried myself into despondency.

Once, when with a heavy heart I came back from my joyless yucca refuge and took my usual place next to my father, he suddenly opened his eyes for a moment and looked at me. My heart skipped a beat. In a wild hope, I grabbed his hand. "Papa," I called. "Papa, can you hear me? It's me, Mila." I thought I felt a light squeeze of his hand. Overwhelmed, with tears streaming down my face, I began talking to him. I told him he was going to be better and soon we'd take him home; I told him I was sorry for being such a bad daughter; I told him he was a great father, the best one in the world. I thanked him for everything he had done for me. I was going on and on, but Papa remained silent.

He died on June 12. The yuccas were still in full bloom.

56: Losing the Motherland

Planes did not crash, and trains did not derail in the Soviet Union. Everything was stable, built to withstand and made to function. There were no massacres, no serial killers, and no riots. Our factories did not burn, our bridges did not collapse, and our mines did not explode. What was more amazing, there were no natural disasters in our country, either—no earthquakes, floods, or forest fires. Our media reported on the plane crash that had killed everyone on board in the USA, a flood that took hundreds of lives in Indonesia, and an earthquake in India with details about the seismic size and number of fatalities. The capitalist world was full of disaster. But we, the Soviet people, were lucky. If sometimes catastrophes like the Ashkhabad earthquake were so enormous that they could not be concealed, the number of victims either was not reported or was grossly understated.

In November 1982, half a year before Papa's death, the Soviet Leader, Leonid Brezhnev, was carried out of the Kremlin feet first. After eighteen years of governing, he left the country devastated, exhausted by the arms race and the war in Afghanistan. He had been our *Gensek* (General Secretary) for so long, that people got used to him as one got used to an old watchdog, who no longer barked or chased intruders away, but lay in the shade and didn't care what was going on around him.

During the last years of his regime, the theft of state property and blatant double standards, which had always been part of our Soviet reality, thrived as never before. It seemed as if Brezhnev's government had entered into a tacit agreement with its people, allowing them to work half-heartedly, to drink and to steal from work in exchange for their loyalty and obedience. People pretended to be working, their leaders pretended to govern, and all were satisfied. Everything was calm but murky, like in a swamp.

While the Soviet government boasted about the country's space achievements, mammoth constructions, and five-year plans, the citizens spent half of their time scouring shops in search of meat, butter, cheese, and bare necessities. Our Communist shepherds, detached from reality, didn't see that their flock had drifted away, insulating themselves with a wall of apathy, distrust, and sarcasm.

Left to care for themselves, the masses used all their creativity in finding ways to improve their existence. Pilferers, with the innocuous nickname of *nesuny*, appropriated anything that *plokho lezhalo* (was badly placed), swiping what they could carry off from their work—meat and sausages from meat plants, building materials from construction sites, office supplies from offices, groceries from warehouses and stores, and food from kindergartens and schools. Further up the social scale, more intricate petty thefts had been devised with cooked books, bribes, or whatever could make life worth living.

The Soviet intelligentsia—doctors, teachers, engineers, people of art—probably was in the worst position. They didn't steal, some on moral grounds, others because there was nothing to carry off from their workplace. A box of chocolates or a bottle of perfume from parents or patients was a grain of sand compared to the scale of state property looting. There were exceptions among them too, like Yulka's father, the head of the Polytechnic college departments, who had been copying old theses and selling them to his students for decades.

Our aged lackluster Leader Leonid Brezhnev became the subject of the nation's ridicule. No one took him or his geriatric government seriously. There were frequent jokes about him. People mocked his inability to link two words together without reading notes (*At the 1980 Moscow Olympics, Brezhnev begins his speech. "O!"—applause. "O!"—an ovation. "O!!!"—the whole audience stands up and applauds. An aide comes running to the podium and whispers, "Leonid Ilyich, those are the Olympic logo rings, you don't need to read all of them!"*); his purely fictitious leadership role and his propensity to vanity (*The phone rings. Brezhnev picks up the receiver, "Hello, this is Dear Leonid Ilyich . . ."*); and his fondness for medals and the highest government awards (*"Have you heard Leonid Ilyich is in surgery?" / "His heart again?" / "No, chest expansion surgery, to make room for one more Gold Star medal."*).

By the time Brezhnev died, every thinking person understood that it was impossible to continue the way we had been living and something had to be done. The new Gensek, Yuri Andropov, who came to power in November 1982, knew it better than anybody else—he was the former Chairman of the Soviet Union KGB. The very first days of his reign he began tightening the screws.

To improve labor discipline, the militia and the people's patrol launched raids on shops, movie theatres, and restaurants, rounding up truants who were shirking their work responsibilities. Stories spread throughout the city how so-and-so had been caught, reported to his or her workplace, and deprived of a "thirteenth salary" (one-month-salary-size bonus), or even sacked. People got scared and laid low. There were also rumors about arrests, political trials, expulsions, and labor camps for dissidents. The laughter and jokes subdued but did not disappear. (A joke: *A new unit of time: One Androp = 10 years in a labor camp.*)

In 1983, Moscow officials launched the biggest criminal investigation in the history of the USSR against alleged corruption in the Uzbekistan cotton industry, dubbed the "Cotton Case," But

Andropov was not destined to see the end of it. He too died, having been in power for only fifteen months. He was the thunderstorm that scared the hell out of people with all its lightning and rumbles and was gone without even spilling a good rain. People breathed a sigh of relief, "Whew! That was close." But despite his short rule, the Russians remembered Andropov as a tough leader who had tried to restore order in the country.

Next came Konstantin Chernenko. (A joke: *TASS announcement: "Today, due to bad health and without regaining consciousness, Konstantin Chernenko took up the duties of General Secretary of the Communist Party of the USSR."*)

Thirteen months later, our morning started with mournful music again. Our new old Leader had slipped quietly, leaving behind no memory, except for the fact that he was one of Brezhnev's decrepit Politburo members who had been dropping dead one after another, like flies. In addition to three successive Genseks within short intervals in time, the country had buried four influential members of its government. When, instead of the expected "Pionerskaya Zor'ka" or "Sport News" programs, we heard slow classical music playing on the radio, someone would quip, "*Opyat' kto-to v Politburo duby dal* (Another of Politburo has kicked the oak box)." More jokes followed.

"Igor Kirillov, the anchor of the popular news program "Vremya" (Time), *is in a black suit. 'Comrades! You're probably going to laugh, but our country has suffered another heavy loss.'"*

"If the morning on the radio starts with mournful music, it means that it's minus one in Moscow."

"The favorite sport of members of the Politburo is hearse racing."

On March 11, 1985, the day after Chernenko's death, the country had its fourth Gensek in two and a half years—Mikhail Gorbachev, the youngest member of the Politburo: dark-eyed, energetic, eloquent, with a pleasant face and intelligent-looking wife at his side. He spoke *bez bumazhki* (without a piece of paper), in a clear voice with a southern Russia accent and looked unlike any Soviet leader I remembered. The contrast was so stark that he immediately became popular. For the first time, I did not feel embarrassed when TV News program *Vremya* (Time), showed him and Raisa, his wife, attending international meetings and conferences. They did not stand apart from Western politicians and their wives, like our previous, stiff-backed leaders, whose wives we had seen in public for the first time only at their funerals.

The first measure of Gorbachev as a General Secretary of the CPSU was a campaign against alcoholism—which immediately split the country into two camps: most women skeptically supported the idea, and men vehemently objected to it. Mama noticed wisely, "Russian women should bow at Gorbachev's feet if this works. But alcoholism is not a splinter; you can't just pull it out and turn the country of hooch hunters into nondrinkers in one fell swoop. It'll take time and patience to change people."

The price of alcohol tripled and sales of it were limited, which led to kilometer-long lines and widespread manufacturing of *samogon* (moonshine). Sugar, needed for hooch-making, disappeared from store counters making every woman angry. Men were furious.

Mama was right to be skeptical. The measures did not work. People poisoned themselves with underground swill, but continued boozing. In addition to all that, the government ordered the vineyards of the southern regions of the USSR to be cut down. That was a blunder for which Russians would never forgive Gorbachev. Eventually, because of huge budget losses and rising popular discontent, the whole plan had to be rolled back. The country continued imbibing.

Soon everyone talked about coming reforms; new words *uskoreniye, glasnost,* and *perestroika* (acceleration, political openness, and economic restructuring) sounded like the key to all our problems.

Sometime in 1989, I heard Gorbachev speaking on TV. I was home, in my own condominium—Papa's last generous gift—at the other end of the city from Mama, ironing my sheets and towels (we used to iron everything, even socks). I can't recollect the exact occasion for Gorbachev addressing the nation. He spoke about the economic and social problems of our country, explaining, admitting mistakes. We cannot live this way anymore; Soviet people need to know the truth, he was saying.

Never before, had I heard any Soviet Leader speak directly to the people so frankly, not hiding behind pompous words and false promises. But it was not *what* Gorbachev was saying that amazed me the most, but the fact that he, the General Secretary of the CPSU, was openly admitting what the majority of Soviet people had already known. It was so unbelievable that I could not contain my emotions. I set aside the iron and sat down on the sofa; tears ran down my face. The contours of our Leader's face blurred on the screen, but his voice sounded strong and clear.

When I heard Gorbachev admit the existence of anti-Semitism in the USSR, I grabbed the phone to call my co-worker and good friend, Larissa Bobman. She and her husband, Aleksandr, were a Jewish couple who had come to Ashkhabad from Ukraine, where, unlike our multicultural Turkmenistan, anti-Semitism had always been a huge problem. From her, I had learned what it meant to be a Jew in the Soviet Union. "I recoiled every time somebody started telling jokes at a party," she once confessed. "They told dirty anecdotes about Jews and bellowed with pleasure seeing our humiliation."

The Bobmans were also listening to Gorbachev's speech. "I cannot believe it," Larissa cried into the phone, "He admitted it."

Exciting things happened almost every day. We called each other with news, "Have you heard they let Sakharov free?" "Can you believe they've stopped jamming "enemy voices"?" "They are going to publish Pasternak's *Doktor Zhivago*!" "Do you know that they've opened unlimited subscriptions on all newspapers and magazines?" "I've just finished reading Bulgakov's *Heart of a Dog*. Now I see why it was banned."

We gathered to discuss the latest events. My refrigerator was empty, except for a little flour and a couple eggs, but I baked a simple cabbage pie and called friends. Half an hour later, they arrived, noisy, with a bottle of wine in hands, and we talked our hearts out until midnight. It was an amazing, unforgettable time; we drank in big gulps and could not quench our thirst for freedom. The stores were empty, there was nothing to eat, but we were happy.

In March 1989, the first Soviet free elections of the Congress of People's Deputies began in all fifteen Soviet Republics. The Congress took place in Moscow two months later. For two weeks, we all turned into eyes and ears, fearing to miss a single word of the people's deputies. Our skepticism and frustration with the Soviet hypocrisy, failing economy, and shortages turned into expectations and new hopes.

Inspired by Glasnost (freedom of expression), the employees at offices and enterprises confronted their corrupt bosses, demanding their dismissal. Bitten by the same bug, the teachers of Music School #2, where I worked at the time, began our own fight for justice. We wrote a petition to the Ministry of Culture accusing our principal—a young haughty Turkmen woman, hung with diamonds—of bribery, mistreatment of subordinates, and using school funds for her personal needs. After the Ministry of Culture conducted a "thorough" review and did not find any violation, the indignant staff wrote a collective letter which Larissa and I were dispatched to take to the major Russian-language newspaper *Turkmenskaya Iskra.*

The newspaper responded in the spirit of the time and assigned one of its best reporters to investigate the problem. A month later, the article about the conflict in the musical school was published, but the result of it was not what we all had been hoping for—the principal remained in her position, but the head teacher who was an instigator of the uprising and several teachers (including me) resigned in protest. A year later, I married a young, handsome investigative journalist who was the author of the article.

In the meantime, perestroika was underway: new laws allowing Soviet citizens to own small businesses were adopted. In the country where no private businesses were allowed and where the Party dictated everything, from the planting of sugar beets to the repertoire of the Bolshoi Theatre, it was unheard of. Thousands of want-to-be-capitalists rushed to find ways to make money. Tiny stalls, tents, and pavilions began springing up in the streets of Ashkhabad, like mushrooms after the warm autumn rain. Newborn entrepreneurs were cooking, repairing, renting, sewing, fixing, and trading. Wholesale buyers shuttled across the country buying goods from cheap sources in border or port cities and selling them at home at threefold prices.

My family also took advantage of the open possibilities. Andrey, my brother, opened a shop with one of his friends; Dima traded metal with someone in the far east of our country; my friend Svetlana and I talked of starting a baking business. The problem was finding ingredients. Through our friends and acquaintances, we spread the word that we were going to bake cakes for family events and holidays using our potential clients' ingredients. Soon people began placing orders, offering their own eggs, butter, sugar, flour, and even milk, depending on the kind of cake they had ordered. Most of our clients had money and connections, but there were those who had been saving eggs and butter for weeks to order a cake for their daughter's or son's birthday. How could you explain to a child why he or she could not have a birthday cake this year? Ultimately, because of lack of time, first Svetlana and then I backed off, and Mama inherited our customers. The baking endeavor did not bring her much profit, but it definitely helped her to survive the hard time.

Everyone tried to somehow make extra money. Those who did not have initial capital, borrowed money from relatives, friends, acquaintances, or acquaintances of acquaintances, promising to pay off the debt with huge interest. New businesses disappeared with the same speed they came to existence. Deals crumbled. Money was lost. Friendships broke. Angry clashes and nasty fights erupted between different groups of petty "capitalists."

The country was slipping into chaos. I felt depressed. Mama comforted me as best she could.

"Imagine a dog that has been held on a chain all his life," she told me. "One day his owner suddenly decides to let it loose. Not knowing what to do with its freedom, the poor wretch will run around like mad, until it falls half-dead from exhaustion. Then, he'll rest, come to his senses, and start living a free dog's life. That's what's going on with our country now. When Soviet people understand that nobody is going to take their freedom away, they'll settle down, like that dog. Everything will be good in the end." I wanted so much to believe her.

But time went by and nothing changed. The country reminded me of an old rusty mechanism—its cogs spun, smoke and steam billowed from the chimney, the motor roared, its body shook, but nothing happened. The engine idled; perestroika did not work. People grew increasingly skeptical. The economy collapsed. Bare shelves in grocery stores looked frightening. Market prices were sky high. On paydays all I could afford at Tekinsky Bazaar was two apples and a dozen eggs. The money was gone.

On top of that, glasnost, like a champagne cork, unleashed pent-up discontent, ethnic tensions, longing for independence, nationalist ambitions and territorial demands, people's dissatisfaction, and decades-old distrust of the Soviet Government.

Seizing the moment, the Baltic Republics (Estonia, Lithuania, and Latvia) and then Georgia, one after the other, declared their independence from Moscow. The Soviet Union began to crack and creep along at the seams, like an old, narrow-shouldered jacket, which had become too small for its owner.

On March 17, 1991, on the initiative of the Supreme Council, a Referendum on the future of the Soviet Union was held in the remaining Republics. The single question was whether or not we, the Soviet people, "consider[ed] necessary the preservation of the Union of Soviet Socialist Republics as a renewed federation of equal sovereign republics, in which the rights and freedoms of an individual of any nationality will be fully guaranteed." Two thirds of the country's population voted "yes." Turkmenistan reported that 97 percent of its citizens had voted for saving the USSR.

In August, 1991, an attempt to remove Gorbachev from power was staged by the right-wing forces. TASS, the Soviet news agency, cited Gorbachev's "inability for health reasons" to perform his duties as President. The coup failed, but it mixed all plans and became "the point of no return."

On December 8, the leaders of three Soviet Republics—Russian, Ukrainian, and Belorussian—signed a treaty dissolving the Soviet Union.

Two weeks later, the leaders of eleven Soviet Republics (Ukraine, the Russian Federation, Belarus, Armenia, Azerbaijan, Kazakhstan, Kyrgyzstan, Moldova, Turkmenistan, Tajikistan and Uzbekistan) met in the Kazakh city of Alma-Ata and signed the Protocol, which confirmed the extinction of the Soviet Union and stated the establishment of the CIS (Commonwealth of Independent States). With one stroke of the pen, they severed economic and cultural ties, fragmented families, and broke the hearts of hundreds of millions of the former Soviet Union citizens.

On December 25, 1991, the first and only President of the Union of Soviet Socialist Republics, Mikhail Gorbachev, announced his resignation. The next day, the Supreme Soviet adopted a declaration on the cessation of the existence of the USSR. People gasped.

I lost my Motherland.

EPILOGUE

My son Dima was eight years old when his father and I officially divorced. After his two years of compulsory military service, Sashka went to Norilsk, the world's northernmost Arctic city where his father, Oleg, lived with his second wife and a baby daughter. From time to time, I received letters from him, first from Norilsk and later from Murmansk where he worked as a correspondent for a local newspaper called *Komsomolets Zapolyaria* (Komsomol of the Arctic). One of the letters came with clippings of his articles.

After a while, he wrote that he got married again and had a son, named after him, Alexander. About a year later, he called, drunk. He said his wife had left him. He blamed me for spoiling his life. "In every woman I've met, I wanted to see you," he told me. Then he hung up and disappeared from my life again. Once a year, a telegram would come for Dima's or my birthday and it always ended with "The gift is on its way." No gifts or money ever followed.

The final call came from a hospital. He said he had been helicopter-lifted from one of the islands in the Barents Sea of the Arctic Ocean where he worked as a ranger. In a weak trembling voice, he informed me that he had a surgery due to stomach bleeding. I suspected it was from alcohol abuse. After that, the letters and telegrams stopped coming. Years later, I learned that Sashka had died.

My best childhood friend, Yulka, was murdered in Moscow during the turbulent perestroika time. Her body was found in early spring when the snow started melting—the Russian militia called the dead found during the spring melt "snowdrops." I heard rumors that Yulka was killed because a man she lived with at that time coveted the condo which she owned. There were many similar cases in those days. The killer has never been found.

Tolik, my first childhood friend made an excellent career in aviation and became a deputy chairman of Turkmenistan Airlines. Life scattered all my friends around the world. Larissa Bobman moved to Israel with her husband; Tolik and his wife Lida have a beautiful flat in Moscow; my son Dima and my brother Andrey reside in the Seattle area, not far from my houseboat on Lake Union.

After the break-up of the Soviet Union, Turkmenistan became an independent country, but nothing improved. Amid all the confusion and chaos, some meaningful changes occurred. One of them turned my life in a direction I never would have predicted. The new country opened its air space for international flights, and the knowledge of English, as a standardized language of ICAO (International Civil Aviation Organization) became essential. I was hired by Turkmenistan Airlines to ATC (Air Traffic Controls) as an interpreter and later was invited to the Aviation Personnel Training Center to teach aviation English to pilots, flight attendants, and ATC controllers.

In 1993, after the President of Turkmenistan bought a Boeing aircraft and was about to buy the second one for his presidential fleet, I became one of five interpreters for the Turkmen pilots who were sent to the Boeing Flight Training Center in Renton, Washington to be trained to fly Boeings. My life split into two disparate worlds. My business trips to the US continued; they were long, challenging, exhausting, but extremely exciting. Back home, my family's existence was not only hopeless but became exceedingly dangerous.

Thoughts of leaving Turkmenistan crossed my mind after two different break-in attempts at my condo and, soon after, the ransacking of my husband's apartment. In all three instances, despite broken doors and windows, the militia refused to investigate, which we knew was meant to warn Vladimir. As an investigative journalist, he wrote articles about corruption in Turkmen legal institutions, such as the militia and the KNB (former KGB). If during perestroika, it was possible, now it became dangerous. More than once he was threatened and attacked. Suspecting that drugs or cartridges could be planted on him—as had happened more than once—he stopped using public transport.

The decision to escape ripened in the fall of 1994 after my son was detained on a fabricated suspicion of murder charge. Dmitry was taken from Mama's house by a group of uniformed officers. He had been interrogated for several hours, while I stood with Andrey and Vladimir, outside the Militia building, helpless and agonizing. Eventually, they let my son go, but warned him to leave the country. Several days later, he left for Russia, but fear and danger hung over us like a storm cloud.

I decided that if I were sent on another business trip, I would not come back. I was the only one who had the opportunity to help my family escape. I knew it was a bold decision, but I had no idea how scary and difficult it would turn out to be. No one knew about my intention except for my immediate family. Mama supported my decision.

In May, 1996, on the last day of my fourth business trip to the US, I packed my small suitcase and fled. I was forty-nine years old and had nothing and knew nobody in the whole country. I had to start my life anew.

A quarter of a century passed. I kept my word. My son, Dmitriy Shebeko, and my brother, Andrey Kondeykin, with their wives and children, one after another, joined me and became citizens of the United States, the generous country which I now consider my only real Motherland. My only regret is that my dearest Mama, could not come. She died at age seventy-seven in Ashkhabad, while awaiting our pending reunion.

Complete information about the Ashkhabad earthquake and its consequences was suppressed for decades. Only in 1978, on the thirtieth anniversary of that event, did the number 110,000 surface as a realistic casualty count: two-thirds of the entire pre-earthquake population of Ashkhabad and 98 percent of the city's buildings were wiped from the face of the earth. But still, the government did not do anything to commemorate the victims.

As more Russian families died off or moved away from Turkmenistan, the old cemetery is abandoned: crosses tilted, barriers fallen, and tombs overgrown with weeds.

Printed in the USA
CPSIA information can be obtained
at www.ICGtesting.com
LVHW061453280124
769963LV00024B/216

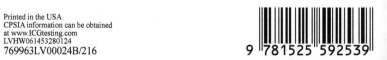